Praise for *The Last Master Outlaw*

"In my professional opinion as a seasoned and trained investigator and former criminal court judge, the case Colbert has made establishing Robert W. Rackstraw as the 1971 hijacker, documented in *The Last Master Outlaw*, is one of the strongest cases I have ever seen. The book, coauthored by Tom Szollosi, invites you along on the five-year hunt, as Colbert's cold case investigators track down old crime partners and coworkers, dig through the records, and log the solid evidence. You are left to ultimately conclude—beyond a reasonable doubt—that he has identified the man America has come to know as D. B. Cooper."

—*Shannen L. Rossmiller*, Montana State Investigator and
former criminal court judge and FBI cyberspy asset

"This book should come with a warning: Don't pick it up because you'll never put it down. I am so pleased that Colbert's efforts to bring closure to this case, which the world has been fascinated by for decades, is ending up in the win column. Credit his talent, time, and selfless attitude for this success. He would have been a great FBI agent!"

—*Jim Reese*, pioneering profiler, FBI Behavioral Science Unit,
and consultant, Silence of the Lambs

"Tom Colbert is the best investigative journalist I know. Tom possesses the curiosity and instinct that have repeatedly led to discovering the truth. All of us who reported the fascinating tale of D. B. Cooper and anyone who savors a mystery must read Tom's superb investigative story. Believe me—and believe him!"

—*Connie Chung*, former network news anchor

"A must-read. I believe this cold case, involving a fugitive many consider to be America's last outlaw before modern law enforcement tools, has been finally solved by an outstanding team of professional investigators. A fitting end to an epic legend of history."

—*Major General Paul E. Vallely*, US Army (Ret.),
Chairman, Legacy National Security Advisory Group

"Tom Colbert has truly made history by finally solving this cold case. His tenacity and zeal in leaving no stone unturned has made *The Last Master Outlaw* a perfect example of how a lifelong criminal like D. B. Cooper can keep running but can never hide!"

—*Rich F. Vigna*, *former Field Operations Director,*
US Customs and Border Protection, Pacific

"Readers will be captivated by the detail and complexity of its content, produced by authors Tom Colbert and Tom Szollosi. Tom and Dawna Colbert brought together a prominent group of cold case professionals from across the country to ensure they left no stone unturned during their extensive investigation. After reading this book you will be able to judge for yourself whether the D. B. Cooper case can be closed 'beyond a reasonable doubt.'"

—*Thomas P. Mauriello, MFS*, *Professor of Criminalistics, University of*
Maryland, one of USA's "Top 15 CSI Professors"

"A great tale of dedicated, dogged determination, and a fascinating story for the public. Tom Colbert's research was excellent, and the resolve to see this case to the end is a testament to his focus."

—*Jamie Graham*, *former Chief Superintendent,*
Royal Canadian Mounted Police

"The determination of Colbert to track down D. B. Cooper is amazing. His cold case team's investigative work to solve this mystery is unbelievable. *The Last Master Outlaw*, with cowriter Tom Szollosi, makes for great reading."

—*Scotty Sang*, *former Port Director, US Customs and*
Border Protection, Phoenix Sky Harbor International Airport

Praise for the Cold Case Team's Investigation

"I usually study reports three times, but my first read [of the investigative report] says yes, he's the guy."

—James Reese, PhD, pioneering FBI profiler,
Behavioral Science Unit, Quantico, Virginia

"It was quite amazing to see the volume of work and care you put into this case. You seem to have turned over every rock [and] followed all the right leads. It sounds like [Rackstraw] is the best suspect so far."

—Jamie Graham, former chief superintendent,
Royal Canadian Mounted Police

"I believe Mister Rackstraw is D. B. Cooper. It's time for him to take credit for what he did."

—Jack Trimarco, PhD, former FBI polygraph manager and profiler,
Los Angeles Field Office

"Based on all the [investigation report's] circumstantial evidence, I believe this suspect should be given a second look."

—Johnny "Mack" Brown, former US marshal,
South Carolina (2002–10)

"If this was a fresh case with this amount of information, you couldn't set him aside."

—Ron Hilley, former FBI agent and polygrapher

"The more I thought of it, the more I realized that Rackstraw had the background and required attributes [to be the hijacker]."

—Jack Immendorf, career private eye
who has been investigating Rackstraw since 1978

"I have dealt with a number of clever sociopaths in court, but he has more smarts and nerve than the rest put together."

—*F Clark Sueyres*, *retired San Joaquin County Superior Court judge and the deputy district attorney who prosecuted Rackstraw in 1979*

"[The hijacking] would suggest that [Cooper] was not only fearless but also had fully prepared a detailed recon of the area from the air. I would propose that of the potential suspects identified by the FBI, Rackstraw fits the mold best."

—*Ken L. Overturf*, *retired lieutenant colonel and Rackstraw's former army commander in Vietnam*

"I believe it would serve justice if the Bureau revisited Rackstraw as a possible suspect."

—*Richard W. Smith*, *former FBI special agent for twenty-five years, twenty of them in Soviet counterintelligence*

THE LAST
MASTER OUTLAW

HOW HE OUTFOXED THE FBI *SIX* TIMES
BUT NOT A COLD CASE TEAM

THOMAS J. COLBERT
TOM SZOLLOSI

Jacaranda Roots Publishing

Jacaranda Roots Publishing
543 Country Club Dr. #B324
Simi Valley, CA 93065
www.jacarandarootspublishing.com

Ordering Information

Quantity sales. Special discounts are available on quantity purchases by corporations, associations, and others. For details, contact the "Special Sales Department" at the address above.

Printed in the United States of America

Cataloging-in-Publication Data
  Colbert, Thomas J., author.
    The last master outlaw : how he outfoxed the FBI six
    times--but not a cold case team / Thomas J. Colbert and
    Tom Szollosi. -- First edition.
    pages cm
    Includes bibliographical references and index.
    ISBN 978-0-9977404-3-1 (pbk.)
    ISBN 978-0-9977404-2-4 (ebook)

    1. Rackstraw, Robert W. (Robert Wesley), 1943-
    2. Cooper, D. B. 3. Criminals--United States--Biography.
    4. Hijacking of aircraft--United States--Case studies.
    5. Cold cases (Criminal investigation)--United States--
    Case studies. 6. Biographies.   I. Szollosi, Tom, 1950-
    author. II. Title.

    HV6248.R235C65 2016   364.1092
    QBI16-1140

First Edition
20 19 18 17 16   10 9 8 7 6 5 4 3 2 1

Cover Design: Michael McGarry

Contents

We thank our remarkable wives, Dawna and Donna, and our children for their patience, support, and love. In this jump into history, they were the chutes.

How I Made the Cooper Connection

Thomas J. Colbert

*"This is just the most outstanding example that
I've ever seen of a professional investigation."*
—Former FBI Assistant Director Tom Fuentes[1]
October 17, 2015, after three days of study

As a boy, my grandfather swapped Wild West tales about Billy the Kid and Jesse James like other people traded baseball cards. With my dad, it was Dillinger, Bonnie and Clyde, and Capone. My generation—I was a teen entering high school in 1971—was captivated by the breaking story of a skyjacker called D. B. Cooper.

Now forty-five years a fugitive, he is considered by many to be America's last outlaw legend. I write "last" because modern law enforcement tools such as DNA, store cameras, GPS, cell phone surveillance apps, credit-card tracking, CSI teams, and national crime databases have made unidentified criminals as rare as rotary phones.

Cooper's stagecoach was a passenger jet, his "stand-and-deliver" weapon was a briefcase bomb, and his getaway horse was a parachute. On Thanksgiving Eve, authorities paid his $200,000 ransom in exchange for the release of the passengers and then watched as he took off with most of the crew for Mexico. But somewhere over the Northwest forests between Portland and Seattle, Cooper jumped out the back exit door of the Boeing airliner and became the stuff of folklore.[2]

News anchor Walter Cronkite called him "a master criminal."[3] *Time* magazine described a "dapper, audacious fellow," while a United Press International writer said he was "incredibly bold."[4] Fans, writers, even a sociologist labeled him a "Robin Hood."[5] But my investigation determined that although he had distinguished himself as a pilot in Vietnam, the man I believe to be Cooper was certainly no hero.

The adventure started on February 2, 2011, with the journalistic intuition of a longtime associate in Las Vegas, cameraman Rich Kashanski. His grapevine in the casinos had alerted him that a former Colombian cocaine runner had a story to tell.

Old drug mules can deliver rich tales, so Kashanski wasn't surprised when he heard the man had a humdinger. But when the tipster offered to take an FBI polygraph test to prove he wasn't making it all up—even to testify in court—well, that cleared the calendar for a rendezvous in Kashanski's home production studio.[6]

With my latest movie find, *The Vow*, in the can and a year away from its premiere, I was enjoying a hiatus from producing real-life stories for film and television by writing a sci-fi novel.[7] A breathless phone call from Kashanski corked that pipe dream on page 66.

I can recall only one word of it: "Cooper."

At first I found myself giving an obligatory eye-roll and headshake, which I'd done when those frantic tips found their way to my Los Angeles news research desk at KCBS-TV in the 1980s, and later, at Paramount Studios. Keep in mind there were more than 130 hijackings in the United States from 1968 to 1972, but the only case that callers wanted to talk about was the unsolved one.[8] The "whodunit" theories were always passionate, but the callers' dreams of catching D. B. Cooper, along with the fame and fortune that would follow, often got in the way of the facts. None of them were easy hang-ups.

When my photographer next relayed that the tipster witnessed the planning of the burial of the $5,800 of skyjacking ransom money found along the Columbia River in 1980, it was like I'd been hit with jumper cables—I fumbled for my steno pad.[9]

Throughout my thirty-five years of chasing true tales, I've been a part-time trainer of law-enforcement members. And I'd long heard cop-shop chatter that the shoreline "discovery" of Cooper cash by the picnicking Ingram family was, frankly, all wet. Nobody, however, had yet proved it had been staged or why.[10]

The former drug runner, Ron Carlson, had no proof either. But when you consider the agent in charge of that riverbank scene had famously speculated, "This is strong evidence that Cooper didn't survive,"[11] a stunt like this would be a hell of a great way to get the feds off your trail.

I knew this development could fire up the conspiracy crowd and sell a lot of tabloids. But without a methodical, proper investigation, it would quickly sink into the crowded swamp of wild Cooper theories.

The mantra of my former college journalism professor at California State University, Northridge, retired network producer Jerry Jacobs, rang through my mind: "Three sources for every fact, two if you know one, or I'll flunk you for life."[12]

I had always taken that maxim like the knuckle-whacks from my grade-school nuns: very seriously. The downside of being obsessively meticulous? You're not on the Hollywood party A-list. The upside? No lawsuits in thirty-five years, a steady

Ron Carlson, drug runner and first to hear Briggs's phony claim to be D. B. Cooper.

stream of referrals from old contacts, and detectives calling to clue you in on cases.

I had no delusions, however, about tackling the Cooper caper. In this search for journalism's five Ws—the who, what, when, where and why—the who was a forty-five-year-old ghost, and the what ended where the trail began: at the jet's rear stairway. There was also my investment of serious calendar time (ultimately, five years) and cash (ironically, the cost mirrored Cooper's ransom bounty).

After eight months of phone conversations, letter writing, and data mining, I had found there was some truth to our tipster's tale: Carlson's former trafficker boss had bragged to his Portland underworld crew that he himself had in fact planted the Columbia River hijacking cash.[13] But the reason why was never shared—he died under mysterious circumstances months later.[14]

Then I learned the dead man just happened to have a secret crime partner friend in California, a bad-ass Vietnam veteran who for a short time had been an FBI Cooper suspect.[15] And he happened to have been cleared of the hijacking charges *the same year* the bureau announced the Portland ransom money was "found" and Cooper probably "drowned."[16]

Do you know what cops, investigative producers, and parents of teenagers have in common? None believe in coincidences.

To complete my five Ws, I still had to answer a big why: if this vet was Cooper, why, years after his getaway, would he risk exposing himself in a complex, two-state plot along the Columbia River? A head-scratcher like this would take old-fashioned digging through dusty file cabinets, delicate microfiche, and forgotten storage containers from the pre-Internet 1970s.

And a whole pot-load of luck.

The answers started coming together in October 2011, thanks to two savvy backroom professionals.

A newspaper librarian at the *Stockton Record*, Delailah Little, discovered what had been tormenting our vet: dozens of forgotten article clippings (1977–80), yellowing photos, and mug shots from the disco era showed he was facing a litany of unrelated local felonies. Other stories documented the Cooper rumors swirling around him and the FBI's curiosity.[17]

My second hero was archivist Shannon Van Zant in nearby Calaveras County, who spent dozens of hours on my behalf diving into crumbling courtroom boxes and squeaky drawers. The result was hundreds of pages of fading court transcripts, the defendant's scathing appeals letters, district attorney memos, and detective briefs that gave a pulse and riveting timeline to the former soldier's decade of unbelievable mayhem.[18]

Between indictments and court dates in Northern California, the mysterious man twice fled authorities by plane; the FBI was involved in both recaptures.[19] He had used aliases along a trail involving more than sixty cities,[20] including multiple stops in his coke-trafficking friend's town of Portland.[21]

Then the feds' interest suddenly and inexplicably went cold.[22]

A 1980 article disclosed our vet was sitting in a California prison, serving a short sentence, when the Cooper ransom money was "discovered" along Oregon's Columbia River on February 10. And that's where the bureau's focus headed, to look for more cash—and bones.[23]

I believe to one isolated convict, those were headlines to die for. A half year later, he walked out of the prison and went quietly off the media's radar for good.[24]

A plausible motive was lining up with his military skill sets and hell-bent personality like three cherries on a slot machine. My gut, for the first time, overruled my cautious brain.

"Damn, this could be him!"

By December, a bounty of fresh documents and witnesses had connected the vet to the hijacking, the drug dealer, and the alleged river stunt.[25] It didn't take a detective to notice that the outline for a planned documentary film and book was also starting to look like the backbone of a criminal case.

As a journalist, I had become adept at cautiously working with local cops and feds during serial killer cases and hunts for fugitives—many times in conjunction with a cold case team. Later, in crisis management classes that I taught for eighteen years at the California Specialized Training Institute at Camp San Luis, I encouraged criminal justice, military, and fire and rescue students to seek out such liaisons with legitimate media.

So this Cooper project would be no different. I planned to approach the FBI and propose an *America's Most Wanted*–style collaborative investigation and television documentary, where the audience would be asked to call in clues and tips to authorities on our vet's last thirty-five years.

On August 15, 2012, the FBI responded to my proposal. While it welcomed "any further information" I—or the audience watching such a television program—could provide, the bureau turned down the opportunity to work together.

Why? The e-mail from headquarters explained: "The 1971 Northwest plane hijacking remains open but is not active. . . . The timing of investigative actions is based primarily on resource allocations among prioritized threats," and "this likely will not complement your own production timeline."[26]

If you think about it, this formal rejection of collaboration made perfect sense—considering today's world of suicidal jihadists, flash-mob robberies, website hackers, lawless borders, and senseless mass shootings. On the FBI's (unofficial) priority list, the hunt for my guy ranked somewhere between Jimmy Hoffa and Bigfoot.

I realized the chances of solving the case through the FBI had vanished as completely as the agents assumed Cooper had. But my epiphany raised a question that I'd previously learned was dangerous to say in front of a mirror: If they're not going to confront this guy, who is?

For guidance on this momentous undertaking, I needed a nationwide cold case team, men and women who had the investigative skill sets and resources of a multiagency task force. So dozens of retired law enforcement and forensic professionals were recruited—old news sources of mine from a variety of government, local, state, and federal agencies—to be my on-call consultants. Then I hired an elite team of private eyes and investigative journalists, all from the pre-Internet, "gumshoe" generation, to knock on doors, conduct stakeouts, dig into forgotten drawers, and shoot the documentary. (Meet them all in the "Acknowledgments" section.)

In short, these more than forty superheroes were instrumental in helping me identify the man who I absolutely believe is our last outlaw legend.[27]

After a half year of futile negotiations for an interview with this "cleared" hijacker,[28] I came to one conclusion: to hook him, we needed to get within casting range. That meant a discreet approach to his home turf, situated on an upscale residential island where his yacht was docked, just a few miles from the Mexican border.[29]

I was up to my eyeballs planning the face-to-face encounter (chapters 18 and 19) when a sudden chill hit me. Even though this vet was beyond retirement age, I had absolutely no idea which man we were about to confront. The tuxedoed husband at society events? The cheery granddad on social media?[30] The convicted con artist?[31] Or the vengeful old warrior fighting his way out of an ambush?[32]

It was time to consult my secret wizard behind the curtain.

Twenty-three years ago, I married the beautiful hero of one of my true-crime stories. When Dawna's personal case got stalled by police policy and jurisdictional red tape, she turned detective and solved it herself—followed by a trial and a conviction. The courage and tenacity she exhibited during those very demanding times still inspire me. That's why, whenever brain lock strikes during my criminal justice research or story development, my first lifeline is a call out to her desk.

After hearing my operational plan, Dawna put her finger on the missing component: security, and lots of it. She also warned she wouldn't give her blessing without it. The macho male in me was about to utter something stupid, like "Why do we need rent-a-cops?" when the reasons came to me with morning hugs—my two young kids.

Once again, my guardian angel had spoken.

With the confrontation's logistics set and armed protection arranged, I finally had the time to methodically study our adversary's mind-set. Being the son of a shrink didn't hurt.

According to psychologist Robert D. Hare, PhD, in his authoritative *Hare Psychopathy Checklist—Revised*, a psychopath shows no remorse or guilt; is callous; is a pathological liar; fails to accept responsibility; lacks realistic, long-term goals; is impulsive; has a grandiose sense of worth; and displays criminal versatility.[33] During the course of my five-year investigation, sources and witnesses branded my Cooper subject with every one of those descriptions.[34]

I realized early in my career that the only way to learn the truth about a subject was to study his or her whole life. In our man's case, that meant contacting people who over seven decades had called him not only neighbor, buddy, classmate, band member, soldier, coworker, crime partner, felon, teacher, and club member but also son, brother, nephew, cousin, uncle, lover, Dad, and Grandfather.

The chapters leading up to our on-camera confrontations with my identified D. B. Cooper—a mosaic of humorous, stunning, tearful, and dark memories—are accentuated by interviews with six of his women: two ex-wives; a Hollywood producer who was also his cocaine-trade crime partner; the "getaway gal" lover who twice joined him on the lam; a befriended college coed; and his only sibling, an estranged sister who gave a four-hour deathbed testimonial as to his guilt.

They have all clarified how a troubled boy genius who took root in the remote woods of California became one of the most brilliant and conniving criminal minds ever nurtured and trained by the US Army[35]—a criminal sociopath who we believe outsmarted the FBI six times, two of them resulting in escapes.[36]

Then he lived, prospered, and grew old to lie about it.[37]

Authors' Note

Four times in the distant and recent past, our subject has publicly admitted he enjoyed letting people think he was the hijacker, but it was all "an act that got out of hand." We, however, have been told by many it is not an act, so the investigation was launched to set the facts straight. This wasn't an easy task, asking about events decades-old—especially when details came from conflicting sources. And if any family members or associates of our interviewees were unintentionally embarrassed or threatened because of the team's approaches, we do regret that. But we put the onus on one stubborn man, still holding the ripcord to the truth.[1]

"Son of a Bitch! You Got Away Again!"

Who in heaven's name would "chain and shackle" a man to his own wheelchair?[1]

This wasn't just any man but the one and only Robert Wesley "Bob" Rackstraw. And to those who had been chasing the bastard around the world, the answer was simple: Who the hell wouldn't?[2]

He was rolled into the Calaveras County courtroom in San Andreas, California, for arraignment on March 14, 1978. Rackstraw claimed to need the wheelchair because of a recurring back injury, but those in this old gold-rush town who knew

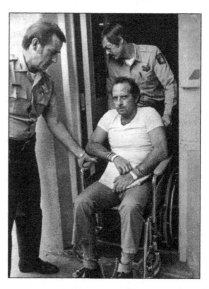

Wheelchair-bound and shackled, Rackstraw during the trial for the murder of his stepfather, Philip Rackstraw, 1978.

anything about him were skeptical, believing his sudden disability to be a ploy for sympathy.[3]

When the case came to trial four months later, Rackstraw's lawyer, Dennis Roberts, turned away assertions that his client was faking it. His attitude was understandable. He did not want courtroom waters muddied by accusations that the defendant was anything other than the forthright Vietnam War hero—with the medals to prove it—that Roberts was planning to demonstrate his client had been.[4]

Rackstraw's combat fame was already part of the court record in neighboring San Joaquin County, where he had faced an earlier hearing for other felony charges. Judge William H. Woodward heard the former Green Beret captain had earned a whopping forty medals in Vietnam, including five Purple Hearts, "several" Bronze Stars, and five campaign ribbons. The judge appeared to be stunned. "This simply can't be true. If this is true, his record will bear weight with this court."[5]

The hearing's deputy district attorney, F. Clark Sueyres, admitted he couldn't prove the medal count was a lie. But he argued, "Perhaps we do owe Mr. Rackstraw something for what he did in a foreign land, but that certainly doesn't give him any right to murder and plunder in this country."

Judge Woodward, of course, reminded Sueyres that Rackstraw was only accused of these offenses and was presumed innocent.[6] Nevertheless, Sueyres decided to initiate a search of military records to verify exactly what honors the veteran had earned.[7]

At the March 14 arraignment in Calaveras County though, Rackstraw stood—or, more precisely, sat—accused of the execution-style murder of his stepfather, Philip Rackstraw. Philip's body had been found beneath three feet of soil, face down, hands bound behind his back, legs bent as they had been when he apparently knelt to take two bullets to the back of his head. He was wearing only a T-shirt and underwear, with his head wrapped in a bloody jacket. The victim had been listed as missing for seven months.[8]

The new owner of Philip's ranch, Kelly Cline, testified that Bob Rackstraw had mentioned an old well "up on a hill where the ground might sink and need refilling" when giving Cline a tour of the ten-acre property. But when Cline, who was well aware of Philip's disappearance, found a second sinking spot there, he told the county sheriff's office.[9]

The second depression, situated under a sagging woodpile by a shed, proved to be Philip's grave. It seemed strange that Rackstraw would think

to mention a sinking spot at all, but it was even stranger that he had ne-
glected to mention the second, far-more-troubling one. It hinted at deception and did little to make Rackstraw look like a straight shooter to
anyone.

But attorney Roberts had a card up his sleeve.

When he had visited the ranch to get a personal feel for where Philip's body had been found, he discovered a piece of physical evidence the
sheriff's department, incredibly, had fumbled. Cline told the lawyer he had
uncovered a pair of bloody Levi's jeans in the shed's trash can and that a
detective had shown no interest in them. Amazed, Roberts told Cline to
put the jeans in a bag and bring them with him to court when he was called
to testify.[10]

It would not matter. Judge Joseph Huberty wasn't about to stop the
proceedings to wait for a definitive answer about Rackstraw's military
decorations or for the testing of blood on the jeans. Smelling an easy win,
attorney Roberts called Rackstraw himself to the stand.

"I didn't kill my father," he told the jury, "but I swear to God that I'll find
out who did and I will bring him here to justice!"[11]

Rackstraw's righteous truculence, along with the defense premise that
Calaveras County Sheriff Russell Leach's department had committed serious
mistakes "in the handling of evidence"—detectives had not only had ignored
the pants, but had inexplicably destroyed the gory jacket wrapped around
Philip's head—led the eight-man, four-woman panel to acquit Rackstraw of
his stepfather's murder after a mere six hours of deliberation.[12]

Attorney Roberts was all smiles—possibly because he knew part of his
payment was going to be his client's 1958 classic Corvette.[13] Rackstraw,
though, faced additional charges for check kiting, forgery, and the illegal
possession and delivery of dynamite.

All of these charges would be tried shortly in San Joaquin County
Court, and because of them, Rackstraw was still being held on $60,000
bail. But the veteran seemed to have friends, and funds were pooled to
meet the required bail amount.[14] While Deputy DA Sueyres diligently assembled his coming case, a judge required the out-on-bail Rackstraw to
sign a consent to release his full war records.

When he showed up in court to do so, the smiling vet strolled in without the aid of a wheelchair or crutches—a truly remarkable recovery by any measure.[15]

A good deal more was remarkable about Rackstraw—or "Airborne Bob," as some called him from his military days as a pilot—such as his well-honed ability to lie and deceive with a straight face, convincing patter, and unflinching eyes.[16]

Local cops had briefed the FBI about his decade of shenanigans.[17] Now, twenty-four hours before his next trial arraignment and return to custody, special agents were coming in to interrogate him.[18] One of them tipped the DA's office that Pentagon records the court was waiting for would indeed show Rackstraw had "highly exaggerated" his rank and the types of medals he'd earned in Vietnam—for example, he was never a Green Beret, his rank was not captain but lieutenant, there weren't five campaign ribbons, and all five Purple Hearts were phony.[19]

Before long, Bob Rackstraw was missing. An experienced, thoroughly tested aviator, he had rented a small plane, ostensibly to visit his divorced first wife and their three children in Santa Cruz County. To make his story more convincing, he had asked his ex to meet him at the local airport.

"He was coming for dinner and the kids got excited," she recently recalled.[20]

And then suddenly everything seemed to go wrong twelve miles out over Monterey Bay. Rackstraw made a distress call, reporting fire in the engine and smoke in the cabin.

"Mayday! Mayday! I'm going to ditch!"[21]

Air traffic controllers directly notified rescue authorities, and five planes from the coast guard, navy, and air force scrambled. For seven hours, three coast guard cutters traversed a thirty-mile span of the Pacific for wreckage or a survivor. But they found no trace of either.[22]

Nothing about the October 11, 1978, emergency call would have tipped off even a suspicious listener—unless that listener was familiar with Bob Rackstraw, in which case what he did not mention would have come under a great deal more scrutiny. For instance, he did not mention that he would actually be turning left and flying below the radar, all the way down to a secret airport hangar in Southern California.[23] He did not mention that his current girlfriend would join him there—just as she had joined him in far-off Iran a year earlier, when he fled to avoid being the main attraction at the trial for the murder of his stepfather.[24] And of course he didn't mention what the FBI was now considering anew: that seven years earlier, for a brief, high-stakes and high-altitude game of "stick it to the man," he may have gone by the more nefarious name Dan Cooper—or, as a wire service reporter erroneously made famous, skyjacker D. B. Cooper.[25]

The late Philip Rackstraw's highly suspicious mother and brother had hired Jack Immendorf, a San Francisco–based private investigator (PI), to find Philip when he'd vanished from his ranch property in 1977. On the day of this Mayday call, Immendorf coincidentally happened to be driving home along the coast with his wife when he heard about the "rescue search" going on in Monterey Bay. His concern spiked into astonishment and rage when the radio announcer said the pilot feared lost was named Robert W. Rackstraw.

Immendorf was convinced that Rackstraw was Philip's murderer, despite the acquittal he and his attorney had wangled. He also felt that Rackstraw indeed could be Cooper. He slugged the dashboard in frustration.

"You motherfucker!" Immendorf hollered. "Son of a bitch! You got away again!"[26]

Indeed, he had.

CHAPTER 2

Blended Beginnings

Circa 1960

Robert Wesley Rackstraw probably remembers Santa Cruz County, California, as the first place he lived as part of a full-fledged family. He was born in Ohio in 1943 and was the older brother of Linda Lee Rackstraw, sharing the same mother but having different divorced fathers. The family wasn't officially brought together until a third marriage, when he was eight and Linda Lee was four. It was complicated. Rackstraw's life, as it turned out, would always be complicated.

The kids had been together with their mother, Lucille, but little Linda Lee was sent to live with her birth father at some point during those first four years, only to be reunited with her mother, brother, and new stepfather, Philip, shortly after he and Lucille got married in 1950.[1]

Together, they were a true blended family. Philip put a lot of importance on the idea of family being family. He said he never wanted to hear the word "step" in front of "son," "daughter," or "father" in his house—and he meant it.

To a degree, the idea was a success. Bob and Linda Lee were close in those early years, but being close with Bob meant Linda Lee was subjected to "a great teaser," she later recalled. Not that she had much choice. They shared a room until she was ten and he was fourteen. The small house had only two bedrooms, so sharing and being teased by Bob were unavoidable facts of her life—a life that was a long throw from anything like an idyllic Norman Rockwell upbringing.

The house, in the rugged Santa Cruz Mountains, was in a little community called Scotts Valley. The property's most desired feature was a secluded creek that meandered around two sides of it, which, with its towering pines, emitted a sense of wistful mystery. The children's first outings were spent learning not to fear the water but to embrace it—with skipping rocks, playing in the mud, and having splash fights. When summer turned it bone dry, the town swimming pool, just over a little mountain, provided relief. But it wasn't the same.

Bob and kid sister, Linda Lee, go biking in happier days, 1953.

Their backyard forest, however, was a year-round playground where kids could be kids, tree-climbing, stargazing, bike-riding, and mischief-making. It was the kind of pastoral setting city dwellers often dream of— minus the borderline poverty experienced by the Rackstraws.

"As I got into my older years, I kind of resented being out there," said Linda Lee, "because your friends are, you know, are from school, and they don't make a trip from the burbs." So with few other neighborhood kids, "it's almost like it's you and him," Linda summed up.

And Bob wasn't shy about teasing—anybody. On rare occasions, when Linda Lee did have classmates over, he would do boy stuff—like find a garter snake and chase them around with it. Linda Lee was careful to never let him know too much of what she feared; he would make her life miserable if she did. "But you know, those are brother things," she said.

But Bob didn't spend all his time teasing his sister and her classmates. He had his own interests, some quite consuming and destined to stay with him all his life. One of them—a big one—was flying. Like many other boys, he built a lot of model airplanes. But with Bob, the hobby was more serious and intense. It was the first evidence of his brilliance at methodically going about something he was interested in until he mastered it.

He'd start by going to the library to get a book, as he did not only with model airplanes but also with armaments. At twelve, he built a small cannon on the property using construction odds and ends that Philip had around the house, most importantly a length of clay pipe. Following the directions he found in a book, Bob worked diligently until the project was done.

When his first cannon broke, he built a second one, changing his method to avoid another failure. Linda Lee remembered being amazed that Bob had managed to also make a cannon ball. It didn't surprise her, however, that he could make his own gunpowder—knowledge no doubt gleaned from the library.

When he tested the cannon, Linda Lee said, "Dad was proud of it." But the widely dispersed neighbors in Scotts Valley—you don't live there to be close to other people—immediately knew whom to come complaining to. The startling *boom* rattled and shook every window in the area and revealed to Bob that not everyone was enthusiastic about his newfound firepower.

It wasn't that he didn't have the chance to observe guns firsthand. The family always had weapons in the house. Living some distance from town, Philip saw them as a necessity. He didn't have the time to just call the police and wait for a response.

The most memorable airplane Bob built was another matter. Unlike guns, there was nothing with wings around the property to use as a rough model except birds. Thanks to yet another book, he made a plane—a glider big enough for a person to sit in and, theoretically, fly.

The idea was to launch it off of a nearby hill, but Lucille drew the line right there. Her son was not, at twelve, going to go floating through the air and slam into something while she watched helplessly. She actually tied the aircraft to the house so it would remain grounded and in her window's view at all times.

Bob's mechanical accomplishments were amazing, however, to everyone in the family. They were a vivid confirmation of what his family had already known, and his teachers had reinforced, about the importance of keeping him challenged. If they could focus his mind on more engaging projects than the rote learning that bored him as busywork, young Bob was someone who could succeed at whatever he wanted to do.

But truth was, those teachers had difficulty keeping him challenged, too. And like his parents, they quickly realized that when he was not challenged, trouble was often only a matter of time.

For example, one time angry neighbors complained about Bob shooting his BB gun outside their house. Lucille didn't want to believe them, preferring to think that it must be some other boy. Part of her, however, knew it was probably her son behaving as he often did when he had too much time on his hands. He knew better, but with nothing else to do he was drawn to what seemed most interesting—namely, something he wasn't supposed to do.

Linda Lee, who was frequently on the receiving end of things Bob knew better than to do, never really thought of him as malicious in those days. He was never mean to animals, for example, and they grew up around plenty of them. But if he was somewhere south of malicious, he was usually north of mischievous.

She remembered one occasion where big brother Bob crossed the line with her and really blew it with their parents. It was the BB gun again. Linda Lee was sitting outside on the porch when, for no apparent reason, twelve-year-old Bob came up to her and pointed the gun right at her: close, face-high, barrel practically touching her upper lip. By this time, Linda Lee was accustomed to his goading, bluffing, and sometimes off-the-rails idea of fun—and that odd, mischievous half-smile of his.

"What are you doing?" she asked.

"I want to see you flinch. Because I'm going to pull the trigger."

She didn't believe he would ever do anything to really hurt her. "I'm not gonna flinch."

"I'll pull the trigger," he repeated.

She knew the gun was empty. It had to be empty. He wasn't stupid. He was just looking for something to do.

"The gun's empty, but I'll pull the trigger if you don't flinch," he said.

Linda Lee knew that he wanted her to think there was a tiny chance that he could be wrong. Everybody knew that people made mistakes and found out only after a gun went off. But she had a stiff-backbone streak of her own, and she didn't flinch.

And Bob, being Bob, did pull the trigger.

He didn't count on the blast of air from the BB gun being as violent as it was. They were both amazed when her lip began to swell as if she'd been punched in the face. There wasn't going to be any way to hide the truth, and it was obvious he was going to be in big trouble for it.

The strange thing Linda Lee would always remember about the incident was that while he did seem sorry, it was more like he was sorry for getting caught than for hurting her. Years later she could see that Bob never really had much sympathy for people he hurt, accidentally or otherwise, no matter who they were. Trouble happened and he went on without any big display of conscience or regret. In truth, Linda Lee wasn't even sure he was that sorry he got in hot water because he didn't seem to care.

"He just kind of . . . did it," she said.[2]

It was a case of an unchallenged mind and idle hands casting about for something—anything—to do. Bob was restless, jumping from one thing to the next—again, just to do something.

Sometimes, in the midst of Bob's increasingly troubled existence, there were moments of clarity. One such time came when the family took a trip to Arizona to visit relatives in 1960.

"We went back there one time, Mom, Dad, Bob, and me, when I was probably about twelve, thirteen years old," said Linda Lee. "Bob would've been [almost] seventeen. I think my parents thought this will be the last chance we'll have the family together and have a vacation."

Her brother's love of flight and airplanes had never dimmed, so he was fascinated when he met his uncle, forty-eight-year-old John "Ed" Cooper, a skydiver who would tally more than two thousand jumps during his lifetime.

"He was a really nice guy," recalled Linda Lee, and "he loved parachuting. That's all he talked about."

Bob followed him around during the trip, hanging on his every word. At one point, the men—Bob, Phil, and Uncle Ed—took off together to do some fishing and male bonding in Baja California. All the teen wanted to hear about, however, was skydiving. By the end of the journey, the teen was hooked.[3]

It's impossible to know the full impact of that experience on young Bob, but seven years after, he became a paratrooper.[4] Then four years after that—in a moment that represented the zenith of his self-assertion, independence, and defiance against everything that seemed unfair and wrong—he would choose to go by the name Cooper. And as he admitted later to a newsroom editor, his Uncle Ed had been the inspiration for that choice.[5] The connection of the name Cooper with the parachute jump of a lifetime for Rackstraw seems almost impossible to misinterpret.

When he was still years away from using the name Cooper, his lack of hesitation to act—or fear of consequences when he did—was already shaping most of his young friendships. He was the leader in most of the actions he did with his peers. He had always been that way, and living in a small town where everybody knew everybody else and lives overlapped frequently, he had earned an almost affectionate reputation as a mischief-maker. People thought of his actions only as mischief because Bob was charming and full of his own special kind of charisma. Despite the trouble he got into, most of the locals loved Bob.

"He was this genius kid," said Linda Lee, "and good in school when he was interested. The teachers never really had complaints about him."

The charm offensive went further than that. One night when he was an older teenager, Bob was driving a buddy home after a night of drinking. Smashed in his own right, Bob plowed right into the side of the friend's house, doing considerable damage to the structure. Amazingly, the boy's parents decided not to tell Lucille and Philip what Bob had done because they didn't want him to get into trouble.

Preventing Bob from facing the consequences of his actions was a recurring theme, and his "charmed life" track record was teaching him that he could get away with bad behavior because of his personality.

He could even get past a confrontation with his mother. Linda Lee said there was a classic teenage moment in the garage, with young Bob wanting to follow his own will and Lucille putting her foot down. It would have been just another mundane nonmoment in memory, but this time his temper came perilously close to getting the better of him. He actually pulled his fist back as if to punch his mother. Lucille, not for one moment afraid of him, immediately stuck her jaw out, her own fists clenched in offended rage.

"Go ahead," she said, her voice even, almost deadly. "You just go ahead."

It would be a cold day in hell before she let her teenage son intimidate her. Wisely, he did not use his fist, instead turning away and storming out of the garage.

Bob's relatively small transgressions, many of which weren't really crimes at all, seemed to leave the door open to bigger offenses. And he never failed to walk through an open door. The little crimes gradually got worse and worse until, inevitably, he would unblinkingly do things that people were put in jail for. The little crimes came hand in glove with the lies he told in mesmerizing torrents, delivered with more and more finesse, so he could get what he desired without actually earning it.

Very often, what he desired involved cash. "Money became a very big thing to him," said Linda Lee.[6]

Seeing no financial gain while sitting at a desk, fifteen-year-old Bob quit school at the end of his sophomore year. It bored him, frankly, as telegraphed in his last Santa Cruz High School report card: four Fs, three Ds, and forty-four class cuts.[7] And then there was the matter of facing a great deal of authoritarian scorn for having made two girls pregnant.[8]

Between the ages of sixteen and twenty, Bob was old enough to go out and do something on his own. His parents couldn't really stop him, or they didn't try, even when he got jobs on building sites by managing to get licenses that said he was older than he really was.[9]

Linda Lee, Philip, Lucille, and high-school dropout Bob, 1958.

For example, at sixteen, he drove a cement truck for the Graham & Son Concrete Company in Scotts Valley.[10] He worked as a hard-hat on other sites. Bill D. Graham, a future five-time mayor, had turned the concrete plant—with its accompanying sand and gravel pit—into his winning ticket in life.[11] It was just the kind of success story to capture Bob Rackstraw's imagination. In fact, whatever it took to make money always captured Bob's imagination because money got him the things he really wanted—especially more girls.

He was good looking, and he always knew how to wield that enticing charm, but now he had money to flash around, too. He would lead the way to partying and drinking and having fun. He was fun.

But when your personality is predicated on little crimes that gradually get bigger, all greased by a nearly unending stream of lies, exaggerations, and just plain old country bullshit, you tend to fall into the pattern that Bob did. Which was to BS even more, particularly with the ladies he liked to be around so much.

"He lied to girls a lot," said Linda Lee. "He wouldn't tell one he was dating another. He didn't seem concerned if it hurt somebody."

She put her foot down when, one day, he pulled out a wedding ring. "He was going to marry his first wife [Gail Marks, not her real name]. I said, you shouldn't marry him. He's already lied to you. He's already got other women."

Linda Lee had been the petite blonde's roommate and good friend before Marks became infatuated with Bob, soon after they had met at a Santa Cruz hot dog stand.[12]

Linda Lee's advice was outweighed by passion, fueled partly by the romantic idea of dating someone who was in a rock band.

At the age of eighteen, the ever-enterprising Bob helped put together a five-member band called—aptly, in retrospect—the Insanos. Sharing the limelight with locals Earl Latham, Linden Coffee, Dick Tranchina, and George Le France, the rockin' quintet traveled to stages in towns throughout the area and beyond, such as Lake Tahoe, Reno, and even Salt Lake City. For a promotional flyer, the boys dressed in black pants, red shirts, and sombreros, and then grabbed their instruments and posed for photos on top of an army tank. The beautiful Marks, only fifteen—and legally jailbait to the older Bob—eagerly came along for some of the fun.[13]

The next year, Bob took a break to be best man for a former Santa Cruz High classmate, William H. "Bill" Eisele. With more than two hundred friends and family in attendance at Grace Methodist Church, no doubt much of the dropout's reception time was spent explaining how big a rock star he was.

Bill and his bride, Patricia, have been married now for more than fifty years. Recently, he unashamedly declared Bob was still his "best friend."[14]

By 1962, truth was becoming road kill to Bob's wants, needs, and obsessions—a casualty that was increasingly buried beneath everything he said and did. Even the people who knew him best, his family, couldn't figure out which part of what he said was true and which was invented. It was as if he had created his own language, one that only Bob could truly understand.

It worked like a charm on those girls, as it did later in life on grown-up women. He spoke every kind of scam so fluidly, in fact, that it naturally came to comprise the bulk of his communication. The more it worked, the more he relied on it, like an addict in need of a fix.

A textbook sociopath, he was never bothered by the fact that his lies and deceptions hurt other people. Tough luck, he would tell you.

Watching Bob's progression as a cold-blooded con man was confirmation to Linda Lee that the episode with the BB gun had been a chilling foreshadowing of events to come. But she noticed a difference now, a purpose to his behavior. He was no longer lying—or, later in life, committing crimes—simply because he was bored and it was something to do. He lied more and more to get something out of it. Whether it was the acquisition of money or the thrill of cheating on a girlfriend or wife, he seemed to love always being one jump ahead of whatever was chasing him—sometimes literally—and to enjoy the sense of superiority it gave him.

He also made a point of justifying his actions whenever possible, presumably to free himself from even the slightest feeling of responsibility.

"He insisted it was always somebody else's fault. Never his own," Linda Lee said, "and how the people he victimized and hurt deserved it, or even asked for it."

Indeed, the one thing Bob Rackstraw would never do—young boy or grown man—was acknowledge that his actions hurt others. He was, as his sister put it, "a person with no moral compass."[15]

However, he was not a family pioneer in that department. In 1961, his mom, Lucille L. Rackstraw, faced a municipal court judge at age thirty-nine when she was caught receiving earnings while drawing unemployment compensation benefits. She pleaded guilty, was sentenced to fifteen days in jail, and was given a fine of $105.

The *Santa Cruz Sentinel* covered both of her court dates, but despite her guilty plea, Lucille soon wrote a letter to the editor to complain about the articles. Under "Correction," in bold print, she explained that "for the benefit of friends," she wanted to clarify the matter because it had all been "a misunderstanding concerning my recent appearance in court."

In fact, correcting almost nothing, she pointed out that she had paid the $105 fine and returned the $42 owed to the employment department.[16]

Despite his persistent transgressions, Bob maintained a very good relationship with his stepfather for a long time. Philip would come to Bob's rescue again and again. When Bob got one of his young Scotts Valley sweethearts pregnant, Philip and Lucille went to the girl's family. Philip facilitated many of the arrangements for the baby to be adopted. He was far from happy about the situation and worried about the family's reputation, to be sure, but he was determined to protect his son.

Lucille told her children more than once that Philip would never let her give spankings, which were still common when Bob and Linda Lee were kids. Linda Lee later speculated that because Philip was their step-father, he was sensitive to overly harsh discipline and that they avoided some punishments they should have received. Instead, they heard "a lot of talk" the vast majority of the time.

Even so, Philip, when provoked, displayed a mercurial temper that could be the equal of Bob's. When Bob, then sixteen, was spending time with a crowd of boys Philip disapproved of, he flatly told Bob, "I don't want you hanging out with them." The fatherly edict was that there would be hell to pay if Bob did not abide by the decision.

Bob paid no heed. Soon after, his parents went out for the evening and the very kids Philip had forbidden Bob to see came over to the house. Getting home earlier than Bob expected, Philip was furious to see the youngsters.

"Dad grabbed one of the loaded guns in the house," Linda Lee remembered. "He warned them to get the hell off his property or he'd shoot them. They could tell he wasn't kidding so they took off, scared to death, convinced he was completely crazy.

"It takes a lot to stand there and pull a trigger, even when you're angry," she added. "My dad wasn't a violent man, but he was angrier than I ever saw him at that moment."

The boys were upset enough about the threat that they called the sheriff's office the first chance they got.

In the meantime, Philip was chasing Bob through the darkness, up a nearby hill and down the other side. Lucille went after Philip because he still had the gun. She was determined to get it away from him before he took a shot at Bob or the gun accidentally went off. She managed to catch up to her husband and persuaded him to come for a ride with her to just get away from the place and cool off. Soon the car was roaring away, their parents inside, and Linda Lee came out of the house.

She knew Bob had gone over the hill and knew he must still be out there somewhere. She yelled for him, telling him it was safe to come back. She was enormously relieved when he did, but he soon became upset again because he said he definitely wasn't sticking around. He hiked off to a nearby friend's house, leaving her alone. At least Bob didn't drive his old deathtrap pickup truck, which he'd bought in defiance of Philip's warnings. The truck itself had been a festering crisis between them, so walking to a buddy's house was just slightly less inflammatory.

Before long, the Santa Cruz County Sheriff's Department showed up. Soon after, so did Philip and Lucille. Despite the fact that he and Bob generally got along, that evening he had simply been set off. It was the only time Linda Lee could remember seeing her stepfather angry enough to do something truly dangerous and irrational. She didn't believe that Philip would have followed through with the gun. It wasn't in his character. As for Bob, well, that was proving to be a different matter entirely.[17]

One of Bob's early drunk-driving incidents—they are a recurring theme in his life—was jaw-dropping in how it played out. Santa Cruz was a really small town when Bob was twenty, and it wasn't unusual for teachers from the high school to log some hours as auxiliary police. One night, two of them spotted Bob driving erratically and couldn't ignore the fact that he had been drinking—not to mention that he carried what they knew to be a false ID. They put him in a jail cell and called his stepfather.

Figuring his son could stand to learn a lesson, Philip told them it was fine if he stayed there. Linda Lee recited the rest of dad's tough-love response: "Keep him there until the morning. In fact, keep him in the drunk tank, he can mingle with the drunks."

After realizing he wasn't getting out, Bob lay down on a cot. Just over an hour later, appearing to doze with a lit cigarette in his hand, he set the mattress on fire.

Bob swore to the police and quickly summoned fire department that he hadn't done it on purpose. He had simply fallen asleep while smoking. He bore a sheepish look, either embarrassed or fearful of what was going to happen to him. But even though he now faced the additional charge of destroying jail property, the truth was that nothing was going to happen to him. The fire had been put out before it could do any real harm.

"Go home, Rackstraw," said one of the officers, fed up.

They didn't have to tell him twice. It was all just another item to put on the list of mischief he'd gotten away with.

Two days later on October 22, 1963, the Santa Cruz Sentinel gave the quiet incident a brash headline—inking him, like his mother two years earlier, as a town outcast: "Youth Has Hot Time in Jail."[18]

You might suspect that in Bob Rackstraw's circles, the article was worth bragging rights, say in exchange for beer. But six years later, the tabloid tattler would become a festering wound in this young man's promising future.

Youth Has Hot Time In Jail

It's double trouble for Robert Wesley Rackstraw, 20, of 306 Nelson road.

Rackstraw was arrested early Sunday morning by Santa Cruz police on charges of false identification. The young man had hardly been in jail more than an hour when jail attendants spotted smoke coming from his cell.

They found Rackstraw coughing and choking from smoke coming out of a smouldering mattress. The fire department put out the blaze.

Rackstraw told officers he must have dropped a lighted cigarette.

Officers dropped another charge on Rackstraw: destroying jail property.

Earliest headline exposure, 1963.

CHAPTER 3

Reveille

MARCH 14, 1964–JUNE 24, 1969

I t was time—well past time, in fact—for Bob to take wing. He saw the military as a way to get out from under intrusive parental control. He was more than ready to embark on any number of adventures that were, to parents Philip and Lucille, outside the lines of acceptability. He was twenty years old. He was breaking familial bonds, and life would never be the same.

On March 14, 1964, Rackstraw and three of his Insanos bandmates joined other high-school graduates in raising their right hands at the National Guard Armory in Santa Cruz. Joining the California Guard, with all of its discipline and clear-cut rules, seemed like the perfect route for the young man.[1]

"The military [was] a good thing for him," said Linda Lee, "giving him structure and focus and then of course, he loved guns. He loved explosives. He loved all of that stuff."

The simple act of enlisting made up for almost everything he could ever have done to make his stepfather angry. Philip, a World War II navy veteran, was military to the marrow and a gung-ho, first-generation American of British heritage particularly proud of his service.

Philip was stationed in the Pacific theater on an island that was overrun by the Japanese. He became a prisoner of war, part of a large group of detainees. In time, as the island was being retaken by American forces, the Japanese threw their captives into a pit and opened fire.

Incredibly, the Japanese gunmen missed Philip Rackstraw, who had the presence of mind to pretend that he was dead. As the fighting raged, Philip had no chance to climb out and escape, too weak from being underfed and long abused by his captors. He was forced to lie in the pile of dead bodies until he was nearly dead himself.

When the Allies discovered the hellish pit, they began pulling the corpses out for their return home and burial. During the course of that grim chore, one soldier jumped in for a better look with a specific purpose in mind. It so happened that he had been a close friend of Philip's and now found himself simply wanting to make sure of what he was looking at.

To the man's utter amazement, the "dead" Philip Rackstraw was still alive. He was also, by that point, severely traumatized and in shock—but alive, indeed.

Philip required a very long time to heal. Most of his family acknowledged that he was forever changed by his experience.

One constant, however, was his enormous pride in being a veteran of the American military. Both Bob and Linda Lee had been reminded often about the virtues of a military career.

Rackstraw's enlistment made the town paper, and Philip was suddenly downright proud of him.[2]

Days later, his son's name was in print again, this time touted in a coming talent show. But the guitar-playing private first class and his fellow soldier-boy Insanos decided to change their group's name to the Stormtroupers, and they quickly hit the club circuit. The quintet's military moniker, however, didn't exactly leave the Greatest Generation feeling nostalgic. Their high-and-tight haircuts weren't winning over the hippies, either. Times, they were a-changin'.[3]

A few months later, memorizing lyrics gave way to learning marching cadences, as the four underwent "advanced training" at Fort Ord and Fort Irwin, California.

The Rackstraws were also very proud of daughter Linda Lee, especially in June 1965. "I was the first one in my family to graduate high school. Bob said he would like to have been there, but he was in boot camp."[4]

No emergency leave was allowed for clan milestones.

Bob's general, however, did send him away for another emergency two months later: his green guard unit was among the thirty-nine hundred state soldiers sent to the Watts Riots in Los Angeles. He would later describe it as the single most troubling assignment he ever had in the military. It was, to Bob, more deeply disturbing than even Vietnam, especially when commanders ordered their soldiers to be prepared to shoot into the crowd.

Rackstraw may have been far from virtuous, but the angry mobs of black rioters were still Americans, he maintained more than forty years later. They lived in the same country he did, watched the same television shows, and bought the same fast food. He could not feel right about marching into their midst, ready to fire.

Many factors can spawn resentment for institutions of authority. Most of the time Rackstraw didn't need much help in that department, but he was not the only member of the California National Guard to feel uncomfortable and to wonder just exactly from whom he was taking orders—and whether he might have more in common with the people he had been sent to confront than he did with those in charge.[5]

But taken as a whole, the military was having a positive effect on Rackstraw. Three months after Watts, his love life even seemed a bit more respectable—at least from the outside, at least at first. Despite Linda Lee's urging Gail Marks to run for her life, Rackstraw married her. All of nineteen, she was the one-time second runner-up in the annual Begonia Pageant in Capitola, California.

Though Marks had been blinded by love, her stare turned steely when she confronted her new groom about the California Department of Child Support Services representative who had come to their front door. Marks knew Rackstraw had fathered a child out of wedlock in high school, but now this official claimed he'd had a second child from another mother. He was able to verbally tap dance his way out of trouble, as usual, but whether he was ever to enjoy his bride's complete trust again doesn't seem likely.[6]

Still, Marks would bear him three children. In a recent candid confession, however, she admitted enduring almost constant verbal and physical abuse: "Bob was threatening and beating me so many times—off the top of my head, I can't give a number. I was scared to death."

In the beginning, because sometimes love didn't need trust to keep the candle burning, she did her best to be an "attribute" to her ambitious young soldier.[7]

Rackstraw, meanwhile, excelled at training in advanced military techniques, such as HALO (high altitude, low opening) parachute jumping. He steadily rose through the ranks, and the all-important element of challenge was constant in his life.

In January 1967, Corporal Robert W. Rackstraw, now in the US Army Reserve, was transferred to Fort Benning, Georgia, where he attended four weeks of infantry jump school, followed by an eight-week class in demolition training at Fort Bragg, North Carolina. By September, he was taking preparatory courses for becoming a sergeant.[8]

During home leave to Santa Cruz County that year, Rackstraw loaded up his band gear and hit the road—perhaps for a nostalgic jam with former members of the Stormtroupers. But when his broken-down pickup forced him to walk for help, thieves helped themselves to his two guitars and amplifier. Rackstraw's rockin' night ended with a Sheriff's crime report, listing a loss of equipment to the tune of almost $2,000.[9]

By summer, Rackstraw had earned his reserve sergeant stripes, so he left Fort Bragg to return to his growing California family. The returning father had another agenda, however: On weekdays, he began microwave engineering classes at Cabrillo College. And on the next forty-three weekends, he practically slummed at the nearby Presidio of Monterey, training with the US Navy Reserve in scuba, underwater demolition, and weapons practice.[10]

Oddly, during this period he got himself a second social security number.[11]

During his rare downtime, Rackstraw's drinking and physical abuse continued. At one point, Marks called for reinforcements. Her two older brothers, Rulon and Donald, confronted him and warned that if the beatings didn't stop, he would have to deal with them.

On April 3, 1968, the *Santa Cruz Sentinel* revealed the miserable mother of two had had enough. In the paper's "Vital Statistics" section, where local births and weddings were happily listed, Marks's public divorce petition was explained as a case of "extreme cruelty."

One can only imagine the hell that followed. The end result was her divorce action was quietly withdrawn from the court clerk's office, without a word explaining if the acrimony had been patched up or patched over.[12]

However, there was one mother Rackstraw couldn't silence—his own. For years, the heartbroken Lucille had heard stories of her son's cheating and violent side, and she passed them on to her daughter.

"He was abusive to his wives. Not all the time, but he slapped a couple of them around," Linda Lee said.[13]

Back then, slapping was a more common marital practice behind closed doors. Weekly references to it on television, such as on the variety program *The Carol Burnett Show*, brought howls. What was happening in the Rackstraw household, though, was well beyond anyone's idea of common.

In July, Reserve Sergeant Rackstraw returned to Fort Bragg for ten weeks of classes at the renowned Special Warfare School, home of the Green Berets. His courses included 140 hours on conducting Special Forces operations and 130 hours of psychological operations.

PSYOP develops operatives who are able to analyze and manipulate information for maximum effect on a population, whether it is meant to cause confusion or win "hearts and minds." Such a population might be quite large—or very small and concentrated. The key is to influence how that population thinks, no matter its size.

Rackstraw had always practiced his own special version of PSYOP, as far as his sister was concerned. What he learned in the military, Linda Lee believed, had "only sharpened his skills." PSYOP, for good or for bad, was a highly evolved form of lying. It was the perfect graduate course for a born sociopath.[14]

While at Special Warfare School, Rackstraw couldn't help but be engrossed by the new Huey "slick," Cobra "snake," Cayuse "loach," and CH-47 "Chinook" helicopters, swarming above his head—they were combat's future and he wanted in. But to get in, he would have to leave the part-time military and commit to the regular army.[15]

Rackstraw called Gail Marks in California with his new plan and then told her that he had also joined the Green Berets. Later when he came home on leave, his wife managed to get a photograph of him posing in the distinctive Special Forces cap. Until she was told the truth during this investigation, Marks had bought his story lock, stock, and beret.[16]

Primary Helicopter School, 1968.

By the end of summer, Sergeant Rackstraw, now a member of the regular army, was enrolled in Primary Helicopter School at Fort Wolters, Texas. By the end of the five-month program, the pilot had his mind set on commanding his own airship in combat, so he headed to Fort Rucker, Alabama, to become a warrant officer. After completing four months of Advanced Flight Training on the Huey slick, Rackstraw took an additional two-week "transition course" to master the loach surveillance chopper.

On May 19, 1969, Rackstraw beamed with pride and satisfaction as his mother, who came all the way from California, attended his advanced training graduation. Following a time-honored tradition, his wife proudly pinned on his wings. Then with a salute and handshake departure from Fort Rucker, the warrant officer was ready for the ultimate testing ground: the army's new airborne war in Vietnam.[17]

Despite the turbulence that had tainted their relationship from the beginning, Gail Marks had dutifully been supportive through every promotion leading to this triumph. In many ways she had endured just as much stress as Rackstraw had in his rigorous training exercises. In some ways, she might well have endured even more—and people at the base where they lived must have heard more than enough screaming and fighting to suggest that was the case.[18]

Still, the pregnant Marks and her two girls were about to be left behind as her husband went off to a war that was raging at full force, both at home and abroad. It could not have been easy for her or her proud mother-in-law. They knew how eager Rackstraw was to face the challenge, but no one could predict how a human being would perform when faced with the ultimate test of do-or-die combat in the hot tropics.

Equally, no one could predict how a serial liar, unruly dropout, jail arsonist, drunk, con artist, sociopath, and wife-beater might react to the unyielding boot of military command.[19]

First wife pinning the warrant officer grad, 1969.

CHAPTER 4

"Airborne Bob"

JUNE 25, 1969–JUNE 21, 1971

On touchdown in Saigon, the first shock that exhausted rookie grunts faced was "the stench of Nam"—the overpowering smell of putrefying raw sewage, charcoal, and rotted fish, aggravated by the three-figure temperature. Relief came on the racing journeys to army outposts and firebases deep in War Zone C as they traveled through postcard-perfect mountains, jungles, and rice paddies, in between bomb-crater bounces and distant explosions in the Central Highlands.

The troop trucks slowed for a platoon guarding the historic French bridge at Song Be (pronounced "bay") River. Below the passage, mines surrounded the pillars to thwart sabotage, while a two-wheeled army "buffalo tank" sucked up hundreds of gallons of water for troop showers. Oblivious local fishermen and farmers, working long poles, navigated their full sampans toward markets beyond the overhanging jungles. And in the middle of the vibrant waterway, an American-flagged PCF "swift boat," deck guns manned, rumbled closer. As it passed underneath, the Brown Water Navy crew's mission revealed itself: a sleeping SEAL team, sprawled on the stern, was getting a lift to classified parts unknown.

As the grunts rolled into a raucous village, everyone's radar went up. Leather-faced store owners held up goods, a drunk defecated at curbside, "cherry girls" flashed their assets, and a kid on a garbage pile scanned for stuffed pockets while oxen hitched to a parked cart took it all in. A stone-faced gunny sergeant, catching a ride back after dropping off a court-martialed soldier, spotted the long stare of a combat-age male in a doorway's shadow—the gunny coolly leaned a finger against his M-16 trigger guard.

When the new army skytroopers were safely inside First Cavalry Division's five-square-mile firebase at Phuoc Vinh on June 25, 1969, they all did the same thing everyone in Vietnam does first thing: learn how to count days backward.[1]

To twenty-six-year-old Warrant Officer Rackstraw, however—the childhood cannon maker, glider designer, and gunslinger—this was a bad boy's nirvana. He took in the ammo piles, fuel smells, and lines of helicopter gunships on the pierced-steel-planked airfield until two F-4 Phantom jets, on full afterburners, turned heads upward. But heavy mass casualties landing at the medevac LZ (landing zone) for the Fifteenth Medical Battalion, met by exhausted stretcher bearers, were a blunt reminder that John Wayne movies were complete bullshit.[2]

In contrast, the madcap madness depicted in the 1970 film *MASH* got war just right. In between the continuous challenges, structured life, and perilous times at Phuoc Vinh, jokers kept it real—through gallows humor; unforgiving nicknames like Bugger, Babysan, Ben Gay, Mad Dog, and Chickenman; and vulgar acronyms like FNG (Fucking New Guy), FUBAR (Fucked Up Beyond All Recognition), FIGMO (Fuck It, I Got My Orders), the Green Beret mantra WETSU (We Eat This Shit Up), and the generals' favorite, REMF (Rear Echelon Mother Fuckers).

In addition, anonymous instigators would toss the proverbial poop into the nearest fan. For example, during nightly movies at the outdoor theater, regulars brought gas masks—not for the daily bunker dives during mortar or rocket attacks but because of a mystery Cobra pilot. Whenever the flyboy finished filling up his snake at a neighboring fuel pad, he'd mark his departure with the drop of a tear-gas canister or two on the film crowd.[3]

In another case, commanders routinely had trouble getting accurate data reports from their weather station. Blame that on the bad decision to assign a platoon of snipers to barracks within rifle range of the weather balloon launchings.[4]

In between alerts, grunts had a mess hall, Enlisted Men's Club, PX (post exchange and store), regular steak cookouts, and rationed beer. But nasty bastards headed out to a Jeep and truck washing spot at the runway's end called Water Hole 10, where female friendlies offered unlimited "ba-me-ba" (#33 Beer) and trouble.

A retired sergeant named Roland Hayes recalled one story on a veterans' blog. A soldier was "having a time with one of the ladies in the bushes when a helicopter flew overhead and hovered over the couple for a minute, then flew on. The chopper belonged to the battalion commander, who later in his infinite wisdom put the hole off limits. Of course, the troops were upset," but the firebase's medics claimed "this dropped clap rates to almost nothing."[5]

First Cav assigned "Rack," as they quickly christened him, to the Eleventh General Support Aviation Group. The "Ash and Trash" chopper pilots of Eleventh GS were the army's version of Uber, on call to provide immediate troop transport, surveillance, logistics assistance, resupply, and chauffer services for any commander, chaplain, dignitary, or VIP needing a lift like yesterday.[6]

Because of Rackstraw's knowledge of mechanics, however, he was diverted to the group's maintenance hangar, where a thirty-year-old warrant officer named Joe C. Schlein, a big Texas roughneck, took him on. Helicopters came to the two-story shed for avionic tune-ups, patch-ups, or a final trip to the boneyard.

Schlein—who became a chopper pilot six months before Rackstraw—already had a checkered reputation, so the two of course got along like a double-barrel shotgun.

One day at the officers' hooch bar, Schlein went ballistic on a fellow aviator, William E. Rosler. The crowd cheered as the men punched, choked, and kicked their way to the ground, rolling in the red dirt. As a witness described it, "Rosler was getting the best of it until Schlein about bit his thumb off."[7]

It's not clear if Rackstraw witnessed Schlein's nibble or heard about it through the grapevine. Regardless, the Californian had certainly been in enough fisticuffs to appreciate his mentor's desperate tactic; their future scrapes would turn the workmates into lifelong pals.[8]

In the new field of helicopter warfare, a lot of advanced training and maneuvers were mastered while ducking bullets, so that naturally meant a higher rate of combat shoot-downs and accidents. For instance, of the 750 Chinook choppers in Vietnam, more than 200 were lost.[9] But the only statistic that resonated with survivors was the number of fellow aviators they watched crash and burn. As former First Cav door-gunner Ron Ferrizzi eloquently blogged, "Even today, 45 fuckin' years later, the loss of these fine men, my friends, is a quiet rage I carry."[10]

To keep the fleet flying, Schlein and Rackstraw became prolific scavengers for spare engine parts, rotor blades, console gauges, and—well, all sorts of things. These included explosives and guns supposedly recovered from wrecked ships or the jungle. In the Bronx, luck like that came with a wink and the line "It fell off a truck."

Fellow pilot Wayne Olmstead, then twenty-one, said he flew and bunked with Rackstraw. "He was fearless, a very likeable guy if a little crazy. He always had unauthorized weapons around, like a Browning Army Rifle, AK-47s and grenade launchers (RPGs). He would also make these satchel [dynamite] charges. Joe liked the action just as much as Rack."

Olmstead said the two wayward warrant officers would regularly fly out on "freelance" missions, hunting for the enemy's hidden tunnel complexes. One excuse fed to air traffic controllers was the need for a chopper-repair test flight. When a tunnel hole was spotted, they'd land, set up a tripod machine gun, and drop in a satchel charge. One guy would mow down the stunned enemy while the other kept the airship revved up for a last-second escape.

Several vets also remembered that Rackstraw and Schlein rode around in a "hot" vehicle—and just not any vehicle.

"I heard Rack had stolen a commander's Jeep" from another division, said veteran Richard G. "Dick" Schlies.

"It was kept around the company area," admitted Olmstead. "I borrowed it a couple of times to go across base to the PX. They mounted a .50-cal machine gun on it."

Pilot Clarence Manley Jr., thirty at the time, recalled seeing "those crazy guys" during unsanctioned combat trips. "They used to take the Jeep out; I saw them at the Special Forces mountain refueling spot near Tay Ninh," twenty-five miles away from their firebase.[11]

Every day out on the flight line in front of Rackstraw's hangar, a truck dropped off a half-dozen unusual soldiers who, frankly, looked like brainiacs who memorized library books for fun. They were the army's best Morse code breakers, fondly called "ditty-boppers" (intercept operators), headed to their backseats inside three Huey slicks—all featuring an odd antenna extending out front, nicknamed the "elephant brander." As the top-secret helicopters took off, they revealed their painted names, each pirated from the title of Clint Eastwood's spaghetti western, *The Good, the Bad and the Ugly.*[12]

These elite airships of "Project Left Bank," along with a sister program featuring high-flying planes, were the most valuable intelligence-gathering resource in the Vietnam War—so valuable, the nationwide operation was kept confidential for another two decades.

Left Bank's six choppers, half with the First Cav, were stripped down to make room for cutting-edge ARDF (airborne radio direction-finding) consoles. Like cell-phone triangulation methods today, these hovering platforms functioned as signal-sniffing tracking stations, with two backseat operators working with the pilot to pinpoint and collect the hidden enemy's radio signals in the jungles below. Then in real time, a pair of

Project Left Bank Huey.

hunter-killers (a Loach surveillance helicopter and a Cobra gunship), known as a pink team, were called in to end their conversations.[13]

Twenty-one-year-old Sergeant Richard A. "Rick" Sherwood was one of the noncommissioned officers (NCOs) running Left Bank's three-room communication center at the firebase. His two dozen linguists, cryptographers, and signal personnel were protected by armed guards, barbed-wire fences, and layers of sandbags thick enough to withstand a direct hit from the enemy's artillery or rocket fire. Sherwood noted that they lived that way because they knew their adversary's capabilities. "Make no mistake, the North Vietnamese army was brilliant. And it was a nonstop chess game to find them."[14]

Even with just a half-dozen choppers working in country, Left Bank brought "stellar" success. In January 1969 alone, the crews called in six massive B-52 strikes, twelve hundred artillery rounds, and a troop insertion, resulting in three hundred enemy dead.[15]

For weeks, Rackstraw no doubt heard about the unit's achievements from the pilots themselves—all of them fellow Eleventh GS flyers—while sharing the same officers' club bar. He soon was dead set on dumping his wrenches and getting in on all the action.

As it goes with war, his opportunity came through tragedy on November 29, 1969. One of the three Left Bank airships—"The Bad," ironically—was shot down, killing all four on board, along with two more in a supporting Cobra gunship.[16]

The loss deeply impacted the unit but especially aviator Wayne Olmstead. The chief warrant officer on the downed slick, Commander Jack D. Knepp, was his mentor and friend.

"Jack taught me most everything I know about flying," reflected Olmstead. "He and I, shortly before he was killed, found the [North Vietnamese 141st] regiment out East of Song Be. We called in a pink team and later jet bombers, got 50 some kills. We [later] thought it was the same regiment that set the trap for Jack."[17]

Signal Maintenance Officer Larry E. North explained: "Our guys got bold and went low to spot an antenna, and were caught in a crossfire of 51 Cals [machine guns]. But it was said an RPG round, through the chin bubble, was what brought [Knepp] down. Fast movers were scrambled and napalmed the area to keep the classified [gear] out of enemy hands."[18]

Knepp's grieving father, apparently with deep army connections, came all the way to Phuoc Vinh to "get Jack's belongings and see where he died," recalled former Left Bank Commander Kenneth L. Overturf. "I picked him up at Hotel 3, then flew him back to the crash site." His copilot that day, Manley, said the dad's solemn moment was at seven-thousand feet.[19]

Overturf, now a sixty-nine-year-old retired lieutenant colonel, remembered the December day when the "charismatic" Rackstraw approached him to volunteer. "He came into Left Bank after the shoot-down. I met him, told him what was involved, and that it required a top-secret clearance. He said, 'I can do that.'"

Because he was already a qualified warrant officer, Rackstraw was given temporary permission to begin his classified training. And he soaked it right up. "I flew with him a few times," Olmstead said. "He was eager to learn, very capable, fearless, a natural leader."

"Great pilot," agreed Dick Schlies, who as an intercept operator, joined him on missions in the backseat.[20]

Overturf said Rackstraw followed the lead of the other Left Bank pilots by flying a "low airspeed, nap-of-the-earth reconnaissance flight, frequently hovering over suspected enemy locations to mark the sites [with smoke grenades] for helicopter gunships."[21]

Com-center NCO Sherwood noted that the classified slicks were actually supposed to be working from two to three thousand feet up—something doomed pilot Jack Knepp had known. But keeping the flyboys away from the "high risk" ground action was a losing battle.[22]

The enemy quickly adapted to the new strategy. Thomas R. McWilliams,

Commander Overturf gets decorated.

a former career Green Beret and chief warrant officer with twenty-three air medals, remembered his time in Left Bank's kill zone. "Fifty knots and fifteen-hundred feet [made us] an easy target for small arms and a lucrative target for their 51 Cal's, 23mm and RPGs."[23]

"In at least three events," noted Overturf, "the enemy detonated hand grenades and claymore mines attached in the upper branches of trees."

The red-hot missions kept Joe Schlein and his hanger maintenance crew extremely busy. Over a two-year period, five shot-up Left Bank slicks were either patched up or completely rebuilt. One of them, piloted by McWilliams, caught fire.[24]

His copilot that day was Tim McCormick, who recalled McWilliams "was flying in my right seat when we got hit with 51 calibers northwest of Tay Ninh. We had one severely wounded tech, fire in back and severely damaged flight controls. I always blamed him for that day—he just seemed to draw fire."[25]

Just six weeks later, Rackstraw's electrifying time with Left Bank came to a sudden end—not because of a battlefield incident but because of incidents back home. Army investigators researching his background for a top-secret clearance had apparently learned of his volatile times in Santa Cruz County, California. It's unknown exactly what they had uncovered— his authorship of two teenage pregnancies, the drunk driving, the fake IDs, his wife's "extreme cruelty" claim in public divorce records, or his front-page jail arson fire. Any one of them, however, would have canceled the Department of Defense security application.

Rackstraw's alerted commander was beyond livid. He had invested countless hours in highly specialized training for this SOB. Every soldier knew that the requirements for such a security authorization were stringent. The pilot had "volunteered, knowing he couldn't get clearance. When I confronted him, he was cavalier, stating, 'I'll do something else.' That made him a con man," concluded Overturf.

Suffice to say, Rackstraw didn't dwell very long on how his past had become a land mine. After his dressing down, he continued his lying, rule breaking, and pilfering.[26]

Olmstead was given a different excuse for his bunkmate's top-secret rejection: "Rack said his family had a construction company, and he drove all these out of compliance trucks [that] had a shit-load of tickets."[27]

Shortly after his mid-January 1970 reassignment to Eleventh GS maintenance, the grounded combat pilot was heading out when he bumped into his former Left Bank commander.

"Hey, Captain, wanna go jump with the ARVN [Army of the Republic of Vietnam]?"

Overturf, also a master parachutist, overruled the temptation. "Rack, you know we can't do that without Command's permission."

Rackstraw responded with a crazy-sucker grin. "Well, I'm doing it anyway!"[28]

The rebel also figured out a new way to use the guns and explosives he'd been "finding." According to both Overturf and Olmstead, he offered to share the bounty with a man from the Central Intelligence Agency. But there was one catch: if there was going to be any action, he insisted on being there. It was a deal.

"The CIA guy used to come into the company area every now and then," Olmstead said, and "Rack and Joe Schlein used to hang out with him in our Officers' Club. He was always in civilian clothes, slight of build, personable."

"Rack started going out with the guy, for days at a time," added Overturf, who saw one of their jungle departures in that stolen Jeep, "loaded with weapons, ammo and explosives."

After a few months of these off-the-book missions, the rendezvous with the agency man came to a brutal close. "Rack said the spook got caught in an ambush, his vehicle had hit a mine," said Olmstead. "He'd gotten out, but the Viet Cong tracked him down and killed him."[29]

Not long after the spy's demise, Rackstraw got wind of a company-wide inspection coming. Everyone frantically concealed their "three Ps": spare parts, pets, and porn. But Schlein and Rack had that hot Jeep with a lot of extra gear and guns and nowhere to hide any of it. Olmstead recalled their desperate move to avoid courts-martial: just before the walk-through inspection, "They loaded all of it in the Jeep, picked it up with a sling under a helicopter and dropped it into the Song Be River."[30]

The waters carried away the evidence—and inexplicably, Rackstraw's devilish behavior along with it. All of a sudden, he was striving to be the soldier his stepdad Philip had always hoped for. His boots carried a deeper sheen, his step picked up, his shaves were baby-face close, and he was volunteering for extra Eleventh GS flight runs. Had he truly decided to clean up his act? Or was another devious plan in the works? Regardless, a whole new level of the brass had their eyes on him. And that brought on his half-smile.

A war zone offers plenty of opportunities for a chopper pilot to be a good Samaritan. So during maintenance duties and routing flights, Rackstraw kept an ear open on the combat frequencies for emergencies in which he could offer his assistance with transport.

On March 1, 1970, Pentagon records reveal that Rackstraw was awarded a Distinguished Flying Cross (DFC), the nation's highest aviation award, for taking a high-risk action—presumably a rescue—where he went "above and beyond the call of duty."

On April 17, he was again recognized for courage, this time with a Silver Star for "exceptionally gallant action." During an intense Viet Cong mortar barrage and ground attack on surrounded American forces, Rackstraw "skillfully maneuvered his helicopter into the firebase and quickly completed" the vital evacuation of several wounded soldiers.[31]

Riding the wave of these brave acts, he was sought after and appointed to be the pilot for Brigadier General Robert M. Shoemaker, the assistant division commander of the First Cavalry. And as such, he was branded with a new nickname: "Airborne Bob."[32]

Within days, he was side by side with his superior in the hovering command-and-control aircraft. Sitting behind them were a lieutenant colonel, a major, and an NCO master sergeant, feverishly working a stack of com-center radios as the division moved forward in "Operation Rock-crusher." This was part of President Richard Nixon's historic "big push" into Cambodia, one of the more aggressive and divisive expeditions of the Vietnam War.[33]

May 1 began with the crackling thunder of a massive B-52 bombardment. Rackstraw observed as thirty-six of the long-distance jets unleashed more than seven hundred tons of bombs, followed by artillery fire and fighter-bomber strikes. Then fifteen thousand US and South Vietnamese troops, backed by tanks and choppers of every kind, moved across the neutral nation's shattered border for what would become a two month-long "incursion."[34]

General Shoemaker pointed out an American armored unit pushing through; then he ordered Rackstraw to land. On touchdown, the troops cheered as the commander ran their way. Like "Old Blood and Guts" General Patton, he believed in surprise morale boosters.[35]

Left Bank, of course, was heavily involved in all the action. "We'd been gathering intel for a couple of months," recalled Olmstead. "You've never seen so many helicopters in the air at one time."[36]

Former Green Beret McWilliams was among the sorties. "Air traffic was so heavy at Quan Loi [refueling] Base, the [lone] air traffic controller announced on the guard frequency, 'Attention all aircraft, the airfield is now closed. Land and depart at your own risk.' He then left the tower!"[37]

Olmstead said his copilot, Jules F. "Buzz" Mier, suddenly pointed at their excited operators. "The enemy radio was going wild. The guys in the back were plotting a strange configuration of signals, and we realized there were enemy transmissions around a square perimeter, about a klick [.62 miles] or more. So we called for pink teams, and as soon as they were in, they called for blue teams [ground troops]. We had found the largest cache of arms, ammunition and supplies ever found by the 1st Cav. The brass [later] called us in and gave Buzz and I a Distinguished Flying Cross," said Olmstead.[38]

It was his second. But everything wasn't always medals and WETSU.

Rackstraw's First Cavalry Division (Airmobile).

A few weeks after the operation's start, an exhausted Rackstraw was shaken awake in his hooch by General Shoemaker's aide. Olmstead overheard the bad news: one of the isolated firebases established in Cambodia had been hit by a massive ground attack in the middle of the night. The commander wanted to go up there and buck up the survivors.

Never mind the danger of putting one of the war's top leaders in the middle of a hornet's nest. This was also the time of year with the I-can't-see-my-own-hand variety of morning fog. But that's why Shoemaker recruited "fearless" Airborne Bob.

Taking off before dawn, they climbed out over the pea soup, which disappointingly stretched for close to fifty miles. Rackstraw got on a frequency for a flight-plan briefing, but it was short: the outpost, on top of a strategic jungle mountain, was in the same weather boat. And he could forget about air traffic controllers guiding him in; all they had was a young radio operator standing by with "a portable radar unit."

As the arriving Rackstraw started his circling descent, the radar man below kept reporting his position and altitude. The blinded pilot wondered, could he trust this kid? What if the enemy started firing wildly toward his noisy, defenseless airship? Sweating profusely, he concentrated on the instruments for both focus and solace.

After what seemed like forever, and just as he'd talked himself into pulling out, they broke clear of the fog—thirty yards above the base. Rackstraw was totally drenched, but the stone-cool Shoemaker never said a word. That was likely because of what lay before him.

The enemy's bodies were stacked everywhere like cordwood; others were twisted like pretzels in the collapsed barbed wire. The only difference between them and the surrounded American soldiers was a pulse. The general shook his head and put on his game face.

In Olmstead's retelling, he called his bunkmate's "heroics" worthy of a DFC.[39]

Rackstraw's bond with Shoemaker over the months became so strong that, on a rest and relaxation (R&R) break in Hawaii, he and his flown-in spouse, Gail Marks, were invited to join the general and his wife, Tute, for a private dinner.[40]

Shortly after the Hawaiian break, an article about Rackstraw's March Distinguished Flying Cross award appeared on the front page of his California hometown paper, the *Santa Cruz Sentinel*.[41] On the surface, the May 17, 1970, feature with his picture looked like any other Pentagon-planted press release, touting a local boy's natural-born leadership skills and courage.

But when a copy of the forty-five-year-old story was scrutinized in the context of what is now known to be the truth of Rackstraw's Vietnam history, investigatorial alarms went off. First, the paper didn't use a standard headshot with a flag background but a private photo from a formal army ball—with Rackstraw's arm-in-arm dance partner scissored out. Then the puff piece itself was filled with unprofessional hyperboles, flat-out lies, and even (at the time) classified information.

It stated that the hero, still in the war zone, was "one of only a few Army fliers authorized to wear three sets of wings—those of the American Special Forces, Vietnamese paratrooper and Army aviator." There were two glitches with that claim: the Special Forces have no such medal, and Rackstraw's jump with the Vietnamese had not been authorized.

The most disturbing passage, though, dealt with Rackstraw's short time with "Left Bank, a top security organization," specifying that "it was his job to make low-level flights over known enemy [radio] positions, pinpointing locations" for gunships. Then his March DFC award was linked to action with the unit. An alleged citation "notes Rackstraw's 'courage and devotion to duty under the most arduous conditions' have provided the Army with a valuable intelligence source for finding and destroying the enemy."

This investigation tracked down his former unit commander to confirm this claim. Ken Overturf was unswerving: "Rackstraw was not awarded any medals for valor during his time with Project Left Bank."[42]

Never mind that Pentagon records claim this DFC action occurred six weeks after he was kicked out of Overturf's operation.[43]

None of that kept him from gilding the lily when he evidently wrote and planted this bogus ego piece in the *Sentinel*. Fortunately, this tiny paper's article never reached the wires, so Left Bank remained a deep war secret until the 1990s. Still, the program's former NCO, Rick Sherwood, was asked for his thoughts on the print story. "Whoever did this, it was flat-out treasonous. Back then, we would've hung him by his thumbs."[44]

The new and improved Rackstraw who emerged after the Song Be River Jeep dumping and all his bonafide heroics that followed appear, in context, to be components of a sociopath's scheme.

He was no doubt enraged when his army career path to top-secret clearance was derailed by his documented youthful transgressions.[45] But when the Eleventh GS base inspection popped up, Rackstraw apparently realized his current company crimes and misdemeanors would lead army investigators back to that Santa Cruz past, all neatly summarized now in a Pentagon file. This time, though, the combination of both might get him booted.

After the deep-sixing of his present troubles, he had an epiphany: the way to bury his past for good was to flood editors with good news—like reports of medals, citations, and promotions. Besides, becoming the next Audie Murphy had side benefits: war heroes got girls, cuts in line, free beer, ripped-up speeding tickets, complimentary dinners, crowd recognition, and most significant, post-army job offers.

That *Sentinel* clipping, as future incidents would document, became Bob's golden parachute.[46]

On June 1, 1970, at the rank of chief warrant officer 2, Rackstraw once again made aerial history. He was awarded another Distinguished Flying Cross (First Oak Leaf Cluster) for "exceptionally valorous action."

When he overheard on his slick's radio that a surrounded brigade commander was in danger of falling into the hands of the Viet Cong, Rackstraw volunteered for a rescue mission. With the "firebase receiving heavy enemy mortar and rocket fire," the pilot "carefully guided his aircraft into the base and safely lifted the general from the area."[47]

Three months later, Airborne Bob left Vietnam for a stateside military assignment. He had become one of the most valued flyboys in the war, and of the fifty decorations he received in the fifteen-month tour, thirty-six were air medals.

On his September 21, 1970, return to Fort Rucker, Rackstraw received a plum test-pilot job, with a royal title to boot: chief of the technology analysis section for Army Aviation. He also received a direct commission to first lieutenant and a new ID photo—which, forty-six years later, would play a key part in this investigation.[48]

Gail Marks and the three children joined their rising star in residence.[49]

By 1971, the ever self-improving Rackstraw decided to apply to become certified by the Federal Aviation Administration (FAA) to fly commercial helicopters and to give fixed-wing aircraft instruction. The accreditations would, effectively, be a backup plan should anything ever go wrong with his military career—not that he had any intention or desire to leave the army.[50]

In the middle of all this flight training and testing, he also found time to teach scuba classes on the weekends in nearby Pensacola, Florida.[51]

His long-suffering and often bruised wife, by this time, had her own ideas about the foreseeable future. Marks was disgusted and disillusioned. Some might call her husband Airborne Bob, but her own opinion came closer to that of wiser souls who thought of him as "Bullshit Bob."[52] She didn't want the rest of her life to be full of the kinds of lies, bullying, beatings, and other abuse that had characterized her marriage thus far. Instead of improving, it had become worse—as had his drinking—after his return from the war.

By the time the couple settled in at Fort Rucker, the exhausted Marks had endured years of his throwing and breaking keepsakes in anger and then tearing phone wires out of the walls so she couldn't call for help. She lived in fear every day that this time, this beating would be the one she couldn't survive.[53]

But all of that was only a prelude to the intolerable day, in February 1971, when Rackstraw was literally choking her over the kitchen sink— his face and eyes red with rage—in full view of their two screaming girls and a one-year-old baby boy. He could easily have murdered her, Marks knew, but in truth, the dynamic between wife beaters and their victims is often more about power than the desire to kill. Choking her was a means for him to establish and keep dominance, to be feared and therefore, in his view, respected. To

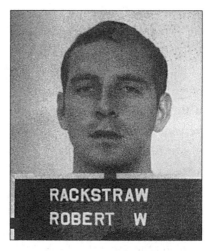

Rackstraw's Army ID in 1970, taken fourteen months before the hijacking.

do it in front of the children was to extend that dominance and power—in effect, to spread the influence.

When Marks sat down with the military police at Fort Rucker, the inclination to overlook the physical abuse of military wives was far more prevalent than it is today. But Rackstraw's commanding officer had become aware of the situation, and he insisted that Marks and the kids be taken to his own residence, where his wife and military guards personally stood between them and anything Rackstraw might try to do.

The report of this choking incident apparently triggered a discreet army investigation that would go on for many weeks, during which time the accused was stripped of his post at Army Aviation and put on special assignment to an executive officer—as one official with knowledge put it, that meant "he was the general's driver."[54] Meanwhile, the commander advised Marks in the strongest possible terms to end her marriage and leave, saying she would be safest if she were far away from her husband.

Marks did encounter Rackstraw one last time in Alabama. When she returned with an escort to the base trailer they lived in to pack up, she told her glum, soon-to-be-ex-husband, "This is all your fault, Bob." With guards nearby, there was—this time—nothing he could say or do.[55]

She headed back to Santa Cruz County, California, with the couple's three young children who had seen far too much. They were strapped securely into their car seats in the couple's VW fastback for the long trip.

Marks's ordeal would not end in tidy fashion, however. After five days on the road, she and the children were jarred awake in a motel room in Burbank, California, during the horrific magnitude 6.6 San Fernando earthquake. The temblor brought Los Angeles, the nation's second largest urban area, to a commercial standstill. Unable to find formula for her baby boy, the exhausted mother was forced to feed him chocolate milk. Desperate to find a way out, in a moment of inspiration Marks went looking for a very specific type of gas station—one frequented by truckers.

As luck would have it, she not only found one before long but also met a sympathetic driver who was willing to help. He told her to follow him and do exactly what he did. He promised to have her heading up the coast in no time.

She drove behind his eighteen-wheeler some twenty-five miles from Burbank to the Pacific Coast Highway, all through clogged surface streets. Many local freeways were impassable and far too dangerous in the aftermath of the quake. It had, all told, been an agonizingly long day, but Marks and her three little Rackstraws were finally headed north on Highway 101.

Somewhere along that famed coastal road, Marks found a pay phone and called her parents to assure them that she and the kids were all right.[56]

Four months later at Fort Rucker, on the very same day that he was certified for commercial helicopter and fixed-wing instruction, Rackstraw got the paperwork for the divorce Marks had filed for.[57]

Then, on June 21, a flood of past deceptions caught up with the twenty-seven-year-old Rackstraw.

The military had questioned everything about the lieutenant. It had been discovered that he had never attended either the University of Southern California or San Jose State University, let alone graduated from one, as he had claimed. In fact, Rackstraw had not even finished high school. What's more, it was established that he had lied numerous times about his military rank and exaggerated the number of medals he had earned.[58]

These sobering truths must have sent ripples of concern through the institution that had trained him—much of the training equal to what is given to their most elite members—because it had, in effect, prepared a chronic, devious liar to be a daunting, possibly dangerous officer. And yet he'd earned his otherwise unlikely rank for achievements in battle.

When Linda Lee heard about her brother's deception—and she only heard years later because he certainly wasn't going to admit the shameful truth to anybody—she wasn't particularly surprised. She knew Rackstraw hadn't graduated from high school. The fake college degrees were just another example of her brother's ability to fabricate whatever he needed out of thin air. It was one more big lie, told with a straight and charming face, only this time to the United States Army instead of a gullible girl.[59]

After seven years of otherwise "gallant and valorous" service to his nation, Rackstraw's record was indelibly stained. He was now a documented con artist, he was compelled to resign in shame from the military career he loved for "conduct unbecoming an officer."

Official documents reveal he received a general discharge under honorable (as in below honorable) conditions, which two county officials, years later, would characterize in his court records as "less than honorable."[60]

An army attorney explained that a general discharge is usually given to soldiers who "have engaged in minor misconduct or have received non-judicial punishment under Article 15 of the Uniform Code of Military Justice."[61]

The biting words of a testifying army superior, read in a Stockton, California, courtroom, branded Rackstraw "one of the two worst lieutenants I have ever seen. His leaving the Army is a great asset to the service."[62]

Rackstraw no doubt had been infuriated about his expulsion—a man bearing a grudge. The day after his booting, the disgraced army liar immediately stopped making payments on his leased car, packed up his belongings, and then took off for the Pacific Northwest, not bothering to let his extended California family know where he was going. As he would at other times in his life when the shame apparently was too great—or was it that defeat seemed overwhelming?—he simply vanished.

The sheriff of Houston County, Alabama, filed a felony warrant for "criminal fraud" against Rackstraw as a result of the abandonment of the car lease agreement. But the fallen officer had already put Fort Rucker in his wake, having decided to use his pilot qualifications to get work in Washington State.

As he would explain years later, his plan was to start a "light plane service for realtors" in the Northwest, enabling them to have aerial photography done to show off their prime properties.[63]

One might argue that it was also the perfect way for the disgruntled pilot to take a thorough, bird's-eye look around the rugged, heavily forested mountains between Portland and Seattle while formulating a bold and grand plan. It was an opportunity to exhaustively survey some of the harshest terrain anywhere in the United States—and analyze what possibilities might be at hand if "someone" were someday to perform a daring, dangerous parachute jump directly into the wilderness around the Columbia River.

The FBI did not learn of Rackstraw's warrant for skipping car payments or the Washington plane service until 1978[64]—seven years after a hijacking in the same location and time frame. At that moment, they became aware of Robert Wesley Rackstraw for a variety of other criminal actions.[65]

CHAPTER 5

Baron Norman de Winter, Grifter

JULY 16, 1971–NOVEMBER 23, 1971

Patty Mott, widow of James C. "Jim" Mott, a strapping six-foot-four-inch former tackle and captain of the Oregon State Beavers football team, sat in her home reminiscing over old pictures. Seven months after Jim had succumbed to leukemia, her smile had returned. She reached into their dusty photo cabinet for another handful of memories—and that's when two envelopes fell to the floor.

It took only moments for Patty to recognize the signatures of "le Baron Norman de Winter," a man her husband had warned her about. And the letters' existence confirmed the biggest secret shame of Jim's hometown of Astoria.[1]

Looking back on it, many of the good folks in the Columbia River town acknowledge that they should have suspected something sooner. For example, some might have taken notice of the stranger's name: Baron de Winter was a gallant character that rode with the heroes in Alexandre Dumas's celebrated novel *The Three Musketeers*.[2]

On July 16, 1971, a man claiming to be a Swiss noble walked into their midst, picking this historic mining, lumber, and fishing town over all others. Delightful and friendly, de Winter, who many described to be in his early thirties, seemed intent on knowing everyone in the community of ten thousand, and he seemed to show up everywhere. Smoother than an elixir salesman, he claimed to have "come to America to walk with the people"—phony European accent and all.[3]

Paul "P. K." Hoffman was a twenty-eight-year-old pottery sculptor, working his vender booth at the semiannual Astoria sidewalk sale, when the easygoing visitor in a suit coat and turtleneck strolled up to admire some of his signature giant clay pots. Without batting an eye, de Winter ordered almost a dozen of the three-foot-wide pieces to be made for his chalet in Switzerland, saying that he would return in a couple of weeks to check on the order. The baron also shared that when it was time to return home, the items needed to be loaded onto his private plane, parked at the town's unsupervised runway.

Hoffman was speechless. The baron's commission would be worth thousands of dollars, his largest ever. With a deep desire to celebrate the fact, the ceramic artist ran joyously into a bar to share the news with a friend, twenty-four-year-old manager Pete Roscoe—a future town councilman and renowned restaurateur.[4]

Subsequent investigation indicated that de Winter's aircraft on the runway was the same plane Rackstraw used to visit his parents at their new home in Valley Springs, California, a small Calaveras County town, population fifteen hundred, in the remote Sierra Nevada foothills. Rackstraw would head there or visit his sister, Linda Lee, in nearby Stockton whenever he pleased—sometimes back in Astoria by nightfall, sometimes not seen for two or three days.[5]

It is believed that, during de Winter's two week absence from Astoria, on July 23, 1971, the isolated National Guard Armory in the town of Santa Cruz, California—the very training facility where Rackstraw's seven-year military career began—was hit by a well-planned and perfectly executed after-hours bombing and burglary. At the time local guardsman Joe Hansmann entered the armory the next afternoon on routine business, the destroyed room had still not been discovered. Hansmann found that a piece of a pipe bomb had penetrated a natural gas line.

As for the burglary, authorities realized that the strategy had been to ruin the communications center within the armory but leave the ammo locker unharmed. Based on the damages, the perpetrators—it had to be more than one person—had resorted to sledgehammers, pickaxes, and chisels to attack the larger target, a walk-in weapons safe.

A "huge cache" of M-1 rifles, .45-caliber pistols, machine guns, and grenade launchers had been completely cleaned out. To the present, the crime has not been solved, although for several years after the incident, the FBI considered Robert Rackstraw a prime suspect. One could argue that his inflamed post military-ire fit was a good match for a motive.[6]

Adding to the evidence piling up and pointing to the disgraced veteran, his sister, Linda Lee, remembered that at the time of the armory bombing, her stepfather, Philip, told her, "Somebody's looking for Bob, so don't tell anybody he's here." It wasn't the first time she remembered Philip lying for her brother, and it did not escape her notice that "in that time period" her brother would "come and go" from their parents' new home base in Valley Springs—just one hundred fifteen flying miles (or thirty minutes) from the National Guard Armory.[7]

On the other end of the commute between Valley Springs and Astoria, it had not even begun raising eyebrows that few ever saw Baron Norman de Winter during the daytime.

P. K. Hoffman's mood was still buoyant when, two weeks later as promised, the bloviating baron visited his studio to watch him working at his kiln and see how the order was progressing. That was the last time Hoffman ever saw Baron Norman de Winter. The artist still has two of the unsold pots (along with this photo, taken at the time by Pete Roscoe) which serve as a daily reminder of a

Artist P. K. Hoffman makes custom-ordered pots for Baron de Winter and learns a valuable lesson.

lesson absorbed the hard way: "That's how I learned to get a third down," says Hoffman.[8]

Wilfred P. "Willy" Wyffels, at the time the twenty-nine-year-old assistant pastor at Astoria's Saint Mary Catholic Church, found de Winter to be agreeable enough when he walked into the rectory that summer. The confidence man explained that he had departed his native Switzerland without any of his money, his belongings, or the support of the "chalet staff" that was waiting patiently for him to return.

When the baron asked for confession, Father Wyffels proceeded with the sacrament of penance. But instead of offering a formal tell-all account, de Winter just gabbed on and on. Finally out of breath, the visitor appeared to be grateful for their (one-way) discussion, even moved—telling the young priest that, in return, he'd "really like to do something nice" for the congregation.

Wyffels probably didn't think too much of the offer until de Winter expanded on his idea, making a promise to charter an entire passenger jet for his planned flight home in December so all of the parishioners could enjoy a wonderful snow-filled holiday at his beautiful lodge in the Swiss Alps, absolutely free.

Father Wyffels was captivated by de Winter. He made a point of talking to many of the prominent church members about the nice visitor, especially his generous air-travel proposal. The priest even alerted his own parents—they, too, had been invited.[9]

De Winter didn't keep his festive Christmas flight plan a privately shared secret with the assistant pastor. For the next three months, the charmer literally showed up on people's doorsteps around Astoria, eager to make their acquaintance. His capacity to weave stories and anecdotes about life in the Swiss Alps seemed inexhaustible. The good people of the town ate it all up—taking turns to invite him to break bread, raise a glass, and then put him up for the night.[10]

Marian K. Soderberg, a lifelong town resident who had once hosted de Winter (she was married to Jim Mott's second cousin at the time), was less impressed than most. When a "totally enamored" local bachelor brought the garrulous baron into her home, Soderberg, a counselor, "could see through this guy." And to her, it seemed that part of his act was to appear gay.

Another guest, attending the same late-August dinner with Soderberg's best friend, offered a similar if less eloquent opinion of the flamboyant de Winter: "He was so full of shit."

Being in the minority though, these two kept quiet. Between wine and multiple courses, de Winter waxed on about his Swiss servants, his small plane parked at the airstrip, and of course his now-famous promise to fly everyone home for the holidays.

But when he brought up that closer, he didn't expect the response of Soderberg's excited girlfriend: she happened to be a manager for Pan Am Airlines and would be happy to make the arrangements for his airline charter trip. For a brief moment, de Winter froze—then he flashed an ear-to-ear grin. Hearing just enough about his far-off hometown and financial state of affairs, the girlfriend promised to bring this to the attention of her carrier's marketing department.[11]

The travel discussions were also enough to make everyone start updating their passports.

Astoria's former mayor, Willis Van Dusen, was eighteen years old then, but he still remembers the town's growing excitement. His parents told de Winter they'd actually be in Europe at the time and wondered if it was okay to pay a visit. The baron smiled and stated, "I'll alert the household for your arrival."[12]

Since that day, members of the Van Dusen clan have used his pronouncement to satirically welcome anyone planning to come over.

In a letter written to football player Jim Mott on September 16, de Winter brought up the coming yuletide vacation as a thank-you for the generosity he'd found in the athlete's hometown. "To express my gratitude, a most excellent holiday is now prepared," he gushed.

A month earlier, Mott had showed de Winter around the woods of nearby Washington State during a pre–hunting season scouting trip for elk. The baron later referenced that hike in another note postmarked in September, writing that he had returned "to the property we had observed together."

They have given a most beautiful expression to us. To express my gratitude a most excellent holiday is now prepared. The months will pass and years, not my treasure of great price. At the proper moment shall I come to share all the wonderful peace that is now mine.

Thank you mon ami walk in truth and love.

Au revoir et bon chance

Le Baron de Winter

Norman

Norman de Winter's Christmas invitation letter to Jim Mott of Astoria, 1971.

Considering de Winter claimed his only mode of transportation was his plane, the view must have been wheels-up spectacular. "A herd of elk were present and elegant. Indeed the place will be most suitable," he wrote, presumably referring to the start of Mott's hunting season.

But de Winter's main interest, as would later become clear, was in a quarry other than elk.

The baron's September letters were written after the nineteen-year-old footballer had gone 171 miles south to Oregon State University (OSU) in Corvallis for his sophomore year. In effect, the grifter was laying the social groundwork for a future move.

Mott was not the only Astorian to accompany de Winter on rustic forays. As the traveler wrote in his September 2 letter to Mott, he had just enjoyed the company of Mott's second cousin: "This week David Palmberg has shared two wonderful days with me. We have worked together upon his dredge in the state of Washington."[13] According to Palmberg, their work trip to the Skagit River in Mount Vernon was to deliver equipment to the docked boat. De Winter only asked for food and a hotel room. On the three-hour drive though, he attempted to persuade Palmberg to bring his pregnant wife, Marian, along on the coming holiday flight.

Marian added that de Winter even suggested they have their first baby, later to be named Darren, in Switzerland "so he could have dual citizenship."

While appreciative of de Winter's help and vacation offer, Palmberg sensed that something was not quite right. "I was always like, 'I can't fully trust him,'" he said.

The baron also left a trail of flowery missives with this couple. Palmberg still has a forty-five-year-old enveloped card thanking him and Marian profusely for hosting his private dinner. "You have given a great treasure. My blessing I give you and every thought is of courage to your excellence."

In addition, de Winter left a copy of James Allen's classic, *As a Man Thinketh*, for Palmberg—with a cursive message on the first page: "Mon Ami (my friend), thank you for your excellent friendship and delightful life."[14]

Was Allen's inspirational 1903 essay, professing the power of thought to increase personal capabilities, a favorite of de Winter's? If so, the baron no doubt appreciated the last stanza of the book's opening: "He thinks in secret, and it comes to pass: Environment is but his looking-glass."[15]

In the last week of September, de Winter joined a hundred workers in overalls at Astoria's Union Fish Company when the gill-net crews dumped their seasonal salmon onto the wharf. While most were tasked with cutting and canning, our stranger was one of two selected to slice out the head cheeks—a fresh delicacy in restaurants and world markets.

While showing de Winter the ropes, Mark Fick, then nineteen, said his new coworker claimed "to be in a royal family, working several jobs" to bond with the common man. The bogus blue blood also crowed that he planned to "save the clothes" from each assignment as a reminder of his American adventure sans silver spoon.[16]

In between harbor shifts, de Winter couch-surfed at the apartment of twenty-four year-old John Mattingly, a generous new bar buddy. He recently recollected that the guest preferred lounging "in a robe, sandals, and beads."[17]

Jeff A. Salo, then nineteen, remembered Fick and de Winter coming over one day to shoot "hoops" with his neighbors. The accented stranger offered to take all the teen basketball players not only to Europe for Christmas but to the '72 Munich Olympics as well.[18]

To the con artist, they were fish in a barrel.

Early in de Winter's visit, bar manager Pete Roscoe tagged along with "the baron" and some locals for a midnight munchies run to a twenty-four-hour diner on the harbor docks.

According to Roscoe, de Winter ordered a fish-stick sandwich and then, with a straight face and bad accent, asked the waitress for some "*sauce de tar-tair*"—eliciting a laugh from all.

There were also de Winter's grand entrances at town saloons, witnessed by the already suspicious Roscoe on more than one occasion. At a joint called the Recreation Tavern, de Winter would routinely carry over pitchers of beer and bags of chips to a table of surprised strangers, declaring "Beer for everyone!"

Trouble was, when it came to paying, "he'd pull out a hundred-dollar bill, which no small-town bartender in 1971 could readily break," Roscoe said. The incidents always ended with captivated locals volunteering to cover for the "embarrassed" de Winter.

After Roscoe witnessed the same ploy a second time in the same saloon, he started to avoid de Winter—and the con man sensed it. As a result, he never met Roscoe's eyes again.

Roscoe ironically now owns that bar and restaurant, which he renamed Fulio's. It was there that humiliated residents, for the first time, chose to tell the story of de Winter to a man named Robert C. "Pudgy" Hunt in

2011. That put Hunt in a uniquely good position to help connect some rather disparate dots.[19]

In the course of sharing many personal details of his life with the residents of Astoria, the baron was often humiliated to admit that he had grossly underestimated the high cost of vacationing in America. Pete Roscoe said when de Winter's hosts for the evening, by then utterly hooked, would hear this awful news, they'd inevitably offer to loan him money. Usually he needed a few hundred. For some time, all the folks who helped him out would keep it quiet, lest the aristocrat be humiliated in public.

In this way, de Winter flitted from foyer to foyer, swindling and bilking at least two hundred victims, according to former mayor Van Dusen.[20]

By the time the gullible people of Astoria finally began talking to each other about the baron and his tendency to leave their homes a somewhat wealthier man than he had been upon arriving, it was late September. De Winter didn't have to be the grifter extraordinaire to notice that some admiring gazes he'd cultivated over the last couple of months had begun turning to steely stares.

Then Pan Am got back to Marian Soderberg's girlfriend with "absolutely humiliating" news: a discreet airline inquiry had found de Winter "was not real, a total phony." In no time, faces turned red with shame and rage.[21]

The baron, however, was a step ahead of the torch bearers. At the airfield, it was found he had already untied his plane and taken off.[22]

Several Astoria residents now believe the con artist in their midst was none other than Robert Wesley Rackstraw. When shown his military ID photo, taken nine months before his general discharge, along with rare news footage shot in 1979, Wyffels, Roscoe, and Mott (a year before he died) vigorously declared that the man they were looking at was, as Roscoe put it, the "slick" de Winter.[23]

The discharged Rackstraw had come to the Pacific Northwest during the exact same time frame as the baron—not for a vacation but for aerial survey work—which could explain why de Winter was rarely seen during the day.

In that same late September, Linda Lee was somewhat surprised to hear that her brother had shown up again at her mom and dad's place in Valley Springs, California, without warning or explanation. But that was normal for him, as was his tendency to take off again without notice or fanfare, essentially using his parents' remote home as his crash pad.

One thing that struck the family was that after years of excelling in the armed service, Rackstraw suddenly had nothing good to say about the army. He made it clear that he believed the brass took advantage of people and that he had become disillusioned with the whole system. He referred to it as "politics as usual," Linda Lee recollected years later. He said the military loved to blame people for events that weren't fair or true, and that his superiors had an agenda that he just didn't fit into.

Linda Lee had never heard that he had been disgraced and forced to resign and would not know why for many years. She thought he had simply quit in disgust.

He also threw out the excuse that because Vietnam was winding down, the army was trying to get rid of people. That, of course, was untrue. But Rackstraw was always one for volunteering information. "He would do that a lot . . . volunteer lies when he didn't have to," said Linda Lee. The truth was that the war was going full blast in 1971, and it dragged on for another four years.[24]

This was Rackstraw's modus operandi: blame someone else. He always had a reason for life not going his way, for failures. He also always had a tough time staying the course on anything he did. It was a pattern that would continue throughout his life because, Linda Lee observed, he really didn't know how to make something work. He'd have great ideas, he'd be resourceful and get himself into apparently good situations, and then everything would just fall apart.

Gail Marks shared her assessment, and it was succinct: "Bob was a jack of all trades but didn't stay a master of anything." From career goals to business start-ups to personal relationships, that indeed proved to be an overwhelming, self-destructive flaw.[25]

Rackstraw had come to his parents' home fixated on the idea of taking his two little girls with him to Disneyland. He pressured Linda Lee to persuade Marks, who had resettled in Santa Cruz County, to let the sisters go on a trip with their daddy. Until he began lobbying for the outing, Linda Lee hadn't seen much of him, hearing the latest "Bob news" mainly from their parents, particularly their mom. But Linda Lee sensed a strange kind of urgency, a real need on his part to get her help so he could take his girls, who were then four and five years of age.

Only twenty-four at the time herself, Linda Lee didn't mind the idea of an all-expenses-paid trip to Disneyland, courtesy of her big brother, who was surprisingly flush with cash. Of course, she suspected—correctly, no doubt—that he was only including her to look after her two little nieces, since he knew nothing about childcare and had demonstrated no interest in learning. Perhaps Rackstraw felt a need to feel as if he had done right by his daughters, that he had not been the entirely blameworthy monster that Marks had made him out to be.

A few days later, Linda Lee memorialized the Magic Kingdom adventure with two photos of the girls, smiling from daddy's lap—both date-stamped October 1971.

One hallmark of Rackstraw's life as a master of misdirection and disinformation was the truths he didn't tell, didn't volunteer, and never would.

Bob and daughters at Disneyland, 1971.

Case in point, he never told Linda Lee exactly how or where he might have gotten the money to pay for the expensive journey, the airline tickets to Los Angeles, and the hotel stay.[26] He no doubt knew that she would not understand and that it would not make him look good in her eyes. He would never be able to convince her that all those rich, smug people of Astoria were self-satisfied and superior. He would never get her to appreciate that they deserved what they got.

It didn't surprise Linda Lee to hear from her parents, as she did in that second week of October 1971, that her brother was gone again.[27]

With Disneyland behind him and the kids back at home with their mother, Rackstraw turned his attention northward again. Norman de Winter had a bit more to do before he was permanently retired from Rackstraw's stable of personas.

"He always had a reason [to leave]. He was 'working with a buddy.' He was 'going to see a buddy.' He was 'up north,'" Linda Lee recalled.

Before he left, however, he let the family in on how he was "flying an airplane for some real estate guy." For Rackstraw—ordinarily a man of mystery—that was an exceptionally specific report.[28]

In the meantime, another kind of misdirection proved a boon for the disgruntled former chopper pilot. The FBI had captured and arrested Charles Noell Hess, twenty-nine, of Salinas, California, with a trove of sixteen machine guns, forty-seven .45-caliber automatics, and a grenade launcher— all of which, of course, had been stolen from Santa Cruz's National Guard Armory, more than two months prior. The convicted cocaine dealer later pleaded guilty to receiving the stolen arms for resale. The location of the remaining weapons, let alone the name of the heist mastermind, was never revealed. The FBI, however, had a good hunch, and agents let Rackstraw's ex-wife, several of his coworkers, and the local police know it.[29]

Jim Mott, living off-campus in his second fall semester at OSU, had been exchanging letters with Norman de Winter in Astoria for the full month of September. So the sophomore was both surprised and flattered to get a telephone call, that second week of October, from his wandering

Swiss pen pal. De Winter explained that, as luck would have it, he happened to be in the area and wanted to drop in.

Corvallis also "just happened" to be another town with an unsupervised World War II airstrip and a wealth of honest, honorable, gullible residents.

Mott was not up to date on the sad turn of events that had transpired in Astoria, so he happily gave de Winter directions to his boarding home, which was walking distance from the university stadium. After the thick-accented confidence man sauntered in, Mott introduced his four roommates, all fellow athletes—crewmember Mike Belnap, cross-country runner Brian Glanville, and teammates split end Greg Mobley and defensive end Tom Oswald. Running on all eight of his BS cylinders, de Winter quickly got acquainted with everybody in the house and, in exchange for a few odd jobs and cooking at night, charmed his way into a five-week, scot-free stay.

Just as in Astoria, de Winter's hosts saw nothing of him during the daytime, but when they returned home in the evening, the affable "Swiss storyteller" would be waiting with drink in hand, ready for a good meal or a trip to town, then a good night's sleep. This went on until the Friday before Thanksgiving 1971, at which point de Winter suddenly—and without so much as a word or thank-you note to his kindhearted OSU roomies—walked out the door and vanished. He even left behind his personal belongings, which the irked Mott put "in storage."[30]

Not that he went very far.

At the corner of Northwest Tyler Avenue and Northwest 21st Street, almost a mile and a half away from Mott's home, de Winter spotted a jam-packed and noisy college party going on in a second-floor apartment and crashed it. Becoming part of the crowd inside building manager Fred Jaross's own pad was no problem for Euro-smoothie Norman de Winter. In an odd coincidence, Jaross happened to be a football teammate of Jim Mott.

Even more coincidental, two years before Norman de Winter arrived in Corvallis, both Bob Rackstraw and Fred Jaross had been stationed at Fort Rucker, Alabama—from May through June 1969—within a mere few hundred yards of one another at different helicopter hangars. It was nothing but luck that the two had never met, because if they had, Norman de Winter would've been forced to leave that party in a hurry.

Jaross recently described Norman as "an eccentric guy with a bad accent," implying that he didn't think the affectation was real.[31]

At one point, an inebriated young woman at the party, Gayle Downing, began flirting with de Winter. Frustrated when he didn't "reciprocate" her approach, she bluntly asked if he was gay.

Smiling broadly, de Winter said yes. Then, perhaps to offset Downing's apparent disappointment, he stayed with her for an hour. That's when he learned the reason for her bluesy bender—her boyfriend had left her for another woman. De Winter promptly gave her a shoulder to unload on.

"He said everything a brokenhearted woman would want to hear, he really did," Downing recently reflected. "For me, at twenty-one, he really was the most charming, polite person that I had ever met. I recall one of my conversations with him about me living on the Island of Hawaii for a year."

When shown Rackstraw's 1979 news interview footage, Downing's reaction was immediate: "The eyes are the same. I'm kind of an eye person, so I definitely remember eyes—and the shape of the face, I remember him.

"It's eerie to look at this and go back all these years. I'm gonna sound crazy now, but this is the first man that ever, ever in my life was so respectful and kind and courteous to me. I'm sorry, but that's the way it was. So that's the emotion coming up, at age twenty one, and now I'm sixty five, and I'm here and feeling it again."

The necklace: Norman de Winter's gift for a broken heart.

After they said their alohas that night in Corvallis, de Winter sent Downing an unexpected gift: a Hawaiian shell necklace.

"It is beautifully made and has an odd, sentimental value for me," Downing admitted. "I have almost given that away many times over the years but couldn't."[32]

Not everyone at the party was taken with Norman de Winter's pose as a gay white knight. Roxanne Jaross—Fred's girlfriend at the time and later his wife—and Dave Jaross, Fred's brother and roommate, didn't buy it. Dave didn't like the outsider at all, in fact.

When Fred awoke on Saturday morning, he found a few guests sleeping it off around the apartment—including de Winter, snoring on the couch in a nightshirt that could have come out of a Marx Brothers movie. Amused by his antics, Fred let him stay in the apartment as his guest into Thanksgiving week.

One stunt, however, almost cut the baron's slumming short.

In the middle of the night, Dave suddenly started yelling, "What are you doing? Get the hell out of my bed!"

Fred ran to the room to find his brother pushing de Winter off his king mattress. "Norman had decided he didn't like the couch. He came out of there fairly quickly," recalled the host.

On another day, Fred and Dave missed their parents' home cooking. But neither "felt comfortable" about leaving de Winter alone in the apartment, so they and Roxanne took the new roomie along for the twenty-mile ride to Lebanon, Oregon. Roxanne recollected how "very impressed" her future mother-in-law, Thelma, was with the flamboyant de Winter.

Then on November 23, the apartment couch was suddenly vacant. The roommates' guest "disappeared as quickly as he showed up," Fred said.[33]

Pete Roscoe, the man who had tracked down nine old Astoria witnesses for this investigation, wouldn't have been surprised to hear that. For him, the breaking news of the Northwest Airlines' hijacking, just a couple of hours away, was too logical to be ignored.

"I was sitting in a tavern, here in Astoria, home from the University of Oregon for Thanksgiving. And I see the sketch on TV, and I said, 'That's that guy that was here this summer. That was Norman De Winter.' And, you know, everybody [was] really [thinking], 'Oh, yeah. Right. I don't think so.'"

Roscoe contacted his mother, his sister, and his artist buddy, the unfortunate maker of big pottery, P. K. Hoffman, and suggested that Astoria's favorite absentee grifter, Baron Norman de Winter, could very well be one D. B. Cooper. But none of them bought his theory either.

"It was like a cry wolf thing, and nobody paid too much attention. I think Norman de Winter was somewhat embarrassing to some people. And because they were embarrassed, they would rather not talk about it. It's that sort of Luther and Scandinavian, 'Don't be embarrassed, don't lose face.'

"I never let this go, but I didn't pursue it. I was pursuing my life path. I didn't care—okay, he got away. You know, the FBI's gonna catch him. They don't need my help."

It would be forty years before Roscoe seriously brought his theory forward again, to far more accepting ears—some belonging to former FBI agents on a cold case team.[34]

Pete Roscoe of Astoria, Oregon, circa 2013.

The day after de Winter vanished from Corvallis, seventy-two flight miles (twenty minutes) away at Portland International Airport, a man calling himself Dan Cooper bought a ticket to Seattle on Northwest Flight 305. He hand-printed his own name on the boarding pass; he had no Swiss accent; he did have a plan.[35]

He had alluded to it, perhaps, at the end of his September 16 pen-pal letter to Jim Mott. In his overblown style, de Winter hinted of something big coming, writing: "It is my desire that you travel mentally with me [in] the next weeks. Many events will happen, I [will] need [your] energy to assist."[36]

CHAPTER 6

"I Have a Bomb"

NOVEMBER 24, 1971–DECEMBER, 1971

Dan Cooper was just one more guy in a business suit—clutching a small paper bag and an attaché case[1]—plunking down $20 in cash for an airline hop from Portland to Seattle-Tacoma. Witnesses later claimed that he looked about thirty-five to forty years old, but the receding black hair, "wrap-around sunglasses," constant cloud of cigarette smoke, and swarthy complexion could have made him appear older than he actually was. One stewardess recently said she believes he was wearing dark makeup.[2]

The Portland ticket agent, Hal Williams, gave him seat 18C in coach, which was at the back of the cabin on the aisle. He then asked the standard question: "Returning?"

"No," the man replied.[3]

Flight 305 was on a Boeing 727-051, with a capacity of ninety-four passengers, but only thirty-seven customers were on board for the half-hour jaunt to Seattle.[4]

Shortly after takeoff, Dan Cooper got the attention of stewardess Florence Schaffner and handed her a note. She assumed it was just one more in a long line of come-ons from men traveling by themselves on business. She stuffed the note in her pocket, unread.

Dan Cooper wasn't quite that easily put aside. When she had to walk past him, he waved her over, motioned for her to lean in close, and then looked directly into her eyes.

"You'd better read that," he calmly informed her. "I have a bomb."[5]

Having gotten her attention, he indicated the soft-leather briefcase he'd kept on his lap. Then he put back on the sunglasses and sat back.

Her demeanor suddenly more serious, Schaffner walked away, taking out the note and reading it. After a few moments, she approached one of the other stewardesses, Tina Mucklow. It was only a moment before the two women went to the cockpit, where Captain William E. Scott read the note. He immediately got in contact with Seattle-Tacoma air traffic control, setting off a chain reaction of alerts to the Seattle police and the FBI.

Agent Gary Tallis, a Northern California native in his first office assignment, was among the bureau men alerted. He was just out of the academy, on the steep learning curve demanded of all rookie special agents.

"I was working fugitives," recalled Tallis, "and so that got me all over the territory, Seattle territory. And I happen to be near the Seattle-Tacoma airport when the call came in that a plane had been hijacked and was going to land."

Tallis was the first agent to get there. He walked into Northwest Airlines headquarters and introduced himself. "And actually," he said, "I believe the plane was just arriving at that time."

Supervisors at the FBI office in Seattle told Tallis to stay put and wait for the reinforcements who would be there shortly. "Normally being the first agent on the scene made you the case agent, but being a rookie, that was not the case," he said.

When those reinforcements did arrive, Tallis was relieved of his responsibility for the time being. He was happy that he had been taken off the potential hot seat, but he would soon be back on the hunt.[6]

Other agents, meanwhile, had contacted Northwest Airlines president Donald Nyrop about the hijacker's demands. The aviation executive did not vacillate—if the hijacker wanted $200,000 and four parachutes in exchange for the safe release of the passengers and many of the flight crew, he would get Northwest's complete cooperation. The alternative he faced was to have the airliner explode.

Captain Scott sent Schaffner back to Cooper, who had taken a seat by the rear window. Seeing this as an opening, Schaffner sat carefully beside him in the aisle seat. She was rewarded with a view into his attaché case, where she saw wires, a large battery, and several red cylinders that looked an awful lot like dynamite.

"Tell your pilot to stay in the air until they've got the money and chutes ready in Seattle," Cooper said calmly.

He knew that it would take a little while to assemble all the money in $20 bills, especially because he had stipulated that the bills had to have random serial numbers instead of being sequential. The FBI honored that request, but did manage to have all the serial numbers begin with the letter L, signifying that the bills had been issued through the Federal Reserve Bank's San Francisco office. Also, nearly every bill was dated 1969.[7]

But the money was the easy part. When he was told the parachutes were coming from McChord Air Force Base in Tacoma, Washington, Cooper turned them down because military chutes open automatically. Using a stewardess as his go-between, the jumper explained that he had to have civilian parachutes that were equipped with user-controlled ripcords. That would allow him to decide when the semibubble would bloom above him.

Frantic phone calls ensued. Finally the Seattle police got the owner of a local skydiving school on the line and persuaded him to lend them a hand.[8] The parachute crisis was averted, although no one could really understand why a single hijacker wanted the extra chutes. Was he going to insist that one of the stewardesses or crew go with him? Those attempting to psychoanalyze Cooper on the fly realized that even in the highly unlikely event that he would take a hostage—they had assumed a jump was his intention because he wanted parachutes in the first place—phony, nonopening equipment would kill not only the hijacker but his possible innocent companion, as well.

The word was finally passed back to Flight 305. Upon landing, the hijacker would be given the ransom of $200,000—twenty-one pounds of $20 bills—to buy the safety and release of the passengers. He was also assured two sets of parachutes, meaning two backpacks and two emergency backup chest packs.

At the eye of this hurricane, Cooper looked relaxed as he chain-smoked Raleigh cigarettes and sipped a bourbon and seven.[9] Sounding perfectly respectful and courteous in spite of the surreal circumstances, he offered to pay Mucklow for his drink. She later disagreed with descriptions of Cooper disseminated by the FBI, which called him a foul-mouthed drunk; she felt otherwise. "He seemed rather nice," Mucklow said, and "thoughtful."[10] He had even insisted that dinner be brought on board for the crewmembers he had kept on the plane with him after the landing at Seattle.[11]

A few of his comments might not have been well advised, however, if Cooper wished to remain a complete mystery. He knew, for example, when the circling jet was above Tacoma and that McChord Air Force Base was only twenty minutes away.[12] These utterings led FBI and police investigators to conclude that he was probably a native of the Northwest.

On the other hand, he could have been the scheming Baron Norman de Winter, who presumably had done his aerial homework during those daytime disappearances from Astoria and Corvallis over a five-month period.[13]

Finally, word came from the ground that all was ready. The landing was a half-hour late. Cooper told the captain to taxi the jet to a brightly lit location far out on the tarmac. He stipulated that one person bring the money and parachutes. When the lone Northwest Airlines employee stopped the vehicle not far from the 727, Cooper directed stewardess Mucklow to lower the aft stairs. He then watched closely as she met the employee at the bottom to take the parachutes and then the cash stored in a bank bag.

According to FBI transcripts taken from the flight crew's testimony, Cooper opened the delivered money bag at about 5:30 p.m., making sure there was no "funny stuff." Satisfied, the robber suddenly turned "childlike"—both Mucklow and Schaffner reported he "jumped up and down."

Cooper lifted the sack to test its bulkiness. "He even had Schaffner hold the bag so she could feel the weight. Mucklow then joked with Cooper about it being a lot of money, and could she have some. Cooper reached into the bag and gave her a bundle." Mucklow was just joking, so she handed the bundle back, saying she could not accept gratuities.[14]

In return for having his demands met, Cooper let all his fellow passengers leave the airplane, along with stewardesses Schaffner and Alice

Northwest 727-100 on runway in Seattle as hijack drama unfolds.

Hancock. But Hancock, the first class attendant, turned back when she realized she'd forgotten her purse.

She sheepishly asked Cooper if she could retrieve it.

"Sure," he said. "I'm not going to bite you."

Hancock noticed he was already "in the process of putting on one of the chutes."

Mucklow added, "He refused [the parachute] instructions that I handed him, saying, 'I don't need those.' He opened one, looked inside, then closed it up before putting it on. And he put it on easily, as if he had done it before."[15]

Bill Mitchell, a twenty-year-old college sophomore who had sat directly across the aisle from the hijacker, was tracked down decades later by the Washington State *Mountain News*, the famous website for all things Cooper. Even though he was forced to move forward after just twenty minutes, the FBI had labeled Mitchell "one of the prime witnesses" in the case. The former student, now a sixty-five-year-old grandfather, has been avoiding American news outlets—until now.

As the flight began, Mitchell side-glanced at his backseat neighbor, not out of curiosity or fear but with envy. Why were the stewardesses hovering around his seat—especially the cute blonde? "I remember being upset that Tina [Mucklow] was paying so much attention to that older guy."

The University of Oregon student, heading home to Seattle for Thanksgiving, continued to study his competitor, noting his "jugular thing"—the turkey-wattle fold of skin under his chin—and his dark hair, which appeared "shiny, as if it was dyed."[16]

The passengers, who were told the landing was due to an engine problem, had never known of the danger, let alone the culprit.[17] Mitchell revealed how they learned the information.

"We started walking toward the terminal, which was a long ways away. Then a bus came and we got on. The FBI started calling names from a list, and they called my name first. Then they called 'Dan Cooper' and there was nothing. No one answered. So we realized that was the skyjacker."

Mitchell's seat proximity and keen sense of detail led to two years of FBI interviews, which included "reviewing at least ten pictures per visit." The twice-a-month meetings in his college dorm room, while awkward, gave birth to the 1972 "B" sketch, or as it is better known, the number two sketch, of Cooper. Most believe it is a truer portrait of the fugitive than the first drawing, based on the descriptions provided by the traumatized stewardesses.

Today, Mitchell has learned to keep it all in perspective.

"D. B. Cooper was romanticized," he noted. "But you have to remember, when people call him a hero, he also had a bomb and was threatening to blow me up."

The experience didn't keep this observer to history away from flying. In fact, for the next thirty-five years, Mitchell worked for the skyjacked plane's manufacturer, Boeing, in nearby Puget Sound.[18]

Meanwhile, Cooper kept Tina Mucklow, Captain William Scott, First Officer William Rataczak, and Flight Engineer H. E. Anderson on board with him.

"You have a grudge against Northwest?" Mucklow asked at one point.

"I don't have a grudge against your airline, miss," came an answer that was to become famous. "I just have a grudge."[19]

Captain Scott told Cooper that an FAA executive had asked permission to come onto the plane to explain the penalty for air piracy.

FBI number two sketch, courtesy of the alert college student Bill Mitchell.

"Tell him to forget it," said Cooper. It was a little late for worrying about what could happen if he got caught.

He had more important worries, like figuring out how to operate the aft stairway. Whether this whole plot came to him while making the plunge in Vietnam or while overhearing a rogue commando at a bar, when it counted, Cooper didn't know the critical steps—literally. It showed an earlier demand of the crew, where he insisted the stairway be left down upon takeoff. He quickly agreed a scraping and sparking stairway under a fully fueled airliner was a really bad idea.

His comeback, though, kept eyebrows up: "That's alright, the captain can do it after we take off."

The cockpit had a stair warning light only, not a lowering button—and the only way to work the ramp was from the exit door. As one FBI official later put it, Cooper obviously "knew little to nothing of their operation."

To save face and bone up, the hijacker asked Mucklow to read the stairway's instruction card out loud. When the stewardess said she didn't believe it was possible to lower it during flight, Cooper considered her opinion, made up his mind, and said she was wrong.[20]

Using what was normally the jet's cabin phone, the hijacker told the cockpit crew precisely what he next wanted them to do. The altitude must be ten thousand feet or less, the wing flaps must be set at fifteen degrees, and the air speed must be no more than 150 knots (200 miles per hour), with the wheels left down and the cabin pressure off—that way he would not be shot into the night like a bullet when the stairs were lowered.

"And Captain Scott," Cooper said, "I'm wearing a wrist altimeter so I'll know what your altitude is."

It was a shrewd warning to the crew, which was restricted to the cockpit for the whole ordeal. Witnesses in the cabin later testified that "no one saw anything on this wrist or in his briefcase that'd lead one to believe he had [an altimeter]."[21]

The flight instructions, however, were what changed copilot Rataczak's opinion of Cooper. As he recently revealed to *Mountain News* publisher Bruce Smith, "When he told me to set the wing flaps at fifteen degrees, I knew he was a smart guy."

The hijacker's exit strategy notwithstanding, his knowledge of the exact parachuting dynamics of the 727, Smith noted, was "uncanny, because in 1971 it was classified information known only to selected Boeing officials and within covert operations in Vietnam."[22]

If Rackstraw was the hijacker, it wouldn't be "uncanny" to him—considering he freelanced in Vietnam the year before with the CIA and Special Forces. Both groups, in fact, were routinely involved in night insertion airdrops—from The Agency's "Air America" fleet of cargo planes and jets, including 727s—out of Takhli Air Base in Thailand.[23]

The skyjacker next told the crew he didn't care which route they took south, as long as they ended up in Mexico. Rataczak quickly challenged that, explaining that such a trip was not possible—not when they were flying at such a low altitude and speed, which would burn up the fuel. Mexico was twenty-two hundred miles away, but Flight 305 wasn't going to be able to exceed a thousand miles. Finally, it was decided that there would be a fuel stop in Reno, Nevada.

The pilots and airline flight operations wanted to take their special passenger out over the Pacific Ocean, but the FAA in Sacramento, California, didn't approve the risky low-and-slow plan. The jet was assigned the other route, down the popular "Victor-23"—an eight-mile-wide forestry corridor west of the most dangerous mountain peaks, which would send the airliner above downtown Portland.

Many experts today describe Cooper's laissez–faire flight instructions as brilliant, believing he surreptitiously directed Flight 305 over predicable terrain that he had planned for his escape route and jump zone—a parachutist holding all the strings.[24]

The last thing Cooper demanded was a refueling to replace what had been used on the flight from Portland. He became agitated when the process took longer than fifteen minutes because he knew this airliner could take on four thousand gallons per minute without a problem. Seattle tower officials told him that a vapor lock had slowed the process initially but now the system was working well. Soon enough, the 727 was gassed to the wingtips.

After two hours on the ground in Seattle, the jet rose into the air once more at 7:36 p.m.

Aloft, Cooper ordered Mucklow to join the rest of the crewmembers in the cockpit. Before she closed the curtains that divided first class from coach—an absurd gesture, considering the circumstances—she caught a glimpse of him working intently, "tying the lassoed bank bag to his waist." Then while adjusting a parachute, he waved goodbye.

Former FBI agent and author Richard Tosaw told the London *Sunday Telegraph* he had pressed Mucklow for details about that last moment. "Tina said he put the chute on as if he'd done it every day."[25]

Mucklow knew that the cockpit door did not have a peephole, and not even the most advanced jetliners back then boasted remote cameras and video monitors. There would be absolutely no way to keep an eye on Dan Cooper. So once she pulled the door closed behind her at 7:42 p.m., the curious crew turned her way.

Mucklow revealed that Cooper had opened "one chute, and [he] began trying to dump money into [its empty] container. Then he began cutting cords from the chute and is tying [it] around his waist, apparently in an attempt to secure the parachute container full of money." That led her to one conclusion: "I think he is getting ready to jump."[26]

Just a few minutes after departure, Cooper tried to lower the stairs—with no luck. The problem was they operated on gravity, not automatically. He called the cockpit, told Rataczak his problem, and asked for them to "slow and stabilize the plane." The captain lowered the speed to about 170 miles per hour and leveled the aircraft.

Shortly after 8:00 p.m., a red light came on at a rarely used corner of Flight Engineer Anderson's instrument panel. Beside it were the ominous words "OPEN DOOR." Everyone in the crew knew that meant the aft stairs were now down. Scott clicked on the intercom. "Is there anything we can do for you?"

Cooper ran back over and answered that everything was "okay."

"Georger," a former college professor and Cooper chat-room sleuth with "both familial and professional" contacts at the bureau, was given discreet access in 2014 to study the FBI's hijacking eyewitness interview transcripts, logs, and testimony. He said for the next five or ten minutes on that freezing stairway, Cooper was "fully occupied and looking for an opportunity to jump."

The crew members did not hear from Cooper again. They did feel, however, a slight dip in the elevation of the jet's nose at 8:13 p.m., a "pressure bump," closely followed by a corrective adjustment in the tail— Geronimo! Captain Scott took note of precisely where they were: very nearly over the Lewis River and some twenty-five miles north of Portland. The crewmembers exchanged looks; the question hanging in the air was so obvious it didn't need to be asked.

"We keep going to Reno no matter what," said Scott.[27] There was no way for them to know if their suspicions were correct without doing what the hijacker had clearly warned against—leaving the cockpit.

As Flight 305 landed at Reno Airport at 10:15 p.m., a shower of sparks flew up as the dangling stairway scraped the runway. Then the plane sat idle as the crew waited nervously and minutes ticked by. Finally Scott turned on the intercom and asked if anyone could hear him. He tried a second time. Since he got no response, he carefully opened the cockpit door, expecting—literally—anything.

The passenger cabin stretched before him, empty of life, the air chilly due to the yawning, wide-open rear exit. Peering all around, listening for the slightest sound, Scott was increasingly certain that no surprise was lurking. Cooper—soon to be erroneously known around the world as

D. B. instead of Dan because of a reporter's mistake—had indeed jumped out of the Boeing 727 in flight.

The crew stood at the top of the aft stairway, looking down to the comforting asphalt of the Reno runway below. They could only imagine what it must have been like to leap from that rickety, lurching tongue, plunging into the night air. The temperature was estimated to have been twenty-two degrees—with wind gusts and icy rain hitting Cooper in the face. Then there were the spiked treetops and jagged mountain cliffs waiting to greet him.

It was a death plunge, you might surmise. But within hours, Washington State residents near Cooper's suspected jump zone reported hearing someone in the hellish darkness who was very much alive—and taking off in a sputtering small plane. Someone, perhaps, with a new piloting job for a "real estate guy."[28]

Did Bob Rackstraw have the specific skill sets necessary to accomplish this daring getaway jump? According to retired lieutenant colonel Ken Overturf, Rackstraw's former Vietnam commander, "I don't believe the question of whether Rackstraw was capable of jumping from a 727 is even pertinent at this point." Overturf pointed out that jumping from that staircase "is much easier than a side door jump. The jumper experiences a lot less turbulence from the rear than from the side. An experienced jumper, or even a really crazy, less experienced jumper, would have no issue with going out the back of an aircraft at an airspeed of plus or minus 200 knots."

Overturf added that Rackstraw "had the intellect and capabilities to determine the best type of parachute and do the necessary calculations to make the jump and arrange for a successful recovery." Finally, the fact that he performed "heroic actions in Vietnam validate that he would have the courage and 'go to hell' attitude necessary to actually attempt the jump" in the first place.[29]

Former *Reno Evening Gazette* photographer Marilyn Newton, now seventy, recollected she was in her eighth year as a photojournalist when a news editor ordered her to rush out and meet Flight 305. As the only photographer on the runway, her exclusive pictures of the parked air-liner, the "very, very tired" crew, and the police K-9 Rommel—sniffing the aft ramp's steps—were immediately picked up by world wire services. Newton noted, "We didn't get many [photo] credits back then."[30]

Nevada State Journal newsman William Kroger was among two dozen radio, television, and newspaper reporters in the terminal, "rotating be-tween the bar and coffee machine" while awaiting the flight crew's news conference. When the four fatigued survivors exited their FBI debriefing at 2:00 a.m. and headed toward the microphones, Kroger noted "the stew-ardess aboard [Tina Mucklow] appears about ready to cry."[31]

One of the crewmembers shielded her from the shouted questions. "Let up on Tina, she has had a rough day."[32]

Sitting for five hours next to the hijacker naturally made this twenty-two-year-old attendant an extremely valuable witness. But the personality description both she and Florence Schaffner gave to agents left the fugitive sounding like a cotillion dance partner.

He was "calm, polite, and well-spoken," said Schaffner.[33]

He was "very relaxed," said Mucklow, and "very courteous" throughout the ordeal.[34]

Maybe he was just on a roll. OSU party girl Gayle Downing, surprised recipient of that Hawaiian shell necklace, had used many of those same words to describe her "charming" Norman de Winter after the Swiss pilot vanished from Corvallis, Oregon—a day before the Portland hijacking and just twenty minutes away by small plane.[35]

Whether it was part of his intent or not, Cooper jumped headlong into the zeitgeist, the popular imagination of his time. Days after the ordeal, a sociologist at the University of Washington, Dr. Otto Larsen, character-ized this first case of parachute piracy as "an awesome feat in the battle of man against the machine. One man overcoming, for the time being any-way, technology, the corporation, the establishment, the system."[36]

Geoffrey Gray, author of the 2011 book *Skyjack: The Hunt for D. B. Cooper*, has thought a lot about the cultural-phenomenon aspect of the Cooper incident. He pointed out how one man, with that single leap, seemed to

The Northwest Airlines flight crew hostages.

alter the moral landscape. Cooper created a situation where, in almost Robin Hood style, many people found themselves rooting for the "bad guy," the hijacker. He had transcended the mundane, everyday existence that people often feel they are trapped in.[37]

Years later, this sentiment would be echoed by Rackstraw himself.

Cooper had taken almost everything he had brought on board with him. His hat, the briefcase "bomb," his overcoat, and one set of parachutes were gone. The cash, in a bag that looked anything but aerodynamic, was also gone, of course. Where they were now was anyone's guess. Left behind were a necktie, a pack of Raleigh Filter cigarette butts, and a signed gate ticket—all destined for analysis and obsessive expert consideration.

Because of the terrible weather, search parties did not set out on the ground until the morning following the hijacking, which was Thanksgiving.[38] What they may have lacked in speed, they tried to make up for in thoroughness. They combed the area for several weeks.

At one point the air force's top-secret SR-71 Blackbird spy plane was quietly called in to assist. Why the fastest plane on earth was dispatched to find a single person who was either dead or traversing the forest floor under a blocking canopy of trees has never been explained. A thick layer of low clouds added to these elements to thwart five different attempts at photoreconnaissance.[39]

Meanwhile, Gary Tallis, the rookie agent who had been first on the scene at the airport in Seattle, was notified that he and a few other agents were being sent south to attend a briefing on the skyjacking. On Thanksgiving morning, he entered a room with a cross section of law-enforcement personnel, including seasoned FBI agents, other first office agents like himself, and sheriff's deputies, state troopers, and police from several jurisdictions. Longtime, highly respected FBI agent Tom Manning delivered the briefing. He showed a map and talked about the route the plane had taken. He then assigned tasks.

Tallis was put into a helicopter because he had modest experience with parachute jumping, which seemed to lend itself to the job of hovering throughout the region and looking toward the ground with the hope of spotting Cooper. Tallis described the area as mountainous, adding, "It was really stormy weather, a lot of cloud cover, fog, that kind of thing. And I remember flying through clouds and then coming out and here's mountains right there."

Tallis did not agree, at least at the beginning, with colleagues who believed there was no chance Cooper could have survived his jump. "My first impression was that we would find his chute and we'd find him with a broken leg. I never thought he had a problem leaving the airplane. And, in fact, I volunteered to jump out of a 727.

"You know, the injury comes when you impact the earth. I really never even considered the fact that he could have walked out or had been picked up. The areas we searched didn't have roads."

Still, Tallis was surprised at how sure others seemed to be that Cooper couldn't possibly have survived—at least for a couple of weeks. Not so much as a trace of Cooper or his bright yellow and red parachute ever turned up. Rather than conclude that Cooper could have simply hiked to freedom, however, Tallis eventually chose to agree, in part, with the prevailing wisdom at the FBI.

When he was interviewed decades later, Tallis speculated that Cooper had been injured when he hit the ground, buried the chute, and, unable to get out of the wilderness because there were no roads, wound up with "his bones scattered all over the world" after scavenging birds and small animals picked his rotting body apart.[40]

The debate over what exactly happened began taking shape almost immediately. While law-enforcement personnel publicly admitted "the hijacking had been carefully and minutely planned," they were increasingly convinced the jump had been a spectacular last act. But a fast-growing faction of Cooper-as-Robin-Hood enthusiasts insisted that the absence of physical evidence negated the so-called splatter theory that was popularized by the FBI's hard-nosed man in charge in Oregon, Ralph P. Himmelsbach.

It wasn't that the FBI wasn't diligent about looking at every possible angle. Agents in the Washington, DC, headquarters spent their Thanksgiving searching the bureau's crime records. If the hijacker had been dumb enough to use his own name, they wanted to grill every Dan Cooper who had a felonious past. One of the people they spoke to was a man who was inconveniently named D. B. Cooper and happened to live in Portland. They soon determined he had nothing to do with the hijacking.

To add a taunt to the FBI's growing embarrassment over turning up zilch, four letters—all mockingly signed "D. B. Cooper"—were mailed to newspapers in the week immediately after the hijacking. The first and fourth envelopes were delivered in Reno, Nevada; a daily in Vancouver, British Columbia, received the second; and the third went to a paper in Portland, Oregon. Each of the letters made a point of ridiculing the authorities conducting the search, with three carefully composed from words cut out from papers and magazines and pasted onto a sheet of paper.

When the authorities originally examined them, they apparently did not notice a possible hint about the sender in the postmarks. The Vancouver and Portland envelopes were rubber-stamped in those towns, respectively, meaning that the writer very likely had been traveling through those areas when they were mailed. But the first and last envelopes, both sent to Reno from Northern California, were another matter.

This investigation discovered that the first was dropped into a mail-box thirty-five miles from the Rackstraw clan's remote hometown, Valley Springs, while the second came from another mailbox, fifty miles from their community. The family's isolated abode is almost five hundred flying miles from the FBI's alleged jump site, making the chance of these mailings being purely coincidental very, very small.

Speaking of flying, the logistics of this five-day, 1,200-mile postal round trip would suggest a writer delivering the envelopes by private air-mail—chiefly considering that letters number three (Portland) and four (Sacramento), 580 miles apart, were both postmarked on the same day.[41]

Recall that in the weeks leading up to the November 24 hijacking and subsequent mailings, both Rackstraw and con artist "Norman de Winter" shared with others in the Northwest that they had a small plane.[42]

One might wonder why the Vancouver letter, the only one hand-written on the fly, so to speak, was lumped in with the three cut-and-pasted notes. Besides the writer's identical mocking tone, he printed the same peculiar sign-off contained in the first Reno note: "Thanks for your hospitality."[43] And it wasn't simply a copycat—the investigation discovered the arriving Vancouver envelope was postmarked at 2:00 p.m. *before* the initial Reno story hit the newsstands, let alone any news wires.

Now a final observation on the handwritten note: This investigation also noticed that the Vancouver writer's printing appeared to have a lettering style matching that of the signature on Dan Cooper's Portland boarding pass—as noted earlier, a signature the FBI believes actually came from the hijacker. Realizing the significance of this, we sought the expertise of an impeccable forensic document examiner.

Dr. Linton Mohammed is a past-president of the American Society of Questioned Document Examiners who has testified in more than a hun-dred trials. In a commissioned forensic comparison of the letter and air-line ticket, he warned any conclusion could not be used in court (which requires originals, not copies). But he agreed, "There are indications of one writer."

So if you have an inkling that the four taunting Cooper notes were sent by Robert W. Rackstraw, this alleged match would unmistakably put him at the boarding gate.[44]

A week after the last D. B. Cooper letter arrived in Reno, another familiar character popped back up in the US mail: Norman de Winter. A December 9 note, written with his flowing baronial hand, arrived at the Astoria home of his former Union Fish Company coworker, Mark Fick. Its tone, however, was certainly out of character: "My friend Mark: With

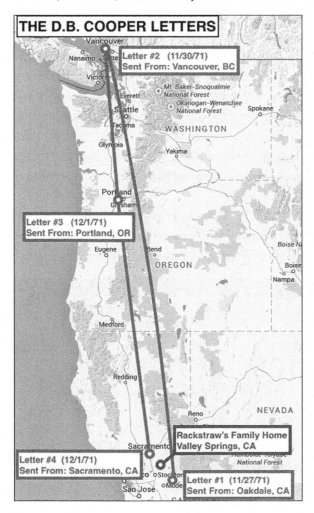

Where D. B. Cooper mailed his taunting letters. Note the proximity of letters one and four to the Rackstraw family home in Valley Springs, California.

great regret do I inform you of the death of my father. The complexity of this event has elected my decision to cancel the [Christmas] voyage to Europa. Most respectfully, Norman."

Pan Am had exposed the Swiss snake in September as a complete fraud, but the scandal had remained a private embarrassment among its victims. Now it appeared de Winter was covering his tracks with the last group of residents he had encountered, down in the Astoria harbor. One might imagine his paranoia had dictated the letter, to nip his friends' curiosity and disappointment in the bud. The last thing he wanted was the two groups of victims crossing paths, comparing notes, and then going public.

A few days later, Fick sent back the response de Winter had hoped for—a note featuring condolences, understanding, and no knowledge of the uptown hubbub. That propelled the grifter to let loose with familiar bravado in a second message, which filled the inside of a Christmas card on December 15: "My dear friend Mark: Thank you for your letter, it has been my delight. You are most kind. Is not it the season to be merry? One thing I regret is I cannot cut salmon cheeks and sing Christmas Carols! Ho, Ho, Ho! My friend, your respect and brotherhood shall warm my heart always. Au revoir, Norman."

This investigation observed that De Winter's return address was that of the boarding house of OSU pen pal Jim Mott—the same pal the baron rudely ran out on in November, after five weeks of free food, room, and board. If

Dan Cooper airline ticket, "Name of Passenger" in Cooper's handwriting.

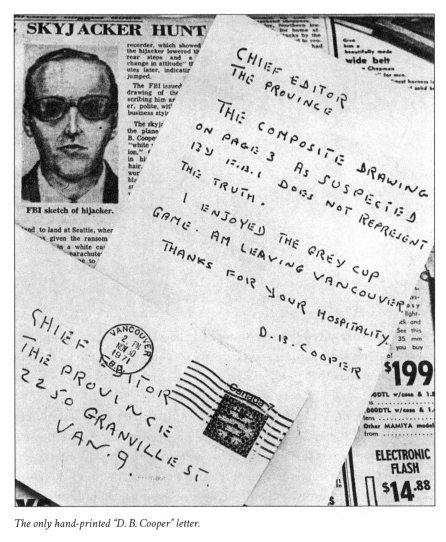

The only hand-printed "D. B. Cooper" letter.

Norman de Winter was a man who covered his tracks, one might conclude he had also returned, hat in hand, to reclaim his "stuff in storage." Why the Oregon State Beaver didn't just slam the door on the prodigal son of a bitch, no one knows.[45] If you believe, however, all three con artists were using the same flight plan, then it shouldn't be hard to imagine how easily Dan Cooper morphed back into Norman de Winter, and then used his inner Rackstraw to charm his way onto Mott's couch—for another week.

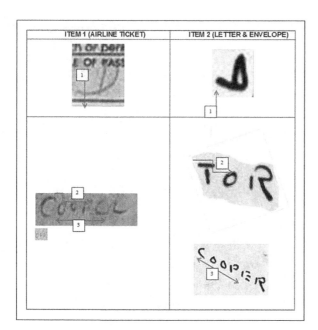

Ticket/letter comparison: An "indication" Dan Cooper survived?

In the years ahead, fourteen more of the veteran's alleged identities would call on that charisma—a charisma so potent, say victims, it could stop a firing squad.[46]

In late December, Rackstraw quietly returned to settle down at his parent's home in Valley Springs, but it was foreshadowed by suspicious behavior almost from the outset. After his June booting from the military, he had instructed his stepfather to not tell anyone he was there. The ongoing secrecy may have disturbed Philip because he eventually told Lucille what her son had said. Soon Lucille told her twenty-four-year-old daughter, Linda Lee.

"That's when I thought, something's strange, now," said Linda Lee in looking back.[47]

For the next year and a half, Bob Rackstraw remained below the radar as much as possible. But remaining below the radar and putting up a truly opaque cover story are two distinctly different matters. Rackstraw left his cover story open just wide enough to let in a ray of light.

Attorney and lifelong Cooper sleuth Galen C. Cook, who has liaised with the FBI, was the one who first saw that light. He doggedly tracked down the four so-called Cooper letters in the case files and their histories in the newspaper morgues, where few had realized they had been lurking for four decades. On June 27, 2012, Cook told a national talk-radio audience that, in his opinion, "The sequence and timing of the letters are very important, as they show the escape route of D. B. Cooper."[48]

And all routes—Rackstraw's, de Winter's, and Cooper's—converge at Valley Springs, claimed Jay C. Todd, an undercover state investigator and ten-year colleague of one of the authors. After studying the investigation's trails of all three, he summed it up with a lawman's wit:

> A master criminal like Rackstraw (RWR) appears in America once every couple of years. Between July and December, 1971, you've documented three within one hundred miles of each other in the Northwest—real estate aerial pilot RWR, vacationing Swiss pilot Norman de Winter and D. B. Cooper, a hijacker with obvious aviation skill sets.
>
> Many NdW eyewitnesses claim he looked very much like RWR; and your investigative team says RWR is a dead ringer for the FBI Cooper sketches. Also, your detailed timeline reveals that whenever one vanished, another popped up—and after RWR went home for good, the other two disappeared forever. It's statistically impossible for three master criminals to all be operating within a hundred miles, let alone three that look alike, have the same flying skills, and their arrivals and departures are synchronized like whack-a-mole.[49]

Bob Rackstraw prudently hunkered down in the territorial triangle between San Francisco, San Joaquin, and Valley Springs—always working, deer-hunting, living, and loving within a hundred miles of the family's remote home base.[50]

Meanwhile, the hunt for D. B. Cooper, who had become a surefire popular story in the news media, blared on around him.

CHAPTER 7

Snake Oil

1972–MAY 24, 1974

Rackstraw was finished with the army. That phase of his life had left him humiliated, and he had lashed out in rage, searching for—and apparently finding—a fitting response to the psychological abuse heaped upon him by what he now must have viewed as an arrogant, myopically exclusive military class.[1]

He had shown his superiors what he was capable of, now that they had trained him and helped him hone his skills and made him into their worst little nightmare. He had shown them, even if they didn't realize it yet.

Gail Marks could go to hell, too, although Rackstraw knew in his gut, as he admitted years later, that she was right when she said he destroyed their marriage, that it was his fault. He knew he would have to ease back on the alcohol; he had become a mean drunk. Although Marks's running to his commanding officer precipitated the avalanche of rejection he had suffered, he could still understand her desire to escape.[2]

Rackstraw, meanwhile, found new ways to demonstrate his contempt for society's rules, regulations, and those that enforce them.

In 1972, Bob Rackstraw killed a deer without a license tag near the Valley Springs family home and failed to appear in court to pay the fine. Stepping in and banking on his own respectability, Philip called the judge, claiming that his son was "in Laos." The $125 fine was paid the following month.[3]

The question of how much the stepdad might really have known about Rackstraw's behavior, let alone his whereabouts, is intriguing in light of his regular "protective dishonesty" on Rackstraw's behalf.[4] Was Philip ever complicit in his son's unethical or illegal behavior? Could he have even helped Rackstraw get out of the Northwest so quickly after the hijacking? In the context of so much willingness to cover for his son, the questions are valid to pose.

On April 21, 1973, Rackstraw encountered the remarried Gail Marks at Linda Lee's wedding in Stockton, California. He handled it very well, appearing cordial—according to a photo of the moment, snapped by someone across the room. The smiling Marks, just feet away, was caught looking deeply into his eyes, as if infatuated. This was just two years after he allegedly choked her over a kitchen sink, and without his forking over a dime of child support yet for their three kids.[5]

When Rackstraw was on his own, he found himself with far too little to occupy his mind. Whereas the army had provided the kind of continuous challenge he had always loved, he was now drifting in the doldrums of unstructured time because he needed to lay low. But he could not stand lingering at home with his parents, so he would take off without warning, just to go, just to do something.

Rackstraw had lovers of convenience in the San Jose area, said his sister, at whose home he'd sometimes crash overnight or stay for the weekend. He also traveled north a lot; he liked it up there. Good memories must have abounded from his great adventure, mingling, no doubt, with a hint of danger that came from entering the region where the pursuit of D. B. Cooper was at its greatest intensity.[6]

The veteran pilot had occasional flying jobs. One of them, however, went very wrong.

Rackstraw was hired on May 4, 1973, by a San Jose aviation company to deliver a new Enstrom F-28 helicopter from its Michigan factory. While flying the civilian airship nap-of-the-earth low, Vietnam style, over Iowa, he suddenly had an engine flameout. Hearing nothing but heartbeats,

Rackstraw and copilot John E. Hannay frantically braced for their only option: a spiraling "autorotative crash landing."

The award-winning combat aviator with more than twelve thousand hours of experience had made a rookie pilot's mistake: he had "miscalculated [his] fuel consumption," as the National Transportation Safety Board (NTSB) later put it.

Farmer Jim Sweeney and his two teen sons were tending to their hundreds of cattle at dawn, three miles from the town of Altoona, when the fast two-seater "came toward them at a low altitude." Then when it "got about 50 to 70 feet off the ground, 'it dropped like a potato, straight down. It crashed just about 100 yards from my feedlot,'" Sweeney told a reporter.

After calling the Polk County Sheriff on the house phone, Sweeney ran out to help. But the crew was already out of the wrecked airship, shaking off the crash and high-fiving each other. "Hannay was reported as saying that they made a good landing," stated the *Altoona Herald*. "But the copter pitched over in the soft ground and the rotor had struck . . . twisting and breaking off the tail section."

Following their nervous introductions, the mysterious travelers became "reluctant to answer questions." The suspicious farmer wondered if they could be "airborne cattle rustlers."

More than four decades later, Sweeney's son David still remembered the dirt-flying crash and the crew's odd behavior. "Were they smuggling drugs? We had no idea."

Hannay, recently tracked down, claimed his pilot ordered him "not to say a word." Rackstraw, usually a man of many words, was stone-faced.

David said their farm driveway was soon "lined with all sorts of cop cars and uniformed men. But some were not regular deputies—seemed like special agents."

Indeed, as an Associated Press wire explained, "Polk County authorities called for the State Bureau of Criminal Investigation and FBI agents."

When Rackstraw saw those shiny-shoed feds, his stomach no doubt returned to freefall. But in short order he convinced them he wasn't the droid they were looking for.

Later though, other feds took an interest in the veteran—"for lies in the FAA report" on the crash, noted Hannay. That might explain the harsh summary that followed from the NTSB: "Lack of familiarity with aircraft . . . Mismanagement of fuel . . . Misjudged speed and altitude . . . [He] thought helicopter had 3HR range; manufacturing guidelines stated fuel range [for] cruise was approximately 2HR."

Seven months after the humiliating ordeal, the Federal Aviation Administration temporarily suspended Rackstraw's commercial helicopter license. But as we know from his army booting, he never was one to rely on a piece of paper.[7]

When his wanderings took him back to San Jose in July of that year, Rackstraw applied for and got the job of managing a Radio Shack. At the end of his shift one day, he dropped by the nearby Red Roof Inn for a drink. That's where he befriended a cute blond waitress named Linda McGarity, a twenty-five-year-old divorced mom from Houston with two young children.

Tracked down back in her home state of Texas, she was happy to give her recollections.

"His eyes and mine met, and it was boom!" laughed McGarity, now sixty-eight. "So he . . . started taking me out and learned I had a house by myself. I'd only had it six months when my ex-husband said he wanted to [go] be a big rock star."

Faster than small-town gossip, Rackstraw moved in and filled the Ward Cleaver roll. Her two young kids branded him Daddy Bob.

"He was just so sweet and a loving person. He loved my kids, he adored me. I'd never had that in my life. It was like, here's your Prince Charming."[8]

Weeks after meeting McGarity, Rackstraw walked into another chance encounter in San Jose. At a

Second wife, Linda S. McGarity

Denny's restaurant, he spotted an old paratrooper buddy, Mike Narro, and gave him a bear hug. It happened that Narro was running his own chemical company, Specialty Surfacing, in the San Francisco Bay area, doing a brisk business creating military ship decks, gym floors, and tennis courts. Obviously fond of Rackstraw, Narro offered the twenty-nine-year-old vet a supervisory job on the spot. Having had enough of Radio Shack, Rackstraw shook hands and accepted.[9]

What helped him ice the deal was a newspaper clipping he had pulled out of his pocket, flaunting his heroics in Vietnam.

There happened to be a couple with Narro—a visiting Oregonian named Robert C. "Pudgy" Hunt, along with a lady-friend. He also remembered seeing that particular article. It had Rackstraw's picture and touted him as "being some kind of medal winner." It was the "treasonous" 1970 *Santa Cruz Sentinel* story plant, doing exactly what it was designed to do: puffing up Bob's credentials in his postmilitary years.[10]

Hunt would eventually get to know Rackstraw about as well as anyone in the years ahead. But on that day, he was doing a good impression of a man who ought to be enjoying life.

Hunt had been a household-name collegiate basketball player at both Gonzaga University in Spokane, Washington, and the University of Oregon in Eugene. His Oregon high-school career scoring record of 2,584 points at Knappa High in 1957 would stand a full fifty years—earning him induction into the state's Sports Hall of Fame. Following school, he went on to enjoy a long and successful career as a contractor and business investor, including partnerships in some of Portland's most successful bars, the most recent being the famed East Bank Saloon.[11]

Hunt turned out to be something of a gatekeeper in Rackstraw's life in those first years after the skyjacking. Besides being present at the chance reunion with Narro, he was also the facilitator for another important Rackstraw connection, this time with a former U of O frat brother and boisterous Portland bodybuilder named Jon Richard "Dick" Briggs.[12]

"A lotta people kinda feared him," said Hunt. "Bench-pressed 425 pounds. And they called him Bugsy [like the 1930s gangster] because he was a little squirrely."

The Hunt brothers at Pudgy's bar.

While frequently scary and a violent drunk, Briggs could instantly switch to seeming like a vulnerable, lost child. His sporadic insecurity and persistent loneliness came from being abandoned as an infant on church steps. Although loving adoptive parents from the parish raised him, they were a constant reminder of his rootless beginning.

"He talked about it a lot," said Hunt. Briggs was troubled by the fact that he never knew his birth parents, and he overcompensated in many ways—not the least of which was having himself chauffeured around Portland in luxurious British limousines.

A master of parlor magic tricks, Briggs was also capable of truly strange behavior. He had been known to attempt to impress women in bars by showing them how he could stick a long, intimidating-looking metal pin all the way through his arm and then remove it without a trace of blood anywhere.[13]

Hunt's wife of more than thirty years, Connie Cunningham Hunt, vividly recalled the first time she met the "human fire hydrant" in the early 1970s. "One of our first dates was at [Pudgy's] unfinished apartment. And there's a knock at the apartment door. And in walks this just gigantically muscular man. Short, stocky, very dynamic. Looked dangerous beyond belief. My husband is just totally engaged with him. And he says, 'Okay, Dick, you want a drink?' Dick does a straight shot of bourbon, and immediately proceeds to eat the glass. Blood is dripping down his face; he's chewing the glass. My husband yells at him, 'My God, Dick, that was my one and only glass!' And Dick begins to cry. His emotional well-being was really questionable at that time."

Then there was the time when Briggs owed Hunt some money. Opening a briefcase filled with sapphires and diamonds, he said, "How about this to settle up the deal?"

Hunt accepted. Some of the gems are now set in Connie's wedding ring.[14]

In the spring of 1974, Linda McGarity, Rackstraw's new homeowner girlfriend in San Jose, enjoyed a couple of "pretty neat" flights with him on a new Bell 47G helicopter, the aircraft made famous in the 1970 movie and subsequent television series *MASH*.

Linda Lee knew the inside story of that whirlybird. Her brother had cut a deal with the head lawman in their parents' mountainous backcountry, Sheriff Russell Leach. In exchange for "flying the helicopter that Calaveras County had bought him" as a volunteer pilot for the "Sheriff's Posse" rescue team, Bob was given the keys. In truth, though, between the rare rural emergencies, both men benefited: while being chauffeured around his thousand square miles by chopper, Leach could channel Boss Hogg, whereas in the off-hours, Bob had something better than a Porsche for hookups.

The family that flies together . . .

The win-win arrangement also had an ominous bonus for the pilot: It came with a badge.[15]

One weekend, Rackstraw suggested to McGarity that they drop her two kids off with his parents in Valley Springs so they could take a getaway jaunt in his plane.

McGarity flashed a big Lone Star smile. "Oh, you have a plane?"

Bob flashed a grin right back. "Yes, I have a small Cessna. You ever been to Lake Tahoe?"

One might wonder where else that plane had been, say, in 1971.

Just before their takeoff for Nevada, Rackstraw had some aircraft safety measures to go over with the "giddy" McGarity. "I want you to learn about Mayday [emergency procedures] ... so you can call in case something happened."

McGarity took it from there: "So we're flying into Lake Tahoe, and he said, 'This might scare you.' We're coming off the mountains and all of sudden he goes straight down [onto] a very short runway, and there we were! He had a car waiting for us from the hotel, told them some big person from New York was coming in. That was a lie o'course, but they treated us like royalty."

Two hours later when Rackstraw and McGarity were in their room, hotel representatives "knocked on the door and said, 'Oh, you're the rock star! We're here to take you down to the show.' And I thought, what? So we didn't have to wait in line and they took us to the front, right close to the stage. That's when I got to learn what Cabernet Sauvignon was, because I'd never drank wine."[16]

Linda Lee remembered her brother's days of living the high life. McGarity's home was "a nice tract house in Cupertino, which is a fairly expensive area. He had that Corvette ... it was a classic, I'm not sure where he picked that up. They lived very well."

Rackstraw began traveling more for Narro, too, because the word on Specialty Surfacing's unique polyurethane floors was spreading. "Everybody wanted their basketball and tennis courts and everything else to be made out of it. They had plenty of jobs," said Linda Lee. The work, however, was dangerous, noting that her brother "would have to wear masks and everything, because it was fairly toxic."[17]

But that was par for the course for a former paratrooper skilled in weapons and explosives.

As might be expected, Rackstraw's wink-wink flying arrangement with Sheriff Leach soured within months. The red-faced lawman briefed Linda Lee that her brother had been "down in Stockton, and he was showing this badge around." He had also "gotten picked up for drunk driving, and he told them he was a sheriff [deputy] in Calaveras County."

The mischievous Rackstraw lost the shield and his gig with the good guys. But to the agency's chagrin, he still legally owned its airship. No doubt whenever the sheriff heard him flying by, he got a loud reminder of his folly.[18]

One day, Rackstraw phoned McGarity from the road about a special gathering. "We're invited to join these friends in San Francisco for dinner and drinks. I want you to feel comfortable and look good. I left you a charge card by the dresser—get one of the neatest outfits you can find. I want you to go to a boutique."

Recalling the shopping episode, she laughed. "I didn't know what a boutique was!"

It was just another chapter in their fairy-tale courtship, said McGarity. "Bob couldn't do enough for me. In fact, his mom even mentioned that he had never showed that much love for anybody."[19]

A few months after Pudgy Hunt was introduced to Rackstraw in the San Jose Denny's, he was on the other side of a fateful first meeting. Hunt introduced his eccentric college buddy Dick Briggs to Rackstraw, who was now the foreman for a Specialty Surfacing floor job at the new Pepperdine University gym in Malibu, California.

Briggs had made one of his odd, dramatic returns into Hunt's life the night before. He had called from Portland, very emotional, explaining that he was in police trouble and asking if his old friend could pick him up at Los Angeles International Airport (LAX).

Hunt obligingly did so, noticing right away that Briggs was in full bizarro mode. He had no luggage and yet managed to grin from ear to ear as he explained that he'd had a terrible fight with his girlfriend.

"He was dragging her up the street by her hair," Hunt said. "He could, he said, hear that her head made a funny noise when it went off the sidewalk and hit the road. He said he knew he was in big trouble"—and that he had to get out of town.

Soon Briggs joined Rackstraw's crew in Malibu, which also included Hunt's younger brother, Daniel, a twenty-seven-year-old state arm-wrestling champion. The workers began doing the town together after work. Drinks flowed fairly freely, which never failed to unleash the inner Rackstraw. This had a particularly bad influence on Briggs, who soon fell in with the foreman.

Both men had a latent potential for criminality, and Pudgy Hunt—whom Briggs confided in because of their longstanding college friendship—remembered that soon "things started happening," and they started "doing jobs" together.

"Rackstraw would do things . . . when he's sober that Briggs would [only] do when he was drunk. Let's put it that way," Hunt said, offering some examples.

"Briggs would get drunk and he would shoot the windshield out of a police car. Or he'd throw a garbage can through a window. Or beat the heck out of somebody. But all these when he was either on drugs or drinking. Well, my recollection is that once he started running around with Rackstraw, Rackstraw planned things. And [Briggs] started following what Rackstraw was doing. And these were all done, you know, in the daylight, and sober. And planned. Briggs didn't operate that way when I knew him."

Hunt later had his own firsthand taste of Rackstraw's tendency to lead anyone palling around with him into risky situations.

"I've seen him operate under extreme conditions. And he's unfazed," he said. "Briggs and I were in his plane one time, in a [thunder and lightning] storm in Northern California. It's just pouring and blowing like a fire hose on the windshield. He was flying blind, strictly on a radio, and it just didn't bother him one bit, just cool as can be. It bothered the airport because he was the only plane up. I said 'Bob, turn this son of a bitch around! I'm not risking my life!' He finally did."

Rackstraw was encouraged by Hunt's arm, wrapped around his neck.

As mentioned earlier, the military had taught the veteran to function in nasty squalls just like this—and just like the one D. B. Cooper had faced in 1971.[20]

In early 1974, Specialty Surfacing had another job in Southern California. This one involved laying cement court surfaces at the Rod Laver Racquet Club, which was atop a ten-story parking structure near LAX.

When the crew's work assignment was complete, Rackstraw led Pudgy Hunt, his brother Dan, Briggs, and a couple of other companions into the ninth-floor club bar for some beers and a tabletop game of foosball. But to their surprise, they actually had walked into "a party, celebrating the [club's] completion. Rod Laver was there and a lot of actors."

Bob Rackstraw's ability to charm and schmooze was soon on full display. Within minutes, he had persuaded Hollywood star Charlton Heston to join them at the game table. Their night with the big-screen legend was later immortalized in a group photo, *with Heston raising beer cans with our alleged D. B. Cooper*. The picture hung on the wall of Pudgy's former East Bank Saloon for thirty years.[21]

A drink with Charlton Heston.

Rackstraw wasn't finished playing genial host and bon vivant with his crew. The Los Angeles Playboy Club had recently moved off of the Sunset Strip to Century City, and he was a new member. After another shift at work, he offered to take Pudgy Hunt and Briggs to experience some bunny hospitality.

Hunt noted Bob "kind of dresses up. He puts on a camel sports coat with his Distinguished Flying Cross."

Their little rented car from Specialty Surfacing looked pretty shabby next to the limos that seemed to be everywhere on the famed Avenue of the Stars in Century City. Hunt was pretty sure they'd never get into the trendy nightspot, but Rackstraw wasn't worried. As the valet parked the car, he led his buddies into one of the many nearby bars for a drink. While the others leaned on their elbows and sipped, Rackstraw dropped out of sight for a few moments, and then reappeared.

"We're in," he grinned.

"What do you mean?" asked Hunt.

"Just follow me," said Rackstraw.

As the floor-pouring crew walked toward the entrance of the Playboy Club, only Rackstraw felt as if what they were doing wasn't hopeless. The line looked even longer than it had before. Rackstraw strolled up to the doorman.

"Bob Rackstraw," he said.

The doorman nodded and smiled. "Right this way, Mr. Rackstraw."

As the men walked in, events really began to get strange. A bunny was waiting for them—ears, fluffy tail, the works—ready to attend to their orders and even join them in a bumper-pool game until a table was ready.

Just as in Lake Tahoe, the rascally Rackstraw had pulled an identity switch. He had called the club from the bar, identifying himself as then-governor Ronald Reagan's personal aide. He then explained that the governor's pilot was on his way over—a fellow named Bob Rackstraw. He said the governor would appreciate it if all possible courtesies were extended to Mr. Rackstraw and any friends he might have with him.

When the bunny escorted them into the main room, it was straight to the front table.

Rackstraw, enjoying every minute of it, heard himself introduced by the emcee as Ronald Reagan's personal pilot. He stood up—making sure his DFC medal on his jacket was visible to all.

"Rackstraw waves to the audience, big grin. I mean he was like a sociopath," said Hunt.

It was a revelation about his friend's ability to manipulate people that Hunt would not forget.[22]

Later that summer, Rackstraw played to another audience—this time through a newspaper, when a reporter documented the foreman and Dan Hunt pouring Specialty Surfacing's chemicals for a new basketball court at Ken Hubbs Memorial Gymnasium in Colton, California.

"What we have used here is Versaturf 360," pitched Rackstraw, while posing shirtless for an article photo. "There're only six people who know how to install polyurethane. There's an art to installing this type of flooring and the material we work with is very toxic. It's a seven-day-a-week, fourteen-hour-a-day job."

San Bernardino floor job.

The self-declared spokesman's next claim to the *San Bernardino Sun-Telegram* newsman—that they'd been working floor jobs worldwide, from "Australia to Portugal"—was recently corrected for the record by former coworker Dan Hunt.

"We never left the country."

Snake oil, brought to you by Bullshit Bob.[23]

While Specialty Surfacing's work took Rackstraw out of town for days and weeks at a time, when he was at home in San Jose, his relationship with Linda McGarity went well. He was "treating me like a princess," she recalled, "and I never sensed an evil side."

But he had never been one to keep matters simple, and he wasn't about to start any time soon.

In April 1974, the multilicensed pilot opened a one-hangar air-taxi service at Palo Alto Airport, featuring a Hughes 500 helicopter—the loach surveillance aircraft he had trained on with the army—and his Cessna plane. The bulk of Rackstraw's flights took golfers and celebrities to Pebble Beach. On those flights, enjoying the reflective glamour of it all, McGarity often came along for the ride. Soon she also was going along to floor-laying jobs for Specialty Surfacing, such as when the crew went back to work out problems that arose in the Pepperdine gymnasium job.

Like he said to everyone else, Rackstraw told McGarity he owned both of these aircraft. The FAA database, however, has no record whatsoever of any aircraft registrations in his name.[24]

Despite her mate's predisposition to privacy and the occasional prank, McGarity put great value on honesty. A Christian, she was extremely gratified when Rackstraw decided to join her and the two children for Easter services at her church, soon after he had launched his air-taxi service. Preserving the moment, she took a picture of Rackstraw, resplendent in a polyester suit, grinning as he posed with the gift she had given him—a chocolate bunny that stood two feet tall.

About a month after Easter, on May 24, 1974, Rackstraw and McGarity were married in San Jose. They held the reception at the site of her old job, the Red Roof Inn, followed by a four-day honeymoon in Carmel, California, overlooking the Pacific. A photo of Rackstraw on the hotel room's balcony showed him in pants that surely belonged to Wavy Gravy—and shirtless again.[25]

True to form for a man who never met a chain saw he didn't want to juggle, Rackstraw soon launched yet another business, Fargo Graphics and Printing, right there in Cupertino. The local financial institutions, none of which would give him a start-up loan without collateral, were obviously wary of his lack of any discernible experience in that field, even if no one else was. But Rackstraw had never been one to let a minor inconvenience keep him from charging forward on a new and exciting adventure. Keeping it a secret from his new bride, he put up her home as collateral, apparently faking her signature on the deed.

Rackstraw also allegedly persuaded the father of their neighborhood babysitter, living two houses away, to invest "most of his retirement money" in the print shop.

There was no way he could keep his double-dealing from McGarity. When she confronted him, "he was just very carefree, like, no big thing, he did this all the time—'You don't remember signing that with me?' And I was like no, I wouldn't have signed over that for your print shop without looking [at] it and seeing the neighborhood [and] everything" on the paperwork.

Despite her understandable flare of anger at the news of his brazen dishonesty, Rackstraw was able to talk her down. "He always had a way of soothing things over," she noted.[26]

Trust, however, was another matter. Justifiably "a little curious" as to what her five-month groom might be thinking of or doing, McGarity went to his locked briefcase, left behind one day. "I found this little key in the underwear section of his dresser and I opened it. I looked [in] and I thought, what in the world?"

Among the business cards and paperwork was a disguise.

After closing it back up, she wondered, "How am I going to discuss this with him?"

When Rackstraw came home, McGarity was direct: Why would anyone need a disguise to do business? With a straight face, Rackstraw told her that he used the brown toupee to conceal his baldness in important meetings.

Not even he, apparently, had the nerve to make up a story about the tape-on mustache.[27]

CHAPTER 8

Song of the Open Road

JUNE 1974–AUGUST 10, 1976

D an Hunt, Pudgy's little brother, was impressed when he first met Bob Rackstraw. More than anything, he was in awe of the man's Vietnam experience. The war stories stuck with the impressionable twenty-eight-year-old, adding to his perception of Rackstraw as a valiant helicopter pilot with the medals to prove it.

On top of that, the thirty-year-old Rackstraw appeared to be a nice guy. Hunt understood that he couldn't really relate to someone who had done so much more than he had in his life, but he was impressed and liked Rackstraw.[1]

"He seemed to have ultimate confidence in himself," said Hunt. "He would do things that I would never do. He could approach anyone at any time if there was something he wanted. Or if there was a goal there that he had his eye set on. He was very confident. Didn't tell the truth a lot, but he didn't tell the truth in order to get . . . what he wanted."

A number of women could attest to Rackstraw's abilities in the lie-to-get-what-you-want department, of course. As Hunt explained, "If it came down to talking to women, well, Bob could get just about any woman. And I couldn't get to first base, you know?"

Hunt fully recognized that this ability was due to Rackstraw's telling them exactly what they desired to hear, even if none of it was real. He did the same in a lot of other areas, such as renting an airplane to fly around the city. He still had his pilot's license, but he'd frequently put down the wrong name on the agreement.

"I don't know what he did that for," said Hunt. "I just was kind of naive and probably in awe of what he was able to do. [He said he] worked for insurance companies to bring back planes during the drug era from Mexico. Did surveillance work. I mean he told me these stories. I don't know if they were true, but they all sounded good. He's very impressive."

Rackstraw and Dan Hunt got along so well that Specialty Surfacing sent them to oversee the company's floor-laying jobs in other states. They traveled all over the country, by air and auto, for eighteen months stretching from 1974 to 1976. Hunt learned you get to know someone extremely well when you travel with him—and when that travel lasts for as long as theirs did, you become an expert.

Rackstraw's alleged double life as a car and weapons thief may have been a colorful byproduct of his Vietnam experience, but on America's back roads, it became an addiction.

"It seemed like Bob always had to be doing something that was illegal and exciting," Hunt said. "We were doing a job in Denver. I remember [that evening], he was dressed up with a sock hat and black sweater. I asked what he was doing, and he said, 'Oh, I'm going to go look around.' It was obvious he was going out and probably stealing."

Later in California, Hunt "was driving with Bob in the truck, back and forth, and Mike Narro [called and] told me not to let him steal any vehicles. And you know, I told Bob that I didn't want any part of that."[2]

In San Jose, new bride Linda McGarity appeared to be the beneficiary of Rackstraw's rolling filched fleet—and each came with a bill of goods. "We would always get like one-year-old cars, Cadillacs, Trans Ams, every six months a new one," said McGarity. Her husband would explain to her, "Oh, this buddy from LA wants me to drop this car. Oh, the window's not going up, I'm going to trade it in."[3]

During an assignment in Cleveland, Ohio, in May 1975, the drunken Rackstraw was pulled over at night for speeding seventy miles an hour down Main Street. When the glaring cop asked for the smiling fool's name, the vet instantly responded "Pudgy Hunt." Then he gave Pudgy's Portland address—to the shock of Pudgy's brother Dan, sitting white-knuckled next to him.

Luck was with Rackstraw, however. An emergency call suddenly blared over the officer's two-way. He gave the men an angry warning and raced away. As Rackstraw put the car in gear, he waved off his partner's very personal concerns. "Ah, they'd never do anything about it."[4]

Rackstraw and Hunt were staying at a nearby Marriott Hotel. The room charge was well above the usual price range at the hotels they stayed in, but Rackstraw managed to get Specialty Surfacing to spring for the extra cost. How he did it was a mystery to Hunt, but he had simply begun to accept such surprises.

Hunt liked to use the television to put himself to sleep. When Rackstraw told him to turn it off that night, Hunt asked if he could watch for "just for a sec" more. In an explosion of anger, Rackstraw threw his glass through the television set.

"What the hell is wrong with you?" Hunt said, jumping up in alarm. "Are you crazy?" Hunt yelled at Rackstraw for about a half a minute until he paused long enough "to look in his eye."

Rackstraw was just sitting there, stone still, utterly cold and calm in the wake of his outburst. Hunt had a chilling realization. He had seriously misread what his companion was capable of because Rackstraw was sizing him up the way a wolf stares at a lamb. He knows he could eat it but has to decide if he's hungry enough to jump the fence and go to the trouble.

"He would kill me," said Hunt. I might physically be able to take him, you know, beat him. Maybe. But he would think nothing of killing me. So I just shut up and went to sleep."

The next morning, cool and in control, Rackstraw cut the rug in front of the television with his knife. Then he went down to the front desk and explained that he'd tripped on the rug the night before because it was ripped. As he did, he claimed, he accidentally threw his glass through the television set. Rackstraw didn't get into trouble. The Marriott, eager to avoid what the staff probably saw as a potential lawsuit, gave Rackstraw and Hunt free tickets to a Cleveland Indians baseball game and the next two nights free.

Hunt enjoyed the ballgame and the free stay, but his opinion of Rackstraw was forever changed. The glass thrown through the television had been a shot across the bow. This devil was hair-triggered.

Strangely, according to Hunt, Rackstraw considered the two of them to be exactly alike—comrades.

Once, in a bar on another trip to Cleveland, Hunt responded to all the tales about Rackstraw's heroic Vietnam exploits—as well as his paratrooper and Green Beret training—by bringing up the fugitive known as D. B. Cooper.

"I asked him, Bob, did you do that? He just kind of had a half-smile," said Hunt. "Didn't say anything."

While Rackstraw had told his sister he quit the military in disgust in 1971, he at least gave Hunt a half-truth—ending with a zinger: "He said he was kicked out of the army because he had an affair with his commanding officer's wife. I found out later that wasn't true."

If Hunt had grown to "respect" Rackstraw's capacity for lies and wanton violence, events the next month left him in absolute awe.

Specialty Surfacing had a contract to lay flooring at a high school in Evansville, Indiana. When Rackstraw and Hunt arrived at the site, they were surprised to find a lone picketing union worker making a lot of noise about closing the job down because it was a nonunion site.

Rackstraw, in the passenger seat, ordered Hunt to drive their car as close as he could to the roadside protester. But he didn't want him to stop, at least not at first. When the optimal moment arrived, Rackstraw let his anger have its way. He swung his door open and knocked the startled picketer down a short slope and into a canal that ran alongside the road.

Hunt came to a halt and Rackstraw leaped out of the car and went to the trunk. Hunt felt a chill as he saw Rackstraw carry a handgun down the slope to the water, wading in. In a moment, he reached the dazed and injured picketer, who was recovering from the full-force blow. Rackstraw pointed the gun at the man's skull, the muzzle resting against his matted hair.

"If you ever come back on this fuckin' job again, I'll blow your head off!"

The union man clearly understood. He gave Rackstraw no argument.

He didn't dare say it, but Hunt nonetheless doubted that this encounter would keep the union from picketing the site. Later that day, in fact, the local union boss arrived at the scene, backed by a muscleman who looked hungry for a brawl.

Rackstraw, however, understood how to deal with boys like these. He pulled a bottle of whiskey out of the car trunk for the boss. Then he challenged the bodyguard to an arm-wrestling contest—with Hunt, who Rackstraw knew full well was an Oregon champion.

Afterwards, there was enough whiskey to make everybody both happy and sick. The faces of the two union men were red with drink as Rackstraw kept the two entertained with war stories, some of which even Hunt hadn't heard during their many months on the road.[5]

Mixed in among the bravado and macho brutality were sour notes that both Dan and his brother Pudgy Hunt would have trouble overlooking. One of them came when Jim Spitznas Jr., a New Jersey–based trade partner of Specialty Surfacing, made nervous phone calls to both Hunt brothers.

The FBI had been calling him with "a lot of questions" about road-trip partner Bob Rackstraw. Spitznas asked Pudgy "where they [Dan and Bob] were going, how long they were going to be there."[6]

The older brother learned Rackstraw was suspected in the theft of explosives—according to the papers, twenty-two cases of dynamite, "two one-thousand foot spools of primer cord," and blasting caps—all taken five months earlier from the Felton Quarry in Rackstraw's old stomping grounds, Scotts Valley.

A green pickup truck had been seen on February 18, 1975, hauling away the cache. As one deputy put it, it was enough "to blow up the county governmental center six times over."

Authorities knew violent revolutionaries and terrorists were after explosives to punctuate their manifestos and protests, and the stock at remote quarries and mines had become easy targets. But one federal expert felt that somebody in this crew's caper was different.

"Someone who knew what they were doing put just enough explosive around the door [lock] to blow it off and not the explosives inside," explained Charles Nixon, a regional official from the Bureau of Alcohol, Tobacco, and Firearms (ATF), to the Associated Press. In addition, only the detonators and fuses that matched the types of dynamite taken were snatched up. "I imagine it was an ex-military explosives type who maybe got in with them."[7]

Was it a coincidence that, within two weeks of the half-ton of quarry explosives vanishing, authorities announced a bombing wave was underway in the San Francisco Bay area—just eighty miles away? Five revolutionary groups there claimed credit for raising the blast rate from once a month to once a week. The most active militant cell, the New World Liberation Front, took responsibility for sixteen attacks, including the blowing up of six Pacific Gas and Electric power-line towers on March 20.[8]

In that bombing, a local district attorney revealed "Rackstraw had been investigated by the FBI for a possible role" in delivering the quarry cache that was used. Agents, in fact, were sharing their suspicions about his new line of underground work with local police, reporters, and even to his sister, Linda Lee.[9]

A year later, the veteran's name came up again when some of the Santa Cruz County dynamite was found at a "bomb factory" hideaway in the Bay Area town of Richmond. And the FBI credited the discovery to a brave mother with two children.

Judy Stevenson had attended a Berkeley "study group" put on by the New Dawn Party—an "above-ground Marxist/Leninist/Maoist organization" operating out of a radical bookstore, claimed one revolutionary newsletter. After hearing of its "support for armed struggle," the twenty-eight-year-old Stevenson telephoned the tip into the FBI. For the next month, she took instructions as a paid informant.

On February 20, 1976, she invited a half-dozen of the key members to move into her Spanish-style bungalow home with her family in Richmond. With the FBI on surveillance, the group arrived with personal items and boxes of radical materials. But then "they put guns on the table [and] are working on explosive devices. One came out with a hand grenade and threatened to blow up the house if anyone tried to stop them."

These New Dawn bookstore operators had double lives in "the terrorist Emiliano Zapata Unit," a recent arrival in the Bay Area that had claimed responsibility for six bombings.

Stevenson found a way to break away and meet with her agent handlers, where she signed a consent form agreeing to the FBI raid on her property. At five o'clock the next morning, both the FBI and Richmond Police SWAT teams crashed in, arresting the half-dozen militants. Four live bombs were defused, and 150 pounds of explosives from the Scotts Valley quarry were recovered.

This young mother's witness testimony proved crucial to the case. Later that year, five of the six pleaded guilty for reduced sentences. (The last was cleared of all charges.)

In court, Judy Stevenson was asked what motivated her courage in calling the FBI. It wasn't the illegal weapons or even the grenade threat against her family. It was a phone call she had received earlier that day, where a doctor told her she had cancer and only six months to live.[10]

Frustration, no doubt, was building at the bureau. Rackstraw, the military bad boy, was now suspected in two high-profile Santa Cruz County break-ins—the first being the National Guard Armory in 1971. But he apparently had good alibis, devoted crime partners, loyal friends (depending on your point of view), and incredibly good luck. No cinematic offense to the FBI, but he was untouchable.[11]

Speaking of Rackstraw's luck, informant Stevenson may have inadvertently revealed another example of it during her pretrial testimony. When the mother first recalled the radical group's arrival, she mentioned, "Some people are in my home discussing a person shot in the stomach."

As noted earlier, Bob Rackstraw never received a Purple Heart in Vietnam. But authorities in the late 1970s knew they had one other way to identify the troublemaker with nine lives, besides through his fingerprints: a mysterious "bullet-wound scar on his left side."[12]

CHAPTER 9

Don't Marry Bad Boys

JULY 1974–DECEMBER 1976

James T. "Jim" Shell was another University of Oregon fraternity brother of Dick Briggs in 1962. But a dozen years later, the two were both divorced fathers and roommates, living bachelors' lives between custody visits, at Shell's new Portland home near the Willamette River.

In the midseventies, Briggs was enjoying a reputation as an enforcer and a barroom brawler. As Shell put it, "If he was your friend, he was your friend for life. But if you pissed him off, you might as well move to a different city, that's really the way he was."

Shell recollected the day a guy at a house party made a comment about his roommate's ex-wife. "Dick just went berserk and literally threw this guy through a plate-glass window. He wound up in the front yard."[1]

After a long day as a loan manager in Portland's financial district in July 1974, the thirty-one-year-old Shell walked in on Briggs in full party mode, entertaining another man with eight bottles of Shell's own wine and cocaine lines on the kitchen table. Between nose wipes,

Dick Briggs, drug supplier and man about Portland.

111

Briggs introduced his Specialty Surfacing crew boss and new friend: Bob Rackstraw.

The Californian and the volatile Briggs would be seeing plenty of each other during the years to come. But Shell said he kept his distance from the intimidating stranger. His first impression that evening was the way Rackstraw never stopped watching everything going on around him.

"He had a linebacker's eyes," said Shell. "The way he looked, the way he acted, he just sat there, didn't hardly say a word."

Jim Shell, circa 2012.

The lifelong accountant added that there was something else: "A duffel bag full of money next to Rackstraw. I just happened to look down there and see some bills, which is, like I'm not supposed to know what's there? I'm not blind and I'm not stupid. But it wasn't my business, so I headed to my room."

Yet the fact remained the veteran had hauled a big pile of cash more than six hundred miles to a cokehead's house. This understandably raised suspicions about the cleanliness of the cash.

During the 1970s and into the 1980s, illegally gotten gains were frequently laundered using South African Krugerrands, throwing an intriguing light onto the possibility of what Rackstraw might have done to hide the 1971 hijacking ransom money collected from Northwest Airlines.

When asked if Briggs was dealing with any gold—particularly Krugerrands—Shell answered yes with an "of course" tone, adding that at one time, "He had two around his neck, if I remember. That's what people did."[2]

Briggs, however, did more than that. A lot more.

The next year, he was pulled over by a Portland police officer. With him in his 1960 Corvette convertible were another school buddy, Bob

Finkle, and his wife, Sonia—all three squeezed into the Vette's two front seats. In the course of the stop, the officer told Briggs to open the trunk so he could make sure he wasn't carrying anything illegal. When the driver complied, the cop found "a load of guns," Sonia recollected. Moving to his squad car, the officer called in to the station and then came back toward the Corvette. The Finkles were astonished when the officer politely shut the trunk and gave Briggs his driver's license back.

"Have a nice night," he said with a nod.[3]

Such was the relationship the party boy enjoyed with the Portland Police Bureau.

In the summer of 1975, Rackstraw raced up the coast of Oregon to hang out with Dan Hunt, his new road-trip partner at Specialty Surfacing. They met in Hunt's hometown of Seaside at a landmark bar called the Seasider, naturally. Their revelry began with a traditional rum-chugging contest. But as Hunt told it, this one had a memorable moment.

At the finale, Rackstraw "lit up his cigarette. However, the 151 [rum] had dripped down his Fu Manchu and it caught fire."

A stampede of drinkers rushed to his rescue, dousing, slapping, and finally smothering the flames engulfing his face and neck. Rackstraw caught his breath and laughed, and more drinks flowed. He proudly showed off his bubbling burns the rest of the night. It's safe to say the next morning's hangover wasn't his only headache.[4]

Forty-two months. That was how long Rackstraw had gone deadbeat on his ex-wife, Gail Marks, failing to pay child support for their three young kids since the day of their Alabama divorce. On October 23, 1975, Marks went before a California judge in Santa Cruz County, seeking the overdue $16,800—while pointing out that her ex-husband was living nicely in the nearby San Jose neighborhood of Cupertino. She went on to say that he had a red 1958 Corvette parked in his driveway—a couple of years younger than the one his crime partner Briggs drove.

It took the court two full years to order the slippery Rackstraw to pay the sum owed, plus future monthly payments, in a timely manner. But

Marks has always claimed that he never wrote her a support check in his life.[5]

While revenge is best served cold, it's far sweeter on a bed of lettuce—the kind that comes in large denominations. In the years that followed, Marks was the recipient of two considerable checks that were otherwise destined for her ex-husband. She claimed the first, in 1977, was a $10,000 worker's compensation injury settlement that was rerouted by the California Department of Child Support Services. The second came in late January 1980. It was $7,000 generated from the sale of Rackstraw's parents' Valley Springs property and was signed and forwarded by his sister, Linda Lee, who was both the trustee of the family estate and the kids' loving aunt.[6]

In the last month of 1975, Rackstraw was circling the wagons in a number of ways. On the business side, he accepted fewer floor assignments and less travel from Specialty Surfacing in San Francisco, instead setting up his own local contracting concern. Called the American Construction Team, it also operated under a second moniker, Bahama Pools.

Deliberately not taking on Narro's company in its own field, ACT listed services in the areas of general engineering, earthwork and paving, solar, building, pool design, and concrete work. But according to Pudgy Hunt, Bob's breakaway move rankled his former employer just the same.[7]

It was an ambitious undertaking, particularly in light of the fact that Fargo Graphics and Printing—the Cupertino venture Rackstraw had funded by putting up Linda McGarity's house, without her permission, and getting a neighbor to do the same—ran dry on July 1, 1976. When the shop closed its doors, Rackstraw defaulted on the loan. McGarity and her babysitter's dad both lost their properties.[8]

At almost the same time, Rackstraw also closed his struggling aviation company in Palo Alto. He sold off its two aircraft but transported the sheriff's former Bell chopper, along with his somewhat shaken wife and her two kids, out to his parents' town of Valley Springs. The family resettled in a hilltop rental home on Heney Court, about five miles from Rackstraw's folks.

Incredibly, McGarity chalked it all up as just a bad business break. Instead of going into a rather understandable rage, she focused on the kids and their new "adventure."[9]

The downdraft that had swept Rackstraw out of two businesses was not entirely spent, however. It was shaping up to be a bad year for him legally, too. First, he was slapped with a $5,545.50 civil judgment in Cupertino-Sunnyvale Municipal Court related to his failed Fargo Graphics and Printing business.[10]

Close on the heels of that action came a legal maneuver that, one might suspect, has haunted Rackstraw to this day.

To prevent the normal five-year statute of limitations on the D. B. Cooper skyjacking from expiring, Oregon-based lead FBI agent Ralph Himmelsbach and Assistant US Attorney Jack G. Collins called together a Portland grand jury and hammered through an indictment in absentia on the very last day. They filed it against a John Doe, AKA D. B. Cooper, "for air piracy."[11]

"Here's a little guy, all by himself, who reached up and tweaked Uncle Sam's nose and took $200,000 from a major corporation," Himmelsbach told reporters. "This was a desperate act you wouldn't expect from a normal man. This was something you'd expect from somebody who had nothing to lose. And he's not a Robin Hood type. He's just a dirty scum criminal."[12]

The indictment, carrying a possible forty-five-year sentence, was meant to be a blade hanging over the hijacker's head, should he be apprehended.

In December 1976, Rackstraw was spending more and more days away from Linda McGarity and the young children.

"I had no idea what he was working on. I was concerned because he'd been out of town a lot since we had married, and I'm out there in the woods" above Valley Springs,[13] with meandering snakes and mountain lions for neighbors.

Rackstraw's mother, Lucille, then fifty-four years old, had become appalled by what she knew now to be her son's seemingly nonstop infidelities. A pious Jehovah's Witness, she could brook his adultery no further. Deeply conflicted, she gave a mysterious post office box key to McGarity, her beautiful daughter-in-law of two years. The Texan steeled herself for the short drive to the mail-drop.

The key opened the box that Rackstraw and his stepfather shared. "There were two letters, one from a lady in New York, and the other from one in California. Well, I got in my car because it didn't say my name on it, didn't say Mr. and Mrs. Rackstraw, just him. I proceeded to open the one from New York. And I freaked out."

It stated, "You're going to leave Linda, aren't you? I've been waiting long enough."

"I just kept reading the letter over and over," said McGarity. "Tears are flowing everywhere, and I'm trying to drive. I went to his mom's house and [showed] her the letters. She said, 'Kick him out tonight!'"[14]

Rackstraw was a thirty-three-year-old man, not a hormone-crazed teenager, and McGarity had expected him to be the honest husband he had claimed to be. She was mildly surprised when she realized her meandering mate was not going to insult her with more lame explanations after she threw the incriminating letters down on the table between them. He could read the return addresses of his two mistresses.

"You're too good a person for me," Rackstraw sighed, shaking his head. "Look," he went on, voice low, eyes evasive, "something's coming down and I don't think you need to be here."

McGarity lost it again. "What?"

He was unequivocal. "You need to go back, you and the children. Take whatever we have in the bank and head home to Texas."

Without another word, she set out to do just that.

"I remember the next three days," said McGarity. "His parents were helping me pack a few things. Bob rented me a U-Haul and gave me $1,100, and that's what I came back to Texas on."

On the final morning at dawn, Daddy Bob gently put the sleepy step-kids in their seat belts and then gave his stone-silent princess one last big hug. "I love you; you're wonderful." Then once again, that admonition: "You don't need to be here; things are going down."

Odd chivalry be damned, the divorce papers from Prince Charming almost beat her home.[15]

One of his secret lovers, twenty-eight-year-old Mary Yontel (not her real name), was patiently waiting for him in San Jose. In an interview, she talked about how the sharing of stepdad stories had made them instant soul mates.

"He was a young man that had a difficult life, like I'd had," claimed Yontel. "My stepfather shot [and killed] my mother in domestic violence. And I know how it affected Bob when this very abusive man came into his mother's life."[16]

Surely his sister, Linda Lee—who had described Philip as a loving father that wouldn't use the prefix "step" and didn't practice spanking—might have taken some issue with Yontel's characterization of their Scotts Valley childhood.[17]

So might have Gail Marks, who you recall sometimes referred to her ex as Bullshit Bob.[18]

CHAPTER 10

Rattlesnake Ranch

JANUARY–JUNE 1977

Rackstraw's close friendship with Dick Briggs included an element of criminality from the beginning. The two became outlaw partners in Southern California shortly after laying the 1973 Pepperdine University gymnasium floor.[1]

A former supervisor at Specialty Surfacing remembers Rackstraw dressing in a black suit and tie and carrying a clipboard, like a free-moving management type, "so he could steal around the San Francisco shipyard. He reveled in it. He was a thief and a gangster."[2]

But now, with Briggs around, Rackstraw was a gangster with a sidekick or, more precisely, with something of an apprentice. Rackstraw clearly called the shots in the relationship.

Briggs was visiting the newly single Rackstraw in Northern California one afternoon in early 1977. While walking in his old Cupertino neighborhood, about two miles from where he had lived with McGarity and the stepkids, Bob stopped in front of a gun shop window. He smiled naughtily.

"I need more guns," he said.

Later that night, Rackstraw stole a pickup truck from a closed car dealership and, with the white-knuckled Briggs riding shotgun, drove the makeshift battering ram right through the gun store's front window. Before you could say Tony Soprano, the pair was loading a truckload of brand new sports rifles. Rackstraw ended the incident after looking at his watch, and they raced away.

Pudgy Hunt said that Briggs had relayed the whole episode to him: "We get back to the hotel, and I'm scared to death. I ask Bob, 'Jesus, what if the cops had come by?' Bob says, 'I've been following them for the last three nights. Every night between 11 and 11:30, they're at this diner out on the other side of town. It takes them six and a half minutes in a fast car to get from the diner to the gun shop, so I knew we had at least three minutes.' The son of a bitch had it all planned out."[3]

What Briggs would not live to know was that guns sometimes float to the surface, years later. Several of the weapons from that Cupertino smash-and-grab were inherited by younger relatives of Rackstraw's first wife, Gail Marks.

Marks admitted that she was circuitously responsible for those hot estate gifts. After the robbery, she allowed Rackstraw—again, the man she had turned in as a wife beater and deadbeat dad—to hide the rifles in her own mother's attic. When the eighty-six-year-old matriarch, Opal, passed away in 1993, the mystery guns became part of the estate. Oblivious family heirs then split them up.

When recently pressed about whether Rackstraw stole those firearms, Marks said, "I'm sure of it."[4]

On another occasion during Briggs's California visit, he joined Rackstraw for a day trip to San Francisco. The true nature of the journey, however, became clear when they stole a parked Volkswagen and drove it right into the back of a two-and-a-half-ton truck. The VW was quickly stripped of parts for resale, and the remains were dumped unceremoniously on a back road.[5]

In Valley Springs, Rackstraw's lover, Mary Yontel, had "moved up to the mountains" to join him in his rental home. And she was having a blast.

"We had a construction business. Engineering jobs, building houses, whatever we could get a contract to . . . have work. I want[ed] to learn, and it's a great way of learning. I remember with Bob, he would put me on a piece of heavy equipment, and he'd say, 'Just feel . . . you get the feel of what it's like to move earth.' This is with a D10 [Caterpillar tractor].

"He was a man that has to have dirt under his nails. He would come home with an engine in his truck. I've been under a piece of equipment with him, handing him a wrench or whatever he needed, doing the mechanics. Bob was amazing. He could build them. He could take them apart."[6]

And he could steal them, if you believed Briggs and Rackstraw's floor-company bosses.[7] But in this remote town of fifteen hundred, that reputation apparently hadn't been driven home yet.

Yontel also talked about flying in a small plane with Rackstraw where he let her take over the controls while he logged the flight plan. "He put time and energy and love into me, and for that . . . I loved him so very much."

Earlier that year, Rackstraw showed Yontel another side of that energy—in a Texas saloon.

"We flew to meet his old Vietnam buddy, Joe [Schlein], I think in El Paso. We're in this bar and I'm sitting on a stool, Joe on one side and Bob's on the other. This guy walks by and he wanted to start something. And I told Bob, 'He intentionally tried to hurt my foot!'

"The stranger goes to the end of the bar and says, 'What are you going to do about it?' Joe and Bob looked at each other and [Bob] is like, 'Do you want him or is he mine?'

Rackstraw stood up and challenged the stranger, and he "takes the bait." As he stormed by, Joe Schlein twirled around and threw a sucker punch.

"Knocked him out with one lick," added Yontel. "And the bouncer came over, and the bouncer was down" from Rackstraw's own blindsider. "The three of us ran for the pickup and we stopped for breakfast, and they were laughing about it. You think about the movies, you see these fights and how they go on forever. I had never seen someone just hit someone one time and they're out on the floor in front of you.

"So it was just something that happened, and it wasn't initiated by Joe or Bob. But they took care of the situation and all."

Not a bad rationalization for a respected senior citizen, now thirty-nine years after the whacking.[8]

Shortly after Briggs's return to Portland, he went from a happy client to a local supplier in the Colombian cocaine trade. The new drug of choice was sweeping the harbor town like a gold rush, with workers quitting their secure day shifts for delivery jobs. The coke carpetbaggers moved from white-collar parties to bars to college games, staking territory and forwarding thousands of dollars to their far-off masters.[9]

Realizing the illicit enterprise would soon bury him in greenbacks, Briggs sought a discreet partner to handle the books. His first choice was his trusted frat brother and former roommate, Jim Shell. After hearing the pitch, the loan company supervisor ditched his neckties.[10]

In February 1977, Briggs's new middleman hired two runners to facilitate distribution for the cocaine operation. They were Ron L. Carlson, then a twenty-seven-year-old "pill-and-pot" pusher, and trucker Verlan C. "Vern" Burke, ten years Carlson's senior.[11]

When Rackstraw strolled into Pudgy Hunt's Portland saloon in March 1977, he was playing the role of garrulous bon vivant, explaining that he was on the way to a floor installation job in southern Oregon and had just come by to say hello. So it came as a surprise to the bar owner a few days later when a very angry Herb Woods called, asking if Hunt might know where that son-of-a-bitch Rackstraw had gone. The inquiry made sense, considering Hunt had brought the two men together.

The saloon keeper had once been a friendly competitor of Woods in the flooring trade. Woods had called Hunt the year before, asking if he knew anyone who could train his sons to operate their brand-new urethane-rubber-mixing machine. Hunt referred him to Rackstraw, his former coworker at Specialty Surfacing in San Francisco.[12]

Mary Yontel remembered joining Rackstraw for this March trip, along with another Specialty Surfacing colleague, Patrick R. Ebert, "to put in a gym in Oregon. We were just working to get this floor down because you gotta work quickly with that stuff; it'll bubble on you."[13]

The bubbling-over Woods, though, was adamant that Rackstraw had another, much more destructive agenda on this recent visit, to which Hunt replied that Rackstraw had only told him he was on the way "to do a job."

Woods said the "job" had actually been a flooring project the two were collaborating on in far-off Lahaina, Maui, but it had unavoidably gone off the rails. When Woods's son Steve, working in Hawaii with Bob, was ordered to come home with his dad's urethane mixer, he did. Seething, Rackstraw packed up and flew to the mainland with revenge against the Woods family at number one on his itinerary.

True to this intention, he had just smashed a car into Woods's closed Eugene warehouse and made off with the same expensive mixer. That was why Woods wanted to find him, have him charged with everything the police could think of, and then sue his ass on top of that.

Steve Woods, now sixty-six and retired, was tracked down for his take on the blowup involving his deceased father. After the training session on the mixer, Steve revealed, the thirty-three-year-old Rackstraw had made a quiet deal to join the family on floor jobs "around the West, more than a dozen over the next half year."

The violent split after the Hawaiian assignment was scary enough. But like Rackstraw's former coworker Dan Hunt, Steve also had fond memories of his wild and crazy adventures with the veteran. He chuckled when recalling how he, at twenty-three, "sat on the beach with Bob, smoking Thai sticks until we couldn't even stand." Then there was the night Rackstraw "paid for two prostitutes in a bar. I'd never done that before."

Steve paused for a moment. "I knew he had a wife. Obviously, he had an interesting view on marriage."[14]

About a month after the Woods family face-off, right around April Fool's Day 1977, Rackstraw made a fateful decision. He was having terrible problems with his fledgling construction and pool design company, ACT, and finally saw no other choice than to turn to his forty-nine-year-old stepfather for help. For most of his life, Philip had made his living as a bulldozer operator, but he agreed to become partners with Bob in a new venture to replace ACT. They filed "doing business as" papers for 3R Engineering Contractors. The three Rs stood for "Rackstraw's Rattlesnake Ranch."

It didn't take long for the collaboration to start crumbling.

Linda Lee had been worried from the start, given her brother's penchant for starting new projects and then failing to make them stick. She feared that 3R could leave her stepdad holding the bag.

Within a few weeks, Philip's regular clients—the ones he had cultivated over years of hard, reliable work—began to complain. They accused Bob

Robby Jr. with Philip Rackstraw—puts Bob at the family home, laying low in June 1972.

of doing inferior work, even "deceiving" them and "lying" about it, and not completing contractual obligations. Philip, a man who believed a handshake was an ironclad bond, and had proven he was loyal to a fault many times, found this to be torture.[15]

Philip told Linda Lee that Bob's violent, increasingly explosive temper was frightening and that he felt he'd made a terrible mistake in partnering with him. Over the next three months, his fears would mount.

Philip had begun drinking heavily in December 1976, after learning his wife, Lucille, had breast cancer. Bob's original reason for moving back to Valley Springs was supposedly to help Philip by covering the accounting chores his mother normally performed. Bob claimed to Linda Lee that he just wanted to keep the business going, but eventually, "he just kind of took it over," she said. The twenty-nine-year-old daughter, in the middle, tried to give her stepfather as much emotional support as she could, but it would have taken a miracle to calm the brewing tempest between Philip and Bob.

Philip had desperately turned to Bob for accounting help. But the stepson had seen one business after another fail—no matter how great his original idea had seemed—and had reached out to Philip for contacts and operational expertise. This combination created a perfect storm.

"I would go up about every other week or call him," Linda Lee said about her stepdad. "We would be in touch. And I was there and there were these bags, paper bags full of papers, sitting on the front porch."

Philip told her they were his business records and receipts, and he planned to take them down to San Jose where the son-in-law of one of his good friends was an accountant.

Linda Lee said her stepdad "wanted him to go through it all and [have him] tell him what was going on, because he wasn't getting a straight answer from Bob. And then those papers disappeared. I don't know what happened to them. I probably could guess, but I don't know what happened to them."

Bob and his stepfather did do a fair job of hiding their growing anger with each other from the dying Lucille. It came out more frequently in sidebars, such as Philip yelling over the phone at Bob's answering machine: "I know you're there, damn it, pick up! I know you, you know, and you need to pick up!"

Linda Lee, as it happened, was at her parents' and overheard the tirade. But despite the efforts to not trouble Lucille, she knew things weren't right.

"They're arguing, and I don't know what Bob is doing," she told her daughter.

This was extremely disturbing to Lucille because she had always taken fastidious care of the books. She worried about what Bob was up to but was too sick to do anything about it.[16]

Philip confided in Linda Lee as well. He told her that he had been seeing "another woman," from San Diego, the sister of one of his Valley Springs neighbors. Linda Lee knew that her stepfather was not the kind of man who could become a bachelor and take care of himself, and she had privately thought that he would remarry within a year of her mother's death.

She understood that he would never be able to look after his life and business without a woman to do some tasks with him and others for him.

"I was all for him selling the property because he had gone into a depression. He would just sit in his La-Z-Boy. I mean, that's one of the reasons I'd go up there and make him dinner."

Linda Lee knew Bob didn't see matters the way she did. He told her that he was hurt and angry on their mother's behalf. To him it was offensive and disrespectful for Philip to be courting his next wife before Lucille was even gone.[17]

This from a son who split his time between marriages and mistresses.[18]

CHAPTER 11

Philip Goes Missing

JUNE 1977–FEBRUARY 5, 1978

O nly six months after her breast cancer diagnosis, Lucille Rackstraw died in the Valley Springs mobile home she shared with Philip. She was fifty-five.[1]

Mary Yontel was with Bob when he quietly arrived for the June 2 service at Peoples Cemetery in San Andreas. Immediately after, he seemed to channel his grief into a growing anger at his stepfather, suggesting the cheating on his mom had been going on for some time.[2]

"Bob told me Philip was having an affair with a sheriff's wife," Gail Marks, his first mate, recently revealed.[3]

This wasn't the first time he'd tried that twisted story line. As noted earlier, Rackstraw blamed his army discharge on an affair he supposedly had with the base commander's spouse.[4]

After having been in near-constant contact with Philip throughout her mother's decline, Linda Lee felt a stab of alarm when she suddenly couldn't reach him on the phone one day. Rackstraw dismissed her concerns, telling his sister that Philip had mentioned more than once that he ought to go to Hawaii to "sort himself out" after Lucille's death. To Linda Lee, this idea was jarringly out of whack with everything she knew about her stepdad.

The loyal daughter kept trying to figure out where he was. She contacted Philip's eighty-seven-year-old mother, the United Kingdom–born matriarch "Grandma Rose" Rackstraw, in San Jose. She had not heard from him, either. Philip's close buddy, whose son-in-law was the accountant Philip had planned to consult, also couldn't help.

Linda Lee's sense that something was really wrong, really troubling, deepened. She could understand that her stepfather might not contact her because he was afraid "I would just rip him one" if he were out on a drunken binge. But failing to reach out to anyone he cared about? Going silent across the board? She simply could not accept that. Something else was happening.

What could make someone like Philip leave his ten-acre ranch, complete with chickens that needed to be fed and his two beloved dogs—even if, as Bob seemed to be saying, everything had been left in his care while the old man was on the beach soaking up rays? Linda Lee didn't understand how her brother could expect her to simply accept an idea like that. She knew her stepfather too well. The story just didn't add up.[5]

Rackstraw continued to maintain the Hawaii line and that Philip had even called him to say that getting himself together wasn't as simple as he'd hoped it would be. A concerned friend named Ben Brooks, however, claimed the stepson gave him a totally different characterization of the widower's island visit: he was just "having a ball" and a "good time," courtesy of a large government check.

The convoluted accounts didn't stop there. Neighbor Pat Lombardi was told Philip's destination was actually the Philippines.[6]

A month after Linda Lee had last known that her stepfather was safe, she heard from Grandma Rose. She stated her other son, Linda Lee's Uncle Bill, had just hired a San Francisco private detective to find the truth.[7]

PI Jack Immendorf documented Bill's concerns in a detailed narrative outline: "Jack, he wouldn't just disappear. It's totally out of character and the family's convinced something's happened to him. Phil would never let his mother's birthday pass without a telephone call. We're a close family."

On September 1, the forty-three-year-old Immendorf put on his proverbial gumshoes to interview "at least two-dozen people who had lived within a ten-mile radius of the missing man in Calaveras County."[8]

Linda Lee was filled with grief stemming from the recent loss of her mother, as well as confusion about why Philip had just disappeared without contacting her. Loss and bafflement—one set of emotions for each parent—pervaded nearly every waking moment of her life, even as she was now raising a little girl on her own.[9]

She would have felt even worse if she had known what Immendorf had seen and heard.

The investigator had gone snooping, in classic private-eye fashion, around Philip's Valley Springs property. The only signs of life he encountered were the man's dogs, still running loose. The older one, Bingo, slowly wandered back and forth, circling near a red shed by the garage, whining and seemingly confused. The animal, as any dog lover would recognize, appeared to be searching for something, for someone—for its master. Finally it lay down in the middle of the hardscrabble yard and watched the man who had been watching it.

Shed at Rattlesnake Ranch, where bloody pants were found in a trash can.

The PI next introduced himself to neighbors who were more than willing to talk. One claimed Bob Rackstraw "had been observed cleaning the stepdad's trailer himself one night, around the time Philip had disappeared." The witness also "recalled a loud shouting match between Philip and Bob at about the same time." Immendorf then "discovered another witness who said that [Bob] had hired some migrant workers to do a thorough 'wash-down' of Philip's trailer."

Immendorf's concern for Philip soon matched Linda Lee's—he could find absolutely nothing in the man's lifestyle to explain the vanishing. "He was the sort who put his dogs in the pickup with him. He stopped paying his union dues. His three-hundred-dollar checking account wasn't used at all," he later told a local reporter. He had also "purchased a beef roast and took it to a neighbor who was going to cook it for a party the next day." Immendorf said that delivery was on the last day he was seen alive: July 25, 1977.[10]

He reported back to his employer, Bill Rackstraw, that nephew Bob had told him Philip was on a bender in Lahaina, Hawaii. Which is why, in late October, the private eye flew there to take a look. After four days of hotel, credit card, and police checks in the old Maui whaling town, all he found was a pile of mail. No Philip.

"Lahaina was small enough so that a perpetually drunken stranger would be remembered, even if he had come and gone," wrote the PI. "I had taken along pictures of both Philip and his stepson, Bob. Interesting enough, I couldn't find anybody who remembered seeing Philip, but two people thought they remembered [Bob]."[11]

That made sense, considering Rackstraw had been working there with the Woods family flooring company just seven months earlier—until the collaboration turned volcanic.[12]

For his part, Bob Rackstraw was behaving in his usual well-oiled-machine-of-rapid-fire-double-talk mode. His moved-in "soul mate" in Valley Springs, Mary Yontel, had grown used to hearing him call her "wife" and telling others the Heney Court rental home was now his—even though Yontel's personal check had paid for it. Those little domestic details apparently didn't matter to her, because for one of the first times in her twenty-nine years, she felt safe.

"Maybe it was unrealistic, but I made this man my . . . my hero," said Yontel. "No one would ever hurt me; Bob would protect me."[13]

If this loyal companion was out for adventure, her timing was impeccable; she would get plenty in the months to come.

It had been eight years since those First Cav "crazy guys"—Rackstraw and Joe Schlein—were tossing satchel bombs down Vietnamese tunnels. But on November 11, 1977, the Californian recruited the Texas bar brawler for a risky new mission: transporting dynamite across state lines.

Rackstraw carefully packaged up a charge of Tovex Water-gel for the trip to Schlein's hometown of San Antonio, courtesy of those UPS men in shorts. The curious Yontel was given an off-the-cuff explanation: "[The] stuff was being used on a construction job. I guess I was naive, I didn't think he was doing anything wrong.

"Bob put it in three boxes," where he separated the dynamite, primer cord, and explosive caps. She surmised that was to prevent the colliding components from going off in the truck.

Or was it simply to stop cargo checkers from putting two and two together? It's a moot point because the whole crazy scheme turned into a dud—not because of poor planning, but poor penmanship.

"Bob has a tendency to scribble," noted Yontel. "One [box] didn't make it, and they opened the package because they couldn't deliver it. They found the caps."[14]

Because the anonymous sender used a fictitious return address in the city of Stockton, that's where the methodical investigation began—involving the US Postal Service, bomb specialists, arson investigators, and handwriting experts, along with a few good guesses.[15]

As with all his mates, Rackstraw didn't share everything he was up to with Yontel, such as a scheme he had been planning involving local banks. It was going to be another blow struck on behalf of the little guy—Rackstraw himself, specifically—against the greedy corporate giants that had come to represent all that was despicable.

A month after the UPS mess, Rackstraw walked into Linda Lee's work office. That was unusual in and of itself, but then he smiled and said, "Here's some money."

He handed Linda Lee a check for "twelve-thousand something-hundred dollars," she recollected. "I'm going up north to do this big job," he told her. "I got a nice, big advance."

She wasn't quite sure what to say. He had known that she wanted to buy a duplex. She had often talked about it as her "big dream." She would live in one half and rent out the other.

Better yet, it was a cashier's check. If it had been a regular personal check, she might have rolled her eyes and tossed it back at him.

"Invest it wisely," he said.

Rackstraw also said to get it to the bank as quickly as possible. When she pointed out that it was probably safe since it was a cashier's check, he reiterated that she should act with due speed. Linda Lee thought his sense of urgency was bizarre, but then there was always the adage about not looking a gift horse in the mouth—and this gift was followed by three zeroes. It also crossed her mind that he might be making up for the time a few years earlier that he had promised to loan her some money but backed out at the last minute, putting her in a bind.

She went to the bank feeling flush and happy, entertaining the well-known notion "that you had to have cash—cold-hard cash—behind a cashier's check."

That was not quite true. After Linda Lee had used the check to open a new savings account, she got a phone call from the local sheriff's department. Apparently, several checks issued by Rackstraw were bouncing off the walls in various places. Three different banks were involved. He had been kiting the checks from one institution to the next.

"Now remember, back then there was no computerization," Linda Lee explained. Her brother "had a printing business, and he took the [fake bank] check, the money from that," to another bank. "One bank didn't know what the other bank was doing. It took phone calls if the transaction was big enough and you wanted to check on it."

This key recollection of Fargo Graphics and Printing's involvement would explain why Rackstraw's company had always been a mystery to former wife McGarity, a company that her falsified signature had secretly funded, three years earlier—during their 1974 wedding month.

"I [had] never been to the print shop, never looked at it, never saw it," McGarity said. "He never let me know anything, or I never discussed finances with him. It was like he made the money and I knew what to do with it," she chuckled.

Linda Lee concluded that her brother had been transferring the phantom money from his account at Bank A and depositing it into Bank B by writing a normal check. That check would have taken ten to fifteen days to clear in 1977. Before that could happen (or not happen, actually), Rackstraw took the money from Bank B and put it into Bank C, which ultimately believed that he had some $87,000 in his account.

By the time banks A and B realized the funds were nonexistent, cashier's checks on the Bank C account had gone out to Linda Lee and others. Then they turned to vapor.

Rackstraw's masterstroke was to persuade the good people at Bank C to write cashier's checks on funds that had not actually cleared. Linda Lee believed his good old charm—the same slippery quality that had gotten him off scot-free so many times when he was a rowdy kid—must have been in full effect.

"So yeah, [sheriff deputies] got ahold of me that the check had no funds behind it. And it didn't surprise me, knowing Bob," she ruefully recalled.[16]

On January 24, 1978, the law came rapping on Linda Lee's Stockton door. In part, it was about those same check-kiting charges. But FBI agent Warren Little was also curious about some other escapades her brother might have been involved with, as she soon found out.[17]

Little's presence in her living room owed much to two dogged Stockton investigators. Police Sergeant Charles Buck and Fire Arson Investigator Michael Murray had gone to their local library with the express purpose of comparing Rackstraw's background and military qualifications to the skill set of a 1971 hijacker, D. B. Cooper. They matched. The investigators also were amazed at the suspect's resemblance to the famous seven-year-old FBI sketches of the jumper.

"There were so many things that seemed to fit," they later told a *Stockton Record* reporter. "It was just a hunch that kept developing."[18]

The two investigators had quietly tipped Little about their suspicions, and the well-mannered agent was soon "unofficially" sitting with Linda Lee. He no doubt was excited about what he had learned: the FBI now knew the former Santa Cruz County man they suspected to have attacked the National Guard Armory and stolen the weapons in 1971, then to have later absconded with twenty-two cases of quarry dynamite in 1975, was a very strong candidate to be identified as D. B. Cooper.[19]

The agent later asked Linda Lee, in a proactive phone call, whether her fugitive brother might have also had a "possible role in a bombing of the Pacific Gas and Electric towers in San Francisco," just a month after the explosives vanished. It would have meant that Rackstraw had provided hundreds of pounds of dynamite to the New World Liberation Front—a leading "fanatical group" with core members in the Santa Cruz Mountains that had claimed responsibility for as many as seventy explosions in the Bay Area.

Linda Lee was ready for that kind of question. She told the G-man, "Bob would do things for money, but he won't do it for a cause." To her, the answer was "Rackstraw 101."[20]

When the ever-curious Little was actually sitting with Linda Lee in her living room, the inquiry came a bit closer to the target.

"Do you know where Bob was Thanksgiving Day 1971?"

She told him that she didn't and was curious about why he would ask. Little inquired if she knew about the missing Northwest Airlines skyjacker.

"That was the first reference to Bob and D. B. Cooper that I had heard," Linda Lee recollected.

Little wasn't done. He told her about an angry letter Bob had sent to United States Army brass after his 1971 discharge at Fort Rucker. The agent felt that it was entirely possible, even plausible, that this anger was at least part of the motive for the hijacking of Northwest Flight 305.[21]

Finally, the conversation drifted to Linda Lee's fears about her missing stepfather. She halfheartedly explained that Philip was supposed to be in Hawaii, although she had become highly skeptical about that. A good deal of time had gone by, and he still hadn't tried to contact anyone.

"I'm not telling you what to do, but you probably need to go up to Calaveras County and file a missing-person report on your dad," Little told her.[22]

Over the last six months, Linda Lee had lost her mother; her stepfather had disappeared; her brother had given her a very large, very bad check; and the FBI was now asking where he had been during the Cooper hijacking.

Nothing seemed clear or reliable. It felt like emotional battery, and a great deal of it seemed to lead directly back to her slippery sibling.[23]

Linda Lee knew the agent was speaking from both experience and instinct when he told her to file a missing-persons report. Battered or not, and exhausted from regularly working overtime at the phone company, the single mom decided to pack up her little girl for the forty-three-mile drive out to San Andreas.

After she arrived there on January 28, 1978, Russell W. Leach, the county sheriff in his twentieth and final year, shook his head after he realized who she was and who she was reporting as missing.

"He's in Hawaii," Leach declared with certainty.

Linda Lee said that might be true, but it was completely unlike her dad to go as long as he had without so much as a postcard or a phone call. Growing perturbed, the sheriff started to tell her just how deeply he disliked her missing brother, rattling off a litany of stupid antics Rackstraw had done in his jurisdiction over the years.

Leach's favorite annoying story seemed to be about Rackstraw's stint as a volunteer helicopter pilot in Calaveras County and all the trouble he brought to the department in 1974. Linda Lee listened, not doubting a single accusation. It all sounded exactly like the kind of incidents Bob would do. Finally, feeling at a loss, she tried one more approach.

"What do I do, then, if [my father has] disappeared in Hawaii? I don't know how to get hold of Hawaii. How do I do that?"

The sheriff considered Linda Lee. She was clearly vulnerable and tired. Add to that the fact that she had been cursed with Bob Rackstraw for a brother.

"Well, we'll kind of look into it, you know," Leach said in an annoyed and condescending tone. "We'll get into it."

Five days later, the sheriff surprised Linda Lee with a phone call to her Stockton home. "He said, 'We need you to come up here and give us some information about your dad's disappearance.' Well, now I'm glad that they're taking something seriously. I said 'I'll come up this weekend.' The sheriff said, 'No, we need you to come up tonight.'"

Never mind it was a horrible winter evening to drive, she'd have to find an emergency babysitter, and she was expected at work in the morning.

The driven daughter headed back up the windy mountain roads to San Andreas.

Leach, however, instructed her not to rendezvous at the sheriff's station. "He wanted me to meet at the local tavern, which is called Black Bart Inn," recalled Linda Lee. "So that's curious. Well, the sheriff and the private detective that [Uncle] Bill had hired was there."

The family's PI, Jack Immendorf, was back from his fruitless Hawaiian search for Philip, and both men were ready to share the results. "They now believed he never left Valley Springs, and we all know what that means," she sadly noted.

"The sheriff conceded the fact that they needed to start looking seriously. So I said, 'Where are you gonna look?' And he goes, 'Well, there's mineshafts and sinkholes all over the place up here. Drop in a body, then throw in a stick of dynamite; you never find them.'"[24]

The silent Immendorf wasn't as hopeless. After months of knocking on doors in both Valley Springs and Maui, the investigator had his own theory. "It was at this point that I became convinced that my client had been correct all along—that Philip, his brother, was dead, and was probably buried not too far away."

The investigator couldn't stop thinking about the missing man's circling dog, Bingo.[25]

Exactly two days after Linda Lee was first approached by FBI agent Little, the Stockton/San Joaquin County Bomb Squad served a warrant to search eight storage bins that Bob Rackstraw had rented at a Bekins warehouse in Stockton. They found fourteen rifles and 150 more pounds of Tovex dynamite, which was enough to level a city block. The two rolls of primer cord found with the unlicensed explosives had the "serial numbers illegally removed," which prevented authorities from tracing it back to the "two 1,000-foot spools of primer cord" and twenty-two cases of dynamite—including Tovex brand—stolen from the Santa Cruz County Felton Quarry in 1975. A crime where Rackstraw had been publicly fingered.[26]

While a suspect for almost a decade, Rackstraw was never charged with either the National Guard Armory burglary or the dynamite theft, let alone providing explosives to any radical groups.

Back on September 1, 1977, Rackstraw had completed a deal to sell Philip and Lucille's ten-acre Valley Springs property, along with the mobile home that sat on it, the two-car garage and a work shed. A young couple named Kelly Dean and Diana Lynn Cline, both just twenty years old, simply had to take over the monthly $277 payments to make the place their own.[27]

When Linda Lee heard about the deal, signed just a month after her dad vanished, she was more than disturbed. What would happen when he came back from Hawaii, which was what anyone would logically presume would happen? Grandma Rose and Uncle Bill were among those who found the land sale to be a red flag and just as appalling as Linda Lee did.[28]

But there was more going on. Mary Yontel put her Heney Court home she shared with Rackstraw on the block, just half a year after buying it. Valley Springs neighbors noticed a Bekins moving van there on December 9, its crew packing and taking boxes out of the home.[29]

On December 21, Yontel was in a San Diego notary public's office, where she signed over power of attorney to her younger sister with instructions to sell her emptied roost.[30] Meanwhile, Bob was in the border town, too, meeting with his old Specialty Surfacing friend Patrick Ebert. Stockton police would later come to believe that the fugitive had left some of his ill-gotten gains from check kiting with Ebert for safe keeping.[31]

The next day, investigators from the Stockton Police Department and Calaveras County Sheriff's Office showed up at Rackstraw's Valley Springs home with arrest warrants, accusing him of check kiting and forging the signature of his still-missing stepfather, Philip. There was no one there, of course. A week later, the lawmen learned Rackstraw and Yontel were themselves in Hawaii.[32]

PI Immendorf had an early hunch where they were headed. He remembered that one of Rackstraw's "casual drinking buddies [had] recalled that Bob had recently talked about career opportunities in the Middle East, regarding the operation of helicopters. I did a little checking and, sure enough, discovered that Bell Helicopter was the only major concern of its type in the Middle East. And they were operating in Iran. I shared the information with my sources" at the Calaveras County Sheriff's Office. They quickly tipped the FBI."[33]

In early February 1978, just a few days after special agent Little visited Linda Lee, the bureau went all-in on the hunt for her brother.[34]

After contacting Bell Helicopter International's security department in Iran, Little discovered Rackstraw was in fact teaching the fine art of piloting in Esfahan, Iran, to men who were going to fly the Bell birds for the shah.[35] The dictator was in his last year of power before the Islamic Revolution.

The FBI informed the Calaveras sheriff and Stockton police that Immendorf was right—Rackstraw and Yontel were posing as husband and wife. The bureau then persuaded Bell to fire Rackstraw, leaving him no choice but to come home to the United States[36]—and justice.

That was easier said than done.

CHAPTER 12

Rounding Up the Usual Suspect

FEBRUARY 6, 1978–JULY 27, 1978

It had been just five weeks, but "Mr. and Mrs. Rackstraw" were beginning to feel at home in Esfahan, Iran. Store-bought furniture had been delivered to their rental home, a new Fiat sports car was at Rackstraw's disposal, and social gatherings were filling up their calendar.[1] Most of all, it was no doubt an overwhelming relief to be situated on the other side of the globe, away from the check-kiting and fraud charges that were soon to balloon into a messy murder investigation.[2]

With just twelve months before the shah's overthrow, those trying to live a "normal" life in Esfahan's best neighborhoods were beginning to notice the stares of Ayatollah Ruhollah Khomeini's revolutionaries, biding their time.

When Mary Yontel arrived just after Christmas, however, she wasn't aware of the culture clash—until her hosts pointed it out.

"Our Iranian friends, they were wearing jeans, trying to make [us] American hamburgers. And when we went out, we were just told . . . there are areas not to go. They were anti-American. At that time, I didn't really see this coming."[3]

On February 6, 1978, everything went to hell—not because of the revolution, but because of a revelation from Bob Rackstraw's past.

In a company executive meeting at Bell Helicopter International, the expatriate was unceremoniously brought in and informed, after just three weeks of employment, that he was being terminated. The reason: "Falsification of his employment application dealing with his education credentials." It was a familiar tune, no doubt, exactly the kind of technicality upon which the army based much of its explanation for his humiliating, infuriating discharge in 1971.

According to a newly discovered synopsis of the tense BHI meeting, that's when "Rackstraw became abusive to the Division Director" of training. He then informed everyone that "under no circumstances would he return to California, in that to do so would probably result in his violent death at the hands of the mafiosa."

The attending security staff, always professional but holding all the cards, then shut down the ex-employee with words and actions that can only be surmised by reading between the memo's next lines: "At this point the consequences of Rackstraw's continued residence in Iran were clearly defined . . . following which Rackstraw agreed to leave Iran as soon as possible."

The company would pay for his and Yontel's flight back to the United States, which sealed the deal for Rackstraw.

He must also have been worried about what might happen when they deplaned at journey's end. Still, he remained focused on how to proceed, enlisting the help of a fellow instructor in Iran that he'd known from his "Air America" days in Southeast Asia, Herbert M. Baker, to sell the furniture and the nifty sports car that seemed to be a mainstay of his personal image.[4]

As noted earlier, Rackstraw was not in Air America, let alone the CIA, during his Vietnam years. But he did "freelance" with the CIA and Special Forces on several jungle jaunts. The story was another example of the con artist manipulating old facts for maximum punch.[5]

Being kicked out of Iran, even politely, was anything but ordinary, even to Rackstraw. Perhaps that's why he uncharacteristically put his foot in his mouth during an exit security interview. Rackstraw made it known that he was expecting to get off the New York–bound plane when it stopped in Paris, saying he needed a little time to 'get his thoughts together' and plan future action." That was a red flag to the Bell security force, which quickly reached out to the State Department, the US Embassy, and the FBI with the information.

Bell security chief Anthony J. Maloney Jr., in Tehran at the time, reminded them all in a memo that "local authorities in California are extremely anxious to prosecute Rackstraw and have offered to pay or reimburse [the helicopter company] for Rackstraw's transportation."

The result was a seamless deception. Two weeks later, thanks to some adroit backstage maneuvering by the bureau, Rackstraw's passport had been canceled without his knowing it, so when he got to the check-in counter to leave Iran, the deal was already sealed. He would be kept on the jet in Paris—a unique and most certainly ironic turn of events for Bob Rackstraw.

For once, he was the victim of a deception, and he was "obviously upset," wrote Maloney, a former G-man. He then "escorted" the fugitive and Yontel to their seats on Iran Air Flight 779 to New York City.

On the last leg of the trip from Paris, "several FBI agents rode on the same flight with him," private eye Immendorf later revealed to a reporter. He had inside knowledge, of course, because he was the one who had alerted federal authorities to Rackstraw's whereabouts.[6]

Yontel remembered the G-men. "They came to check that we were in our seats. I tried to get [Rackstraw] off the plane in Paris and couldn't figure out how to do it."

Upon touchdown at JFK Airport on February 20, 1978, Rackstraw knew that what was coming "would not be pretty." Yontel was told to exit without him.

"I went to the baggage claim to get the luggage and a flight. Well, I was approached by the FBI and I was taken to this room. They said they didn't have anything on me," so the agents "arranged a flight so I could come home."[7]

Meanwhile, nothing if not consistent, Rackstraw refused to get off the jet. The bureau men were more than happy to drag him out bodily. He was soon asked, point blank, "Are you D. B. Cooper, Mr. Rackstraw?" With the waters deepening around him, the suspect demanded a lawyer. That, for the time being, stopped the line of inquiry.[8]

When Rackstraw landed in a federal jail cell, it was almost a stroke of luck. He met a talkative, friendly drug trafficker named Stan Hamilton (not his real name), who would prove vital to Bob's subsequent legal dealings. Hamilton explained that he was also, not incidentally, a movie producer. One can only imagine where Rackstraw's mind raced in the face of such information.

In 2014, Hamilton's former production partner, Vivian Jones (not her real name), explained that in exchange for Rackstraw's invaluable "advice," Hamilton had "pleaded" for her to get in touch with her longtime "friend, a top criminal attorney named Dennis Roberts." Roberts was practicing law in Oakland, California—an hour's drive from the Stockton courthouse where Rackstraw would eventually be transferred.

Roberts didn't let Jones down. "Dennis detested feds," she explained.

Soon after, the Oakland lawyer formally agreed to take Rackstraw as his client. "For $10,000 and his Corvette," Jones recalled.

She and Roberts already had plenty of shared history, first meeting in the early 1970s when she came home to Oakland from a Vancouver, British Columbia, hippie commune with her draft-dodging first husband. Politically aware, she was soon involved in civil rights. It wasn't long before she got into trouble, needed a lawyer, and found Roberts.[9]

He was a "movement attorney," boasting an array of famous activist and radical clients from the '60s and '70s, including defendants in the Chicago Seven conspiracy trial, American Indian Movement leader Dennis Banks, avowed communist professor Angela Davis, the Black Panther Party, Huey Newton, and Cesar Chavez and his United Farm Workers Union.[10]

Imagine being a fly on that waiting room wall—or, for that matter, a hidden bug.

Roberts, as it turned out, wasn't the only one loyal to old friends. Trafficker Hamilton, when told in New York federal court that "he'd get thirty years" if he didn't "give up people he was associated with in Oakland," answered, "I'll take thirty years," according to Jones.

"Those thirty years were slashed to only five, and finally to one year for good behavior. Then I got him out," said his partner.

Jones had a vested interest herself, as it happened. Hamilton's film projects were largely funded on the backs of cocaine dollars—"creative financing," she chuckled. And those movies were as much her dream as they were his.

They called their company Abracadabra Productions and thought of themselves as producers. "I had race horses back then," she reminisced.[11]

In those days they weren't even being that fanciful. They were hardly the only ones in Hollywood sweetening their professional lives with coke.[12]

Rackstraw's interrogators in New York first focused on what he had told Bell security about why he fled the country in the first place. The suspect opened up about purported "mafiosa" contractors in Calaveras County who were angry about his undercutting their business bids and had shot out his car window (a gunshot that San Joaquin district attorney investigators would later determine was fired by Rackstraw himself); the corrupt Calaveras County sheriff's office, which wouldn't investigate the purported incident; and the banks that suddenly wouldn't cover his business checks. On and on he went, blaming everything on someone else, as Linda Lee said he had always done.[13]

Family PI Jack Immendorf had been pushing the sheriff's office to dig on Philip's land for months, especially where he and the new landowners, Kelly and Diana Cline, had seen Philip's old dog Bingo "hanging around near the garage and shed." When a two-year-long drought in California finally broke with heavy rains in late February, the gumshoe alerted the detectives: now was the time to look for any water-caused sinkholes that might be a grave.[14]

Fugitive in American custody.

The county investigators found Kelly Cline in town, having lunch with his mom. They asked him to meet them on his new property.

Cline beat them there, so he walked all ten acres until he found a "depression in the ground." It was camouflaged by a pile of wood near Bingo's red shed.

After removing the wood and showing it to the arriving Calaveras County detectives, Cline volunteered to poke through the soil with a telephone guide wire. He soon hit something that clearly wasn't soil. Grabbing his shovel and digging carefully, he encountered what he first thought was "a horse's ear"—then, after tugging, realized it was the sleeve of a jacket. The detectives, taking care to proceed by the book, went to get a warrant.

Cline, tracked down for this account, recalled the morbid body recovery: Philip had been buried only three feet down, on his stomach, clad only in his underwear. His legs were bent at the knees and his hands were positioned behind his bullet-riddled head, which had been wrapped in his blood-soaked jacket.[15]

Calaveras County sheriff Russell Leach, the same lawman who'd been so condescending to Linda Lee, would later order the bloody jacket destroyed before the trial, eliminating what could have been a key piece of evidence.[16]

One can only imagine what went through Philip's mind as he looked down into the freshly dug grave that was not much different than the one GIs had miraculously pulled him out of in World War II, the only prisoner to survive a Japanese massacre.[17]

The destruction of the jacket wasn't the only egregious blunder made by the investigators. A week after Philip's body was removed, Cline found a pair of bloody pants at the bottom of a trash can in the work shed. He notified Calaveras County detectives, which culminated in a conversation with Bud Lawrence. To Cline's amazement, the investigator told him the department had no interest in the jeans.

"We got enough evidence," Lawrence said.

Cline followed his gut instinct and did not throw the pants away. They were later introduced at trial by Rackstraw's defense as evidence of the sheriff's office's incompetent handling of physical evidence.[18]

On February 28, 1978, Stockton Detective Sergeant Marvin Krein and Calaveras County Sheriff Detective Armond Rossiter walked into the New

York FBI offices and charged Rackstraw with Philip's homicide. Agents signed off with the release of their rather gabby D. B. Cooper suspect, with the understanding he would face the murder charge first. They planned to revisit the touchy skyjacking subject once Rackstraw was residing in a state prison.

That strategy, however, began to collapse just hours later, when Rackstraw literally fell to the floor during the Manhattan court hearing about his extradition to California. The con artist told his suspicious local lawmen it was an "old back injury."[19]

On March 6, 1978, Rackstraw, "chained and shackled" to a wheelchair, was rolled into Stockton's municipal court for arraignment. Deputy DA Clark Sueyres eyed the man with disbelief; the prosecutor had just received a report that county doctors could not find anything, new or old, wrong with Rackstraw's back.

That might explain why, a week later at his Calaveras County arraignment, he came up with a brand-new excuse—telling a newspaper "he was stricken by some malady during the last few days that left his legs useless."[20]

San Joaquin County got first crack at him, though, because it had coordinated and paid for his return from the Middle East. The defendant heard his charges involving check kiting, forgery, and three counts of illegally possessing dynamite. But those trials would follow Calaveras County's far more serious case—a case not mentioned at this hearing.[21]

Mary Yontel had flown in from her far-off home state to support Bob. But when she saw him enter the courtroom in that wheelchair, her greeting from the seats stopped dead.

"Here was this man that made me feel protected, and when I saw him in an orange jumpsuit and chains around his ankles, my image kind of dissolved. You know, how could this be happening? I was in shock that my dream was just . . . just collapsing around me. Then things were surfacing that I did not know about. His stepfather's death, the unlawful flight to avoid prosecution, check kiting. And it just kept snowballing."

As he had done countless times with his disillusioned girlfriends and ex-wives, Rackstraw somehow wormed his way back into Yontel's good graces. It may have had to do with a peculiar piece of information he later revealed to her in a private jail conference room.

"He held a legal pad up against the window that said, 'Do you remember this? D. B. Cooper.' And I said yes. He said, 'Well, they're trying to prove I'm that person.' And that was the first time that this came up."[22]

While Rackstraw contemplated the charges stacked up and waiting for him in two counties, attorney Roberts was contacted by the FBI. Without explanation, they asked the startled lawyer for his client's palm print. The lawyer's response was instantaneous.

"Are you crazy?" he asked. "I'd be pretty stupid to do that!"

Indeed. Although Roberts could not have known it at the time, a Cooper case agent in 2011 revealed there were "one or two prints" in another part of the hijacked Northwest Airlines jet that the FBI believed could have been the hijacker's. One might imagine a palm print, say, near the rear exit door or in a restroom.[23]

Back in the grim reality of what had gone on at Rackstraw's Rattlesnake Ranch, it took longer than normal for Philip's remains to become available for burial. By the time everything had been settled with the coroner, the police, and other agencies, Linda Lee decided to forego the funeral and, consistent with the intensely private and taciturn nature of her stepfather, proceed with the burial. It was a responsibility that she, as the youngest child, had never contemplated facing.

Then came the phone call from Bob, who was in jail in Stockton.

"I was not expecting him to call at all. I almost hung up right away and he must have known it because he goes: 'Don't hang up. Don't hang up, Linda. Don't hang up because I didn't do it. I didn't do it.' He goes, 'Honest, I didn't kill Dad.' And he goes, 'Please don't hang up on me.' So, I didn't."

The idea that Rackstraw might have killed their stepfather had never come up between them, but here he was telling her emphatically that he had not done it. She thought he must have brought up the possibility preemptively because "Dad was dead. So, I mean, I guess that seemed like the obvious conclusion—that he had done it—to everyone."

They next spoke when Linda Lee visited Rackstraw in jail.

"He repeated a lot of the stuff. The stories became very confusing," Linda Lee said, after she reminded Rackstraw that he'd insisted that Philip was in Hawaii. "He said: 'Well, somebody said this and somebody said that.'"

Rackstraw also maintained that Philip's dogs had just disappeared.

"He went up there one day and they weren't there," he told Linda Lee. "But at that point in life I always knew that with talking to Bob, you're only gonna get part of the truth. You just have to figure out which part," she laughed, shaking her head. "So I . . . just sat there, and he talked and I listened."

Being the passive listener was much easier than when she was asked to talk—pretty much required to talk, really—during fact-finding interviews by lawyers from both the murder case's defense and its prosecution.

The "bad-mouthing" during these grillings left her feeling horrible "because a man had died." When one particularly relentless investigator focused on her brother's character, she reached her boiling point.

"We're not talking about Bob! We're talking about my dad!" Linda Lee fired back.

She desperately wanted to believe her brother was not guilty. He had been accused of murdering their stepfather, yet he was the only real family she had left. Uncle Bill and Grandma Rose had never treated Linda Lee and Bob as family because neither of them was Philip's child by blood.

Still, even Linda had a line she simply would not cross. Supporting Rackstraw was one thing; twisting the truth was another matter. Knowing the way he manipulated people, she told her brother not to expect her to lie for him.

"No, well, I don't expect you to lie," Rackstraw replied.

"Not even partial untruths—anything. Whatever I'm asked I will tell them," she said.

And Rackstraw never did ask her to concoct a story or make up anything that might help his defense.

Linda Lee continued to travel to San Andreas for Sunday jail visits with her accused sibling, before and during the murder trial. Gradually, the situation seemed to mellow between them. It got easier to reminisce; at times Rackstraw seemed almost sorry for some of the events he had done. Linda Lee ascribed his changed demeanor to all those idle hours he was spending in his cell, perhaps humbled by the reality that the old Rackstraw charm wasn't going to have any impact on his circumstances.

They even got around to talking about the D. B. Cooper skyjacking. When she actually asked him the question—"What about it?"—Rackstraw was vague, saying that he knew of "guys that could have done it."

It wasn't lost on Linda Lee that her brother was actually benefiting from the speculation that he might be Cooper. "He was a celebrity. I mean, the prisoners thought he was great. Even the guards thought, 'You could be D. B. Cooper? Cool.'"

And she was sure her brother ate it up.

She was also sure the wheelchair he took into the courtroom was a ruse—pure Rackstraw. "That's the way Bob is. He would do that to make everybody else's life miserable. He was mad at everybody. But he would do it for sympathy. He knows how to play those cards."

Yet she still tried to believe in his innocence.

"I can't say I was ever 100 percent," she said. "I wanted to believe it. I tried to believe it."[24]

Mary Yontel recollected another conversation she and Rackstraw had about the hijacking, be it a pointed one. To help her beau's coming murder case, Yontel had acquired his military record. "I got it all for his attorney so he could present it to the court." But Bob was upset. "He said, 'You should have just flushed it down the toilet, because all of this just proves I could be this [Cooper] person.'"[25]

Defense attorney Dennis Roberts flew in for the July 12, 1978, trial in his own small plane, bringing Vivian Jones along for the ride. Roberts spent a lot of the flight free-associating, thinking out loud, using the producer "as a sounding board" for ideas on his strategy.

When she got into court, Jones said she quickly saw how the small-town judge, Joseph Huberty, absolutely "hated Dennis."[26]

Two weeks later, Rackstraw was acquitted of the charge of murdering Philip. The county sheriff's office tersely told reporters that the outcome "leaves investigators with no other suspects."

It will never be known whether the jury felt Rackstraw was flat-out innocent or found the prosecution's case simply too weak to clear the hurdle of "beyond a reasonable doubt."[27] Linda Lee was among those who felt the case was full of holes and should never have been presented the way it was.[28]

Roberts obviously agreed. "Bobby's homicide trial was fabulous," he shared in a recent e-mail. "It was the worst stack of circumstantial evidence I've ever seen." With his dry sense of humor, Roberts added, "I love trials in rural America."[29]

Private investigator Jack Immendorf, now eighty-two, still remembered his face-off with the wheelchair-bound Rackstraw from the witness stand—and his firm opinion of the defendant's culpability. "He looked, as I testified, like he'd do to me what was done to his stepfather."[30]

The verdict, of course, permanently fractured Rackstraw's family. Philip's last living sibling, ninety-three-year-old sister Betty, had only twelve words to say recently, before hanging up—but it was more than enough. "I don't want to talk about that kid. He killed my brother."[31]

The question that lingers is whether or not the people in Bob Rackstraw's own corner believed him. When recently reminded that many close to the case still think Bob got away with murder, producer Jones took a dramatic pause. In a low, sandpaper voice came the unsettling response. "We all knew he killed him."[32]

Bob and his grinning attorney after Bob's acquittal for the murder of his stepfather, Philip Rackstraw, 1978.

CHAPTER 13

No Hollywood Ending

JULY 28, 1978–FEBRUARY 4, 1979

Attorney Roberts was well aware his old friend Vivian Jones was resourceful about dredging up money. So right after Rackstraw's July 27, 1978, murder acquittal, he reached back to the producer. "I took this case, but Bob needs bail."

Jones was nothing if not a team player. "I talked to Bob," she recalled, in perhaps a masterpiece of understatement, "then I personally signed and guaranteed it" by putting up every cent of his $60,000 bond.

"Talking to Bob" must have included promises and horse-trading. Jones, it seems, had written a movie script called *Going Down*, an intentional and unfortunate double-entendre. When he was released from custody, Rackstraw would be "consulting on the script" because it was about a pilot—who also had to jump. The story included characters based on Jones, Rackstraw himself, producer-partner Stan Hamilton, and even good old Dennis Roberts. The plan was as straightforward as it was crooked—a combination perhaps most easily achieved in the film business.

"We were going to fly a plane into Lima, Peru, and shoot the picture right there, with our own aircraft," said Jones. "Bob said he had friends in the CIA" who could arrange "for a refueling spot for us on an island" along the forty-two-hundred-mile route.

Rackstraw also told Jones he could repaint the plane and give it a new tail ID number. That was a really good idea from her perspective since the

151

whole enterprise really had two purposes: It was going to be "a shoot and a drug run."[1]

Jones's *Going Down* script, it turned out, was not the only horse in the race. On the evening she and Hamilton bailed out Rackstraw, Rackstraw and his sister Linda Lee headed off for a dinner with another "Hollywood couple," as Linda Lee later referred to them. This pair wined and dined the siblings at a restaurant in Stockton and then held up a film poster for all to see. As Linda Lee dryly noted, they, of course, were "so thoroughly impressed" with her brother.[2]

In truth, the meal could merely have been a return favor for the veteran's paid editing help in reworking *yet another* screenplay about skydiving. That theory blossomed from a newspaper interview the next year, where Rackstraw bragged that, months before his murder trial, he was given a script for actor Robert Redford "called *Delayed Reaction*, about flying and parachuting."

"Mouth crinkling with amusement," as the article described the encounter, he claimed the screenplay was "laced with errors," and he told the reporter to "get a hold of Bob [Redford] and tell him I said the script has problems."[3]

Rackstraw wasn't quite finished giving advice. Soon after that celebratory dinner, he made time for Jones and Hamilton to get more details on their planned adventure in Peru. To their delight, he was enthused about the project, agreed to be a partner with them, and, furthermore, wanted to be the pilot. Jones explained that she had another man in mind for that and indicated Bob would be copilot.

What Rackstraw said then left her astonished.

"He's expendable," he said, referring to the pilot. "Do you have a problem with that?"

Jones, just days after the end of the brutal murder trial, quickly responded. "Yes, I have a problem with that!"

A dark realization about Bob Rackstraw unavoidably filled her mind. "For a minute there," she reflected, "I thought *I* might be expendable!"[4]

Within days of his court-ordered bail release, Rackstraw's disabling back injury was somehow "cured." He lost the wheelchair his sister said had made "everybody's life miserable" when he departed Calaveras County for good. Sheriff Russell Leach's embarrassingly bungled murder investigation would be forgotten by the time of his twentieth year retirement dinner on December 2.[5]

In contrast to Calaveras, the pending case regarding the felonies in neighboring San Joaquin County for check kiting, forgery, and illegal possession of explosives looked a great deal stronger to observers—including the defendant. At a September 15, 1978, hearing, a no-nonsense judge ordered Rackstraw to give up his full war record and then to turn over his private collection of twenty-five historic guns to someone for safekeeping.[6] When he volunteered his sister, she wasn't thrilled.

"I went down to the police department and [was given] a trunkful of rifles and handguns." said Linda Lee. "I don't know one rifle from another, so I couldn't even tell you what they were."

The police inventory document she was handed listed more than two dozen rifles and pistols—Winchesters, Marlins, Remingtons, Rugers, and even old war weapons—which turned her small duplex into a veritable armory.[7]

As Rackstraw left that courtroom, he may have sensed that future proceedings weren't going to be a cakewalk. But when his public defender, Gus Guinan, told him that at the October 8, 1978, pretrial Judge William J. Biddick Jr. "indicated that the defendant would be sentenced to prison should he enter a plea" (as in any plea, it didn't matter), Rackstraw began seriously entertaining other plans.[8]

When Linda Lee heard the news about her brother's purported crash on October 11, 1978, she did not believe his rented aircraft had gone nose first into Monterey Bay—not for one second.

"I knew he took off," she said. "Bob's too good a pilot to have a Mayday [emergency]."[9]

Backing her intuition was a timely radio alert from a lone sailboat, *Dawn Tredder*. The crew reported "seeing a plane in the area of the call, flying at about two-hundred feet, but told the Coast Guard it did not appear to be in any trouble."[10]

Also, in what might have been a telltale sign, two handguns from Rackstraw's gun collection were missing from Linda Lee's Stockton duplex. She admitted to officials "her brother happened to be in her house that day she brought home the pistols."[11]

Linda Lee had been in Rackstraw's corner during the murder trial—more or less—but she had not lost perspective on his character.

"Murder is one thing. Disappearing on these charges that he knew he might not be able to beat? That's another. That's Bob."[12]

When Uncle Bill heard the news, it gave him a chill, said PI Immendorf. "He called me first thing in the morning." Because they had both testified against the murder suspect, "he suggested that we should take some precautions because 'dead' Robert might be lively enough to put us in danger."[13]

On the night of Rackstraw's disappearance, the knock at ex-wife Gail Marks's door in Santa Cruz County got their three children screaming with excitement. But it wasn't their daddy arriving for his prearranged dinner, the first in over a year. It was the FBI, revealing the ongoing ocean rescue search for his missing plane and asking questions. Marks was already angry with her ex—as part of the charade, he'd asked her to be standing by at the nearby Skypark Airport to pick him up. Now, six hours later, she realized he'd just used her and their kids as pawns in the escape.[14]

Marks wasn't the only one fuming. Vivian Jones quickly surmised Rackstraw had screwed her—and worse, it was almost as an afterthought.

Her production team was all set and "ready to go" with Rackstraw to Lima, Peru, along with "research, maps, and everything." Of course, there was a second part to Jones's fury. "He left me with the $60,000 bond on his bail."[15]

And there was a third person irate over the latest disappearing act. The next morning, San Joaquin Deputy District Attorney Clark Sueyres had Rackstraw due for arraignment in the upcoming check-kiting trial. Instead, the prosecutor got a 9:00 a.m. call from the coast guard saying he was missing in the Pacific.

Sueyres knew better, telling a reporter, "Mister Rackstraw could be flying to San Diego and then walking across into Mexico."[16]

Mary Yontel was the only one left smiling—she would later rendez-vous with the fleeing Rackstraw in Southern California. And despite news reports to the contrary, he flew away alone, something the girlfriend was certain of.

So why did he fake his death and run?

"Because we didn't have any more money and he was going back to jail again," explained Yontel. "I think somehow he felt like . . . you know, maybe it's time that this man disappears."

After all, it had worked for Norman de Winter—and Dan Cooper.

"He found a place, and his [Specialty Surfacing] friend Patrick Ebert, the three of us lived together in Laguna Beach."[17]

Rackstraw's miffed courtroom adversary, Deputy DA Sueyres, also had a special distaste for Ebert. In his October 12, 1978, court summary of the events surrounding the bogus Mayday call, the reason came up in the last sentence: "Our concern is that Rackstraw's plane had sufficient fuel to reach beyond the borders of California, even San Diego, where a friend, Patrick Ebert, holds $12,000 for Rackstraw which was part of the proceeds of the [1977] bank fraud here in Stockton."[18]

While Rackstraw was on the run, an elk hunter named Carroll Hicks discovered a plastic-encased emergency procedures card in the Washington wilderness on November 1, 1978. It was quickly traced back to the jet from which D. B. Cooper had jumped, seven years previously. The FBI estimated it was "six flying minutes" from the point where Cooper jumped to the spot where the card turned up, factoring in the plane's altitude and air speed.[19]

Just before Christmas, the Hollywood couple who had hosted the celebratory dinner showed up unannounced at Linda Lee's Stockton duplex. When she sat with them in her living room, they quickly ended the small talk: her bail-jumping brother owed them a considerable amount of cash, too, and they suggested that, as executor to their late stepdad's estate, Linda Lee should pay them any share that might be owed to Rackstraw.

"Well," she told them, "it's Bob's debt, not Dad's. But you can make a claim if you want." Getting nowhere, the couple quickly shifted subjects. Possibly forgetting that they had already done so in the restaurant, they again showed her their movie poster, using it as a segue into the idea that, if she was reasonable and would merely give them his gun collection, they "could be used to solve Bob's debt."

Linda Lee wasn't about to be hustled. In her characteristically forthright manner, she told them to "shove off."

"I didn't like 'em anyway," she said. "Never liked 'em."[20]

Just after New Year's 1979, the subject of the gun collection came up once more when the still-on-the-run Rackstraw called Linda Lee. When he learned she had been driving the weapons around in her trunk—because, as she explained, "it's the only secure place there is"—Bob told her he'd have somebody pick them up.[21]

That somebody turned out to be Vivian Jones, who said "Bob felt bad" about stiffing her on the bond money and told her that his gun collection was hers to claim. Wasting no time, Jones arrived in Stockton, signed Linda Lee's official paperwork on January 8, and then left with the remaining rifles and handguns. They still fell short of $60,000 in value, so the outlaw paid the producer the balance in gold "Krugerrands from South Africa."[22]

Perhaps he had acquired them from the Bank of Briggs.[23]

While Jones and Hamilton never made it down to Peru for their "shoot and a drug-run," Jones says "creative financing" did help get one film to screen. Appropriately on April Fools' Day 1980, Avco Embassy Pictures released a movie about pool-hall hustlers, *Baltimore Bullet*, starring James Coburn and Omar Sharif. But online databases show no credits listed for Rackstraw's former producer-partners or their Oakland-based company, Abracadabra. The pair left the picture business and became husband and wife in 1985.

Incidentally, on Rackstraw's thirty-eight-year-old police gun inventory list, there was a clear indication of the location of at least one of the missing weapons in question. Next to the crossed-out eighteenth gun—a 1963 Sturm-Ruger Hawkeye .256 mag pistol, worth $2,000 today—someone had scribbled "Dennis Roberts has."

Maybe he kept it in the Corvette.[24]

The Corvette-less Rackstraw, meanwhile, was in the fourth month of his new life in Orange County, California. He, Mary Yontel, and their favorite relocation man, Patrick Ebert, were renting a trailer in the old Treasure Island mobile home park, perched on the scenic cliffs above Laguna Beach.[25]

To locals, the heavily bearded Bob was known as Robert Eastman, a thirty-six-year-old native of Oklahoma. The makeover, also involving some weight gain, had no doubt helped him land a construction superintendent position on a senior citizens housing project, thirty miles away in the town of Fullerton—right across the street from the police department.[26]

Being within shouting distance of potential pursuers might have motivated his next action: to set up an emergency escape plan. First, he procured another social security number.[27] Next, the rented Cessna 182 he'd stolen in the Mayday stunt—now with new brown paint and a phony tail number—was standing by in a hidden hangar, twenty minutes away.[28] And finally, he created a fake FAA pilot's license and medical certificate for his Eastman alias.[29]

On January 27, 1979, Rackstraw's cover imploded when he forgot a basic rule in American towns: streets surrounding cop shops are extremely loyal to their protectors.

Superintendent Eastman surely had his jolly face on when he walked into a nearby photocopy store and left his work order. But when the vigilant business owner noted his request entailed duplicating FAA licenses—a violation of federal law—he quickly called his awesome neighborhood watch.

A short time later, the returning customer walked into waiting handcuffs. He insisted his name was Eastman, even after Fullerton Sergeant Bud Lathrop's men searched him and found "a pilot's license issued to Rackstraw" and some "matching peculiarities, including a bullet wound scar on his left side" that officials knew to look for.[30]

It took two days to get his fingerprints from the state capitol to confirm what everyone in Fullerton and Stockton already knew.[31] The Okie accent instantly vanished.

Once more, Mary Yontel tried to help Rackstraw. That's when things got complicated.

"I went to see Bob and I took an attorney. They put me in a cell . . . I told them I didn't have any information to give them. To keep calm, I talked to them about nutrition because that's the only thing I could think of. At a certain point they said they didn't feel that I knew anything."[32]

San Joaquin County sheriff's sergeant Max Benitez, one of two officials who came to drive Rackstraw back to Stockton, told a *San Jose Mercury News* reporter how they got him to give up the missing stolen plane: "He thought we were going to lock up his girlfriend. He seemed to really care about that girl."[33]

After making a deal with the assistant district attorney, Clark Sueyres, not to charge Yontel, the fugitive told officials exactly what went on in the aircraft. Then "using a map drawn by Rackstraw, investigators went to Meadowlark Airport in Huntington Beach."[34]

The FBI, which "requested and received fingerprints of Rackstraw during his stay in the Fullerton jail," closely monitored his high-security trip home. An FBI agent told the Fullerton Police that the bureau was investigating whether Rackstraw "is this person [D. B. Cooper]."

It was the first of almost a dozen leaks to the press about the bureau's interest.[36]

Sergeant Benitez and his road-trip partner told a reporter they couldn't wait for the Rackstraw hand-off in Stockton to be done. "Try driving with him in the back of your car for 10 hours at a stretch. He was like a cobra coiled up and ready to strike."

Upon arrival though, the sergeant admitted, "there'd been no trouble, he just wanted to wrap it up and lead a straight life. I told him he was either the biggest con artist in the world or an honest man."

Another officer who spent many hours in Rackstraw's company described their charge as "a free spirit, friendly, polite."[37]

Nevertheless, the chameleon was put in solitary confinement as a precautionary measure.[38]

During his months on the run, Rackstraw had plenty of time to develop a rationale for the sham crash and fraudulent Mayday call. And he practiced them on his sister, Linda Lee, who this time visited him in the Stockton jail.

"He goes, 'the owners really were okay with the airplane. They get to collect the insurance,' and he's pointing out how that's the good part of his stealing the airplane to the owners. Here's my extremely intelligent brother, and I'm thinking you really did something dumb to get caught. And then he said, 'You know, you get tired of running.'"[39]

That was the first time the sibling had ever heard him say anything like that, so perhaps she could be excused for not perceiving the kicker that might have been lurking under his lament. Rackstraw's entire thought was probably something like "You know, you get tired of running . . . so you set things up in advance to work in your favor."

During the four months before he was cornered, Rackstraw's main order of business was indeed just that—conducting advance work. His escape to Orange County, though ultimately exposed by his bungled print job, was just a way station for something bigger and bolder up the road.

In the last month of 1978, the scruffy Rackstraw had brazenly ridden a motorcycle all the way to Portland to visit his old Specialty Surfacing coworker and clandestine partner in crime, Dick Briggs. As the two men stood in the driveway getting reacquainted, one of the two sons Briggs shared in a custody agreement, thirteen-year-old John Briggs Jr., stared out from his bedroom window. He couldn't take his eyes off of the stranger's "semi-chopped, green 900cc Kawasaki."

The boy loved anything with wheels, and being too young to have a license didn't bother his dad at all. "I would ride around by myself on motorcycles or drive any of his [father's auto shop] cars, carte blanche," John recently recalled. "Anytime a cop would try to catch me, I would lead them on a chase back to my dad's. Somehow I would never get in any trouble. Nor would he."

That green bike was calling him, so he hustled outside. Soon, Rackstraw happily obliged the boy's curiosity, telling him to hop on the back.

By John's description, the bearded stranger took great pleasure in "scaring the hell" out of him. Rackstraw ignored the screams and pleas of his young passenger as he raced, skidded, and popped wheelies—all at up to ninety miles per hour. Finally, the boy's yells to take him home were heeded. As they pulled into Briggs's driveway, John launched himself off the Kawasaki and sprinted without a word into the house and up to his room, utterly traumatized. On the way, he heard Rackstraw gleefully tell his dad, "I gave him quite a ride."

Now the two men could get down to business. Rackstraw, in this sixteenth documented trip north, had an elaborate, two-state scheme to plan with his loyal henchman—a scheme that would generate headlines, lower the heat on Rackstraw, and make the FBI look foolish, all at the same time. With the timetable in place—and, like four years earlier at middleman Shell's house, with a critical exchange of money—Rackstraw headed back to California to await the results.[40]

Of course, he wouldn't be doing it from a beach chair in a Laguna trailer park.

Rackstraw's new reality in solitary confinement likely kept him oblivious to a February 2, 1979, headline in the town's own *Stockton Record*: "Is Rackstraw D. B. Cooper?"[41] The story, which highlighted his two "wild escapes" from Northern California custody, was quickly matched by the *San Jose Mercury News*—his former hometown paper with second wife, Linda McGarity. Editors labeled him a "World-Hopping Daredevil," while their writer launched the opening salvo: "Whether Robert W. Rackstraw is the mysterious D. B. Cooper or not, he has plummeted headlong in a streak of infamy."[42] All of these journalistic gems, of course, were quickly mined by the hijack-hungry national wire services.

Days before, DA Joseph Baker helped fuel the rumors when he told the Stockton paper the Cooper caper would "match [Rackstraw's] profile. He's a very daring and cunning man." Prosecutor Sueyres added, "He's a helluva conman. You'd buy a used car from him every time."[43]

Record reporter George Hoeper, reflecting on an interview he'd done with the bail skipper the previous year, said his ego was "almost appalling." With a straight face, the subject had claimed "the FBI considers him 'a James Bond who had gone wrong.'"[44]

A few weeks before, Rackstraw had been just as bold during his murder-case interrogation with Calaveras County detective Bud Lawrence: he had "claimed to be CIA."[45]

The Seattle bureau agents in charge of the hijacking case were trying their very best to bat down all the internal leaks and media frenzy surrounding Rackstraw. A spokesman begrudgingly responded to the *Record* and "acknowledged that friends and relatives had been questioned." But he "declined to confirm or deny" the California outlaw was under suspicion.[46]

The FBI then swung the bat at one of its own. The local agent who had once sat with Linda Lee and later coordinated the escapee's elaborate return from Iran, Warren Little, had spilled to an AP wire reporter that "he believed he [and two Stockton investigators] had established a link between Rackstraw and D. B. Cooper." That unsanctioned disclosure got him shipped back to a remote outpost in his home state of Montana. When a journalist tracked him down there shortly afterward, Little said, "The FBI won't let me say zip."[47]

A day after the wires had taken Rackstraw national, a story in the *Seattle Times* threw water on Stockton's original Cooper scoop. Citing unidentified "law-enforcement officials," the writer claimed those in charge of the seven year-old FBI skyjacking case had officially "ruled out" Rackstraw.[48]

But twenty-four hours later, the *Record* newsroom fought back by putting its own local bureau man on the front page. Senior Agent Thomas Kinberg told a reporter that Rackstraw "remains under investigation" and "information developed by investigators here is still being forwarded" to the Seattle case team.[49]

Meanwhile, there was nothing for the subject of all the headlines to do but stare at the walls of his cell. Rackstraw had no way of knowing that Uncle Bill, Philip's brother, had told the FBI he hadn't the foggiest idea where his nephew was in 1971, but for some time "he was all over the country and in and out of trouble wherever he went." When the bureau bluntly asked if he thought Rackstraw could be the hijacker, Uncle Bill "dismissed the question with a laugh."[50]

The jailbird also had no way of knowing that in Houston, Texas, ex-wife McGarity had been watching the evening news with her family when her ten-year-old daughter pointed at the television and shrieked, "There's Daddy Bob! There's Daddy Bob!"

Rackstraw's bearded mug shot glared back at McGarity, her parents, and her new husband as the anchor told the audience he was a D. B. Cooper suspect. During their four years together from 1973 to 1976, McGarity said she never had the slightest clue of her husband's criminal propensities—not even after discovering the fake mustache and wig in his briefcase, let alone her forged signature on the loan application for that suspicious print shop.[51]

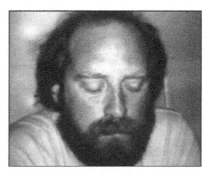

Busted again in Fullerton, California, six months after the murder acquittal, for fleeing a subsequent bank fraud trial.

When former coworker Dan Hunt spotted Bob's mug shot on the same national broadcast, he had quite a different reaction. It had been four years since the veteran ignored Hunt's skyjacking inquiry in that Cleveland bar. But now, "here comes a picture of Bob Rackstraw, suspected of being D. B. Cooper. I said my golly, I'm probably right about that."[52]

After Mary Yontel was freed by the authorities in Fullerton, an FBI special agent investigating her boyfriend came to meet her at the mobile home they and Patrick Ebert had shared in Laguna Beach. During a private walk along the ocean, the G-man adopted a paternal tone. "I'd like to give you some advice. We have nothing on you, but if you were my daughter, I would tell you to get away from this man before you get in trouble."

His timing couldn't have been more perfect, Yontel recently admitted.

"Bob was very good to me, and when [he] got in trouble, it wasn't in my nature to run away. I tried to help him until the point that . . . well, we were out of money. And I realized I was not protected. I started thinking, this was the time when I needed to change my life.

"I still love Bob, but that was a very, very emotional . . . it was a hard time. Through the years, I've had to look to my mind and say, did he love me as much as I thought he did? How did all these things happen that I didn't know about? I'm not saying I was a completely innocent victim, but I didn't know the full extent of any of this."

The former girlfriend was finally confronted about Rackstraw's biggest secret. "I asked him one question directly," but Yontel said she would "not discuss the answer. If I knew he was D. B. Cooper, I would never discuss [it] until he had died."

Moments later though, the sixty-seven-year-old retiree slipped up—revealing that when "things like this have come up, [Bob] would say to me, 'Angel, don't talk to the psychologist, don't talk to anyone because there's no statute of limitations on skyjacking.'"[53]

To one consulted lawman, Yontel's statement sounded like "a testimonial smoking gun."[54]

Rackstraw's other secret, which many believe he had put in play himself during that motorbike trip to Portland, was launched with a subtle action his buddy Dick Briggs had taken—just six days after the Cooper-related headlines first hit the national wires.

CHAPTER 14

Cooper's Town

FEBRUARY 5, 1979–FEBRUARY 7, 1980

L ife was popping for Dick Briggs. Like the Krugerands around his
neck, the Portland cocaine trade was in a golden swing. With a
tucked-away pistol and middleman-buddy Jim Shell chauffeur-
ing him around town in a British Racing Green Bentley or white Rolls
Royce—depending on his mood—it was clear the former enforcer had em-
braced the underworld lifestyle of power and panache.[1]

The new "private Dick," though, had become too much for his four-
year girlfriend, Bev Nevin, who had split the year before. She lambasted
her own gullibility: "Late phone calls, closed-door meetings, suitcases of
jewelry, cash, guns, the cars at our disposal. I now use the excuse of na-
iveté, but was I really that ignorant?"

During their final quarrel, "all of a sudden he shoots one [gun] off, just
out of anger. That's when I had to get out of there."[2]

To Rackstraw, on the other hand, Briggs was precisely the type of crime
partner he required. After seven years of tough tutelage, he had developed
a discreet protégé in the town where new mischief was set to begin.[3]

No doubt Briggs had seen the *Oregonian* and television news coverage
of Rackstraw's recapture a few days earlier. He would have been acutely
aware that his slippery mentor was now being considered Portland's most
wanted fugitive.

He did not have to be told that the time had come to implement the plan that Rackstraw had personally delivered on his motorcycle. The way he chose to do it, though, was pure Briggs all the way.[4]

The trafficker had never met the two men that Jim Shell, his vital Number Two, had hired to do the actual drug running two years before. To the middleman's mild surprise, he was told to round them up for a face-to-face nighttime meeting on February 5, 1979.

So it was that Briggs got acquainted with Ron Carlson and Vern Burke in the backseat of his Bentley. The two men had distributed the supplier's product to buyers as far away as Phoenix, and it was time their efforts were acknowledged, he told them. White powder was divided into "humongous lines" on a burlwood tray table between them.

With the impossible-to-miss vehicle speeding through Portland, complete with the obvious snow festival easily visible through the windows, Carlson counted seven police cars pointedly ignoring them. "We're doing eighty, eighty-five miles an hour, and it's like two o'clock in the morning. Up and down the I-5 [freeway], and they wouldn't even look. We were about the only dang car on the road."

Briggs confirmed he had "immunity" in Portland, "but he couldn't leave the city."

Shell kept his eyes on the road and his thoughts to himself when, virtually out of the blue, Briggs confided something quite remarkable to the two drug runners. He lowered his voice slightly and told them that nobody knew it, but "I'm D. B. Cooper."[5]

Burke said he immediately "thought it was bullshit." But the partners, well-practiced in the art of the poker face, did not display their skepticism.[6] The more analytical Carlson weighed the evidence.

He was familiar with the first 1971 FBI sketch of the hijacker, gleaned from the descriptions given by the flight crew. But he couldn't avoid seeing that Briggs was much shorter, much bulkier, and, most significant of all, had a face that did not even remotely resemble the one released to the media. He then wondered, what was his game?

Nonetheless, for the next year Briggs spun a convincing, ongoing tale of his life of danger and adventure. It wasn't hard for Briggs to reproduce

Rackstraw's highly memorable stories from Vietnam—of the Green Berets he had trained with and the various combat medals he had earned—probably with an embellishment here and there. And he repeatedly held forth about surviving the jump from Flight 305 into the wilderness near the Columbia River.

Shell continued to hold his counsel. If Carlson or Burke looked to him for any hint that Briggs was exaggerating—or flat out lying about his colorful past—they didn't get a thing. But the trafficker must have suspected that his two runners remained suspicious, so he began to pull aces from his sleeves. Convincing them he was the badass he said he was was central to the Briggs-is-Cooper plan. It was time for the tour of his bachelor pad.

"He took us over to his house and it was beautiful, over in the southwest part of Portland," recalled Carlson. "And he started pointing out these pictures along a stairway going up to the second floor. I'm no art critic, but he had paintings of artists that I recognized. All the way up, fine pieces of art. It was kind of a contradiction, never would've believed it if I hadn't seen it."

But on the second floor, Briggs's dark side returned. He proudly showed the astounded Carlson and Burke "hundreds" of military weapons—rifles, machine guns, and rocket launchers—laid out on display tables, as if it were a swap meet for gunrunners.[7]

The hardware before Carlson and Burke was quite possibly evidence—should anyone be able to connect the dots—that Briggs and Rackstraw had been their usual busy selves in collaborative criminal activity. In fact, shortly after Rackstraw's Mayday call from Monterey Bay, FBI agents who visited Gail Marks in Santa Cruz County mentioned that they suspected her ex-husband had been involved in a nearby armory break-in, during which a large number of military weapons had been stolen. Neither Rackstraw nor Briggs was ever charged in that crime, however.[8]

On November 24, 1979, Briggs suggested a trip to the Eighth Annual D. B. Cooper Day celebration in Woodland, Washington. "He told us he had gone up the year before," said Carlson, "and this year he wanted me to go with him."

Upon arrival in Woodland, Briggs put on a T-shirt he purchased with "I'm D. B. Cooper" emblazoned across its front. As he mingled with a sizable group of Cooper-legend devotees, Carlson watched him carefully. He never broke character: the "real" D. B. Cooper secretly rubbing elbows with the faithful.

"All he kept telling me was, 'I just want to tell these people who I am.' We spent the whole dang day and night, and all he wanted to do was jump up and say, 'Hey, I'm here!'"

The next time Carlson was in a crowd with Briggs, it was at a jammed-to-the-walls party on February 7, 1980, in Shell's apartment building on Portland's Hayden Island.

Spotting something he'd been looking for, Briggs took the still-skeptical Carlson and Burke aside. "I'm gonna prove to you that I am who I say I am," he said, pointing discreetly to a couple across the crowded room. The pair looked like a nervous "hippie couple," out of place, Carlson recollected.

"Before you guys get to Phoenix, they and their little boy are going to find some of my money," Briggs said. He then walked to a window overlooking the Columbia and pointed. "Over there, on the Vancouver side of the river."

He then gave the runners a "meaningful" stare to make sure they knew exactly what money he was talking about. Their expressions told him they did.

Carlson and Burke didn't know what to say, each thinking this was a gigantic load of malarkey, even for Briggs. Moments later, he wanted to introduce them to the couple, but the runners somehow managed to decline and leave the party without incurring Briggs's wrath. Their boss, it seemed, had really gone over the edge this time, and they were relieved to get away. Besides, they had work to do—they were loaded up for one of their Arizona distribution assignments.[9]

Asked for his recall, Shell confirmed hearing his boss, over that year, bragging to be the missing hijacker—something he never believed. But the middleman asserted that his party-hosting duties that evening had, unfortunately, kept him from witnessing the key exchange between Briggs and the runners.

Shell did have a sense, though, for several weeks that "Briggs and Rack-straw were up to no good." After witnessing over the years how his old frat brother had gone increasingly astray with each of their southern rendezvous, Shell had developed little love for the Californian with, as he put it, "a linebacker's eyes."[10]

CHAPTER 15

Rants and Rubbish

FEBRUARY–JULY 26, 1979

The jailed Rackstraw received some sobering news: the Stockton aircraft theft could multiply his years, perhaps up to a ten-year stretch, if he were to be convicted of all charges pending against him in San Joaquin County. Even he must have known his chances of acquittal were slim to none. But the California State Prison system consisted of no-bullshit, hard-time penitentiaries, and he told friends he truly feared for his safety.[1]

One of those he reached out to for help was his former Specialty Surfacing boss, Mike Narro. Before creating his floor business, Narro had conducted noteworthy stints as an investigator for both the California Alcohol Beverage Control (ABC) and the Bureau of Narcotic Enforcement. He was so impressive, then rookie governor Jerry Brown tried to recruit him in 1974 to head up the state's ABC. Dan Hunt, coincidentally in Narro's office for the governor's call, heard him turn down the offer because he "was making too much damn money."[2]

Shortly after his Fullerton recapture in 1979, Rackstraw called Narro with his own request—asking for him to intercede on his pending state sentence. The response cut to the bone: "Bob, no, I can't do anything for you."

Narro told Pudgy Hunt his answer left Rackstraw mad as hell.

Years later, Hunt and his new wife, Connie, went to visit Mike Narro at his Nevada house. Pudgy remembered, "It was a beautiful home up on a ridge, swimming pool out over a canyon. And we're sitting out on the patio and a private plane comes down close to the canyon, and I kiddingly said, 'Oh, Bob Rackstraw, huh?' Mike and his wife looked at each other, and Mike turned white. I mean he was like really scared about it."[3]

With no state prison help from friends and power brokers, Rackstraw began to lobby the FBI, seeking a way to transfer to a federal cell. Former FBI agent Himmelsbach, who had heard about Rackstraw's 1979 relocation efforts all the way up in Portland, revealed that his personal club-fed plea was turned down: "That phony, he just wanted better treatment in a federal pen."[4]

One might assume the "phony" label had something to do with Rackstraw's fingerprints. Within a week of receiving them from the Fullerton Police Department, many of the agents who had quietly leaked the Mayday man's name to the press were now joining Himmelsbach's camp.

A confidential source with bureau connections recently confirmed the fingerprint issue was in fact the game changer on Rackstraw. Referring to his "extensive" old file, he explained that agents had "compared fingerprints found in the '71 jet that may have been Cooper's, to Rackstraw's. It cleared him."

In reality, though, the alleged prints of the skyjacker may *not* have been the robber's. In 2013, two former senior agents, including the esteemed 2007–2010 case agent, Larry Carr, publicly admitted to *Mountain News* journalist Bruce Smith that the identities tied to the recovered seventy-seven prints are "far from complete" and "highly suspect." So in hindsight, our bureau source said he agreed that what was believed in '79 to have been the anonymous hijacker's prints "could've been from a mechanic or a passenger on a connector."

Most of the "major" prints that the FBI trusts today came from the plastic cups that stewardess Tina Mucklow had gathered and "put aside." But would Cooper, the master outlaw who had "carefully and minutely planned" everything, have insisted on getting his bomb note back and taken all he had come with (except the tie) and then left behind his prints on his bourbon and seven for forensic experts?

As former special agent and author Richard T. Tosaw noted in his well-documented 1984 book, *D. B. Cooper: Dead or Alive?*, the skyjacker "seemed to be particularly conscious about leaving behind evidence that might be incriminating. The agents found nothing on Cooper's glass" other than "the prints of the two stewardesses."

And what about the aluminum staircase railing or on the handle that lowered it?

"The prints that they found were too smeared to be identifiable," wrote Tosaw.

It is worth highlighting that a week after the hijacking, the four alleged D. B. Cooper letters—the first and last being dropped in mailboxes near Rackstraw's isolated family home in California—were "dusted for prints" by the FBI. And none were found, claimed the respected Cooper researcher, attorney Galen Cook.[5]

Before the 1978 acquittal in his stepdad's murder case, Rackstraw had given the *Stockton Record* an exclusive interview. On February 6, 1979, he once again called up the paper, looking for public sympathy. The prisoner put on a bizarre performance, recounting army battles in Vietnam, airing his grievances toward "the political-legal system," and calling himself a "political prisoner" in the process. When the D. B. Cooper question was raised, he denied the association "with a flippant smirk." The reporters noted that Rackstraw related to the outlaw, just the same.

"He identifies with the spirit of D. B. Cooper, a person he says 'challenged the legal system and beat it,'" they wrote. "'I think I stand for the American people,' said Rackstraw. 'I really do.'"

That's an interesting shift in perspective. First Rackstraw denied being the hijacker. Then he said, "I stand for the American people, I really do."

One more vignette: The article subject asked the reporters to bring along some Kool cigarettes, but his next phone-call demand raised eyebrows.

Bob spins a tale over a jail phone.

"He added, 'Now don't laugh, you son of a gun,' and requested a package of Raleigh filter-tips" (the 1971 hijacker's smoke of choice).[6]

In reality, all of Rackstraw's ink didn't raise a stink among the fifty-thousand newspaper readers in sleepy San Joaquin County. So he set his sights on the ultimate arbiters of fairness and understanding, "the American people." And the way to reach all of them, he now believed, was through national television.[7]

On March 7, 1979, Rackstraw telephoned NBC News in Los Angeles but found himself forwarded to its local station, KNBC. In pleading his case, he first had to persuade Pete Noyes, a no-nonsense editor who was the inspiration for the gruff character that actor Ed Asner made famous on *The Mary Tyler Moore Show* and *Lou Grant* television series. The real one, however, threw typewriters.

It would take a bombshell to get the old pro's attention, Rackstraw must have realized, and he delivered one. Over the phone, he admitted for the first time that he was, in fact, D. B. Cooper.

After a moment's silence, Noyes snarled, "Prove it!"

Rackstraw was ready.

He explained that he had chosen the name Cooper in honor of his skydiver-legend of an uncle, John "Ed" Cooper, who, with more than two thousand jumps, was still actively flinging himself out of aircraft. Uncle Ed, who you'll recall Rackstraw met during his family's 1960 vacation in Arizona, had apparently made quite an impression.

Noyes asked a green researcher in his Unit 4 investigative team, Don Ray, to verify the story, and the Vietnam veteran started his search for Cooper from scratch. Directory assistance turned up many Ed Coopers, so Ray called them all; none was the man he was looking for.

"Eventually I had to think, who would know where skydivers are?" recalled Ray.

After a few more calls, he learned jumpers in the area liked a desert airstrip at Apache Junction, east of Phoenix. It was literally an airstrip and nothing else. A farmer who occasionally leveled the dirt runway told Ray he happened to know the pilot who taxied the skydivers to their midair jump point, an old 1930s barnstormer named Charlie Merritt.

"So I called this guy [Merritt] up and he answered. I said, 'Hey, I'm doing a story about a sixty-five-year-old skydiver I'd heard about—an old guy who's got thousands of jumps and he's still jumping.'"

"Oh, you mean Ed Cooper," came Merritt's answer.

"Absolutely," said Ray, "How do I get in touch with him?"

The hunt wasn't over, however. The address the researcher was given didn't have a phone, and neighbors revealed Cooper had gone camping. So Ray had someone post a note on his door. Then he waited.

"The next day, sure enough I get a call from him. Nice guy. And I said, 'Look, the reason I'm calling is that there's a guy that we're talking to, we're interested in him, and his name is Bob Rackstraw.'"

"Yeah," said Cooper, "he's my nephew."

"Ah, fantastic," said Ray. "He said he's honoring you by using your name in some stuff that he's done. In fact, he claimed that he is D. B. Cooper."

Cooper let out an audible sigh and then said, "I don't know anything about that."

Ed Cooper, Bob Rackstraw's skydiving uncle and the inspiration for the name Cooper in his infamous alias.

After Ray delivered the confirmation of family lineage, Noyes was officially curious. He called an FBI friend whose opinion he trusted, Special Agent Roger "Frenchy" LaJeunesse. The Los Angeles–based G-man tried to talk Noyes out of having anything to do with Rackstraw.

"This guy is a con man; he's not D. B. Cooper," he said. "You know, you're off on the wrong trail again, Noyes."

But Noyes had often been on the right trail, as well, such as the time he personally led the Los Angeles Police Department to the 1969 hideout of serial killer Charles Manson. And he had a feeling about Rackstraw, too.[8]

On March 21, 1979, Noyes met up with his Sacramento-based television reporter Doug Kriegel and a video crew at the Stockton municipal court. After shooting the morning's hearing regarding Rackstraw's recent plane theft, they sat him down in a back room.

What Noyes had not counted on was Rackstraw being Rackstraw.

Kriegel started by going for the jugular: "Do you think it's legit that you could be one of the [D. B. Cooper] suspects? One of the thousand?"

Earnest and seemingly candid, he replied, "Oh yes, if I was an investigator, definitely so. I wouldn't discount myself . . . or a person like myself."

Kriegel asked if Rackstraw had been in the Washington State area. The suspect admitted he was there "a number of times" around the 1971 hijacking date. "The FBI verified all that, that's one of the reasons they keep hounding me. I'm sure of that."[9]

Sources did confirm to the bureau that Rackstraw had told them he was flying a plane for a Washington State real estate firm during that period.[10] That, and the noted fingerprint discrepancy, apparently had helped lower the FBI's suspicions.

The year before, however, Rackstraw had given Stockton Police an alibi that was 653 miles away from what he told the feds: The just-arrived prisoner from Iran claimed to two city investigators that he was holed up at San Francisco Bay's Fort Cronkhite during the Cooper caper—in fact, his own army brass had asked, a few days after, if he had done it.

It didn't take long for the Stockton lawmen to find holes in the tall tale. At the time of the Thanksgiving Eve skydiving, it had been five months since Rackstraw had been kicked out of the army at Fort Rucker in Alabama. This first alibi was featured in an exclusive *Stockton Record* article on February 3, 1979, but the crucial details were buried in one paragraph on a long jump page. One might wonder if the FBI ever heard about this obscure alibi.[11]

KNBC reporter Kriegel looked down at his notes and began rattling off qualifications Rackstraw had—and Cooper would have needed—to pull off the skyjacking.

"Pilot's license, explosives . . ."

And then Rackstraw, nodding, took over. "Engineering contractor, amateur scientist, specialist in underwater explosives, demolitions, underwater operations, air, sea, land. Try—"

Kriegel interrupted. "Some people say it adds up."

"Oh, certainly," said the defendant, but then he wagged a stern finger. "But not for crime, not for crime."

Finally, Kriegel tried again. "Are you D. B. Cooper?"

Rackstraw looked torn. "I, I can't talk about things like that. I can't talk about any of that sort of thing."

The story that aired that night on KNBC was entertaining, good television. But it most definitely did not deliver what Noyes and his Unit 4 team were after: a confession.

"You know, he started talking about one thing and another thing and he didn't kill anybody and he didn't cheat the bank and, you know, all these charges were bogus," said Noyes recently. "He was not unlike several other Vietnam veterans I had met who came back very troubled and got into trouble over a multitude of things."

Noyes was well aware that Rackstraw was blowing a good deal of smoke into the camera, and yet, "he was interesting to listen to because he had a gift of gab that was beyond belief. He would talk about his war stories—but then when you ask him about D. B. Cooper, he would become very elusive on that. And he would like to create the impression that he was, you know, that he might be. He wanted you to leave with a lingering doubt that he was. And my interest solely involved the fact that he was a HALO jumper in Nam. These were . . . paratroopers sent in at night to make low level [openings] that couldn't be detected by the enemy. They couldn't just be an ordinary GI, and I had known one other HALO jumper and had been told of all the extensive training they went through. So [Rackstraw] would fit the profile because virtually all the suspects the FBI had talked to were ex-military paratroopers."

Noyes still has a grudging admiration for Rackstraw's sheer imagination and ability to adapt.

"I'm sure he's still in a con today, whatever he's doing. He's mesmerizing some bank officer or some old lady. I guess I wouldn't have had much of a career if it hadn't been for people like Bob Rackstraw."[12]

Many people, especially the ones investigating Rackstraw in 1979, did not share that admiration.

On April 29, 1979, to show the danger of the dynamite the suspect trafficked in, the San Joaquin County District Attorney's Office blew up a car with the exact amount Rackstraw had tried to ship to his veteran friend, Joe Schlein, in San Antonio, Texas—just before the escape to Iran. The prosecutor's plan was to show all the detonation pictures in a sequential display, like a giant flipbook, to a jury at his coming trial for illegally possessing and distributing the explosives. The proud detective who produced the exhibition mailed a copy of the thirty-seven photos to Noyes at KNBC's Burbank newsroom.[13]

The court, however, decided to try Rackstraw first for the complicated check-kiting scheme involving several banks. On May 19, 1979, he was found guilty of five counts of grand theft and issuing bad checks. While the defendant had earlier been warned he was going to receive three years if found guilty, he would have to wait two months for the official sentencing hearing.

In typical fashion, Rackstraw instigated several incidents during the weeklong trial, searching for ways to postpone the ultimate judgment, to wriggle away from the consequences of his actions yet another time. At one point he tried to enter a revised plea of "innocent by reason of insanity" to delay the proceedings for a psychiatric examination.

Later, in the words of a reporter on the scene, he "verbally attacked [Deputy D. A.] Clark Sueyres when the jury managed to return only a partial verdict. 'Sueyres had his way!' Rackstraw yelled, 'I am going to prison for three years! My life is ruined! My family is ruined!'"[14]

Soon after, Rackstraw went on the offensive once more, firing off a scathing, sometimes bizarre, letter to the appeals court. His target was the man who had prosecuted him, Sueyres, whom Rackstraw described as "a mentally deranged Psycho-Pathic [sic] Communist liar," as well as "a rampant criminal traveling under the title of Deputy District Attorney."

He was far from content to leave it at that. In his six-page screed, he called Sueyres's case a fiasco, frivolous, a farce, and a sham "solely due to the incompetent, scatter-brain jack-ass, two faced lying destructive lunatic, who derives a state of mental masturbation from exercising his ability to ignore the law of the land and get away with it."

Rackstraw even warned the appeals court that "Sueyres is making a 'FOOL' of everyone, at their expense! And you're letting him do it. It's just beginning. Respectfully submitted, Bob Rackstraw."[15]

Sueyres, who went on to become a judge, will never forget contending with Rackstraw almost four decades ago.

"I have dealt with a number of clever sociopaths in court, but he has more smarts and nerve than the rest put together," he recently maintained. He also had a comment regarding what happened in the neighboring county the year before—stating it was "highly likely" Rackstraw had killed his stepfather. "Why else would he leave Calaveras County in such a rush?"[16]

On May 31, 1979, Rackstraw came to the conclusion he had to plead "no contest" to the remaining charges involving possessing illegal explosives, stealing a plane, and writing more rubber checks. It earned him two more years in jail, but that sentence was to run concurrent with the check-kiting sentence of three years.

Because these pleas eliminated Rackstraw's testimony, there unfortunately would be no way to determine if the 1978 explosives found in his Bekins storage unit in Stockton, along with the 1977 Tovex charge shipped to Texas, had come from the 1975 Felton Quarry dynamite theft in his old hometown of Scotts Valley.[17]

Three months after introducing himself on the phone to KNBC editor Pete Noyes, Rackstraw reached out to him again. This time it was in the form of two expletive-laden letters, mailed on June 26 and June 27, 1979. They revealed a somewhat different and decidedly more frustrated Rackstraw.

As in his appeals letter, he spewed venom on his probation officer, the judge who had presided over his trial, and the district attorney who had prosecuted him. But in the next breath, he bragged about the cunning legal maneuvers he had employed to slow and hamper the proceedings. Nothing seemed beyond Rackstraw's grasp, so vast was his grandiose vision of himself. Soon he was reviewing world headlines and rendering solutions.

"If I ran this nation," he wrote Noyes, "I'd take over the entirety of Central and South America!"

Having solved the problem of turmoil in the Western Hemisphere, Rackstraw asked Noyes for a job in his newsroom.

"I could go for one of those overseas assignments, Pete," he wrote. "Those jerks wouldn't stop my ass from getting the truth!"[18]

Noyes did not write back, but the letters may have rekindled his interest in a man he viewed as fascinating and larger than life. He knew that Rackstraw was due for sentencing on July 24, and he planned to be there.

On the day before he was sentenced, Rackstraw was granted a probation hearing. In a final bizarre tactic, he rose to address Superior Court Judge Frank Kim and said he wanted "to confess he was not D. B. Cooper." He explained that in January 1979, when rumors that he might be the hijacker had surfaced in the media, "I decided to go along with the idea" because "I knew it would trigger press reaction."

He never said what he thought he would gain by it. One might assume it was all simply for profit or ego—or yet, perhaps part of a sophisticated, multilayered disinformation campaign that a Green Beret–trained PSYOP soldier like him could have timed with Briggs's Cooper-related antics in Portland.

On the subject of probation over prison, Rackstraw reminded the judge of his outstanding service record and lectured about each of his medals, as well as about all of the "prosecutor's lies." To the probable dismay of everyone in the courtroom, his oratory continued for three full hours.[19]

The following day, Rackstraw was sentenced to three years for bank fraud, but factoring in the May 31 concurrent judgment of two years and time served, he faced only two years in state prison.

Before he was led from the courtroom, however, he was forced to endure a bit of bluster-puncturing truth. Probation officer Darryl Datwyler stood before the bench and reported that Bob Rackstraw was a "chronic liar and manipulative." He was not a Green Beret captain with five campaign ribbons who flew gunships but an Army Airborne lieutenant who piloted transport helicopters during a fifteen-month tour. Datwyler then clarified those often-claimed military decorations, explaining that while Rackstraw had earned a good quantity of medals, his five Purple Hearts were all fiction. Furthermore, he had falsified attendance records at two California colleges and lied about earning a degree.[20]

Noyes and Los Angeles–based anchorman Warren Olney had positioned themselves outside the court, hoping to snare Rackstraw as he went by. To their delight, despite the shattering of his façade, the felon was more than willing to sit down for another interview.

The first thing Olney asked was a mistake. He wanted to know what he had missed in court—in particular, "Were there any specific references . . . to the Cooper incident?"

Like the proverbial gift that keeps on giving, Rackstraw quickly deducted that the out-of-town news team was not aware of his "I'm not Cooper" statement to the judge the day before, which was now featured on Stockton newsstands. Shifting into his familiar skyjacking tap dance, he took on a serious expression.

"Uh, only indirectly, in chambers. You know, you get the side-glances and things," he said.

Olney then directly asked if Rackstraw was the skyjacker. Used to being in the defendant's seat by now, Rackstraw cracked a devious smile.

"I'm afraid of heights," he said.

Undeterred, Olney went after his military skills. "You have parachute training and, as you mentioned yourself, your background suggests that you could have been D. B. Cooper."

The defendant looked downward. "I coulda been . . . coulda been."

"You don't want to commit yourself one way or the other?"

"No, I, uh, I can't commit myself on something like that, Warren." Rackstraw struck a pose reminiscent of Auguste Rodin's sculpture *The Thinker*. "You say with a story like that, should it be fiction or should it be fact? It's primarily up to the American people someday, how that comes out."[21]

On July 26, 1979, Olney's exclusive nonstory was beamed into Southern California homes. But the network's national editors in New York killed the tale for several reasons.

Bob Rackstraw at his sentencing on multiple charges, one year after his acquittal for murder.

First, the FBI was adamantly telling any media willing to listen that Rackstraw was too young in 1971 (he was twenty-eight) to have pulled off such a complicated hijacking. Furthermore, he couldn't be trusted for a moment because he was a justifiably disgraced army liar. In addition, as one of the authors can personally attest (as a ten-year network researcher in Los Angeles, starting in 1979), the celebrated news organizations of ABC, CBS, and NBC and their nightly news programs—the only national television news outlets at that time—were unwilling to gamble their buttoned-down reputations on the unsupported claims of a jailed local con artist.[22]

After recently rewatching both of his reporters' 1979 video stories, retired KNBC editor Noyes was candid.

"Sometimes you have doubts about whether you should put a story like that on the air. Were we being used? Yes, we were being used. We wanted to be used.

"I had a great deal of respect for the FBI's Los Angeles office and [special agent] Frenchy LaJeunesse. [But] when he told me this guy wasn't D. B. Cooper, I wanted to believe he was wrong."

If this *is* the trail to Cooper, Noyes will have the redemptive last laugh.[23]

CHAPTER 16

Take Me to the River

FEBRUARY 12–DECEMBER 12, 1980

E
xactly four days after Dick Briggs told Carlson and Burke about the impending discovery of some of his D. B. Cooper cash on the Columbia River, the sleeping drug runners, along with two road-trip girlfriends, were in the Sands Regency Hotel in Reno.

After waking with a shower, Carlson turned toward something on the television—then froze.

"Wake up, Vern!" He nudged the gangly Texan without taking his eyes away from the screen. "Get up; you gotta see this!" Carlson and Burke both sat on the bed, looking at each other, saying in unison, "Son of a bitch!'"

The screen showed a network news alert, featuring the "hippie" couple their boss pointed to at the river party. Only this time, Dwayne and Patricia Ingram were in front of cameras and microphones, along with their eight-year-old son, Brian, explaining how they had discovered the ransom money buried in the sand on the Columbia's north shore.[1]

William M. Baker, the assistant special agent-in-charge in Portland at the time, recalled how those events unfolded.

"The day before, Mister Ingram called and told employee Marge Gillem his son had found a packet of money while digging on the banks. Serial numbers furnished by Ingram matched the ransom bills. I handled the media, but it was our entire office that sprang in to organized pandemonium."[2]

The Ingrams visit the FBI office to explain how they "stumbled" upon Cooper's hijack money on the banks of the Columbia River at Tina Bar.

The FBI confirmed for a crowd of reporters that it had recovered approximately $5,800 of the skyjacker's missing loot, broken into three bundles of twenty-dollar bills with decomposing rubber bands still in place.[3]

Stunned by the February 12, 1980, breaking news, Carlson said he and Burke were forced to reconsider Briggs and all his claims. "We actually started believing he must be Cooper."

He then kept the river stunt secret for more than thirty years.

Now sixty-seven, the tipster and former runner who sparked this inquiry is among those today who believe Rackstraw was pulling the strings all along, with one goal in mind: like in Vietnam a decade earlier, he sought to be reborn at the water's edge—this time freed of his high-flying original sin.[4]

Allegations of a shoreline setup didn't start with this investigation. As noted in the *New York Times*, "At first, there was speculation that the money might have been deliberately stashed there. Late in the week, the FBI said the loot had probably been deposited by the river's currents, not by Mr. Cooper or anyone else."[5]

The bureau's lead Oregon agent, Ralph Himmelsbach, took it further in a newspaper article: "This is strong evidence that Cooper didn't survive, but we have no proof of that."[6] Another senior G-man on the river, Dorwyn Schreuder, bluntly told a reporter that Cooper is probably not alive. "If he were, I think he'd be with his money."[7]

All the excitement triggered the FBI to quickly move investigative resources to Oregon, which of course was followed by a swarm of Cooper-obsessed reporters and amateur treasure hunters. The search of the beach at Tina Bar for additional cash and the hijacker's bones was on.

It didn't seem to matter to anyone at the river when a fisherman, eighty-year-old Sid Tipper, told a visiting *Seattle Times* reporter that the feds' theory of the Cooper money just washing up and burying itself in the sand was beyond belief.

"I've been going up and down this river for ten years. If it had been here, I think we would've seen it," said Tipper.

Tina Bar was in fact the bearded fisherman's favorite daily spot; he told a wire service the only days he'd miss were during Christmas time, when he was "playing Santa at a local store." Tipper also confirmed "he was there the day the boy found part of Cooper's loot."[8]

Other locals told the FBI they were just as skeptical.

Georger, the retired chat-room professor with bureau family connections, was given access to the 1980 incident records. He posted in 2008 that local farmers Joe, Jack, and Albert Fazio, owners of the Tina Bar shoreline, emphatically told agents that they recently "ran their cattle on that beach for water, and they said there was no way that the money was on that beach more than a few days or weeks. Farmers know their land."[9]

In 2011, Brian Ingram himself, all grown up at forty, was interviewed for this investigation. And he still remembered Sid Tipper. During the two-year period when his family lived nearby, "the older fisherman was always, always there, a big old long beard, and I remember we'd go out and he'd be there like clockwork. No matter when we came out, he was there."

Then Ingram went public with his own doubts. "I firmly believe that the money was placed there, and it didn't float by natural means to that location," Brian revealed.

That led to a tough question: if evidence was found the money discovery was staged, as runner Ron Carlson had claimed, would Ingram entertain the thought his parents were lying?

The camera caught his brow come down.

"Would I entertain the thought? Well if, if there, if there's, if there's, you know, tangible evidence pointing, pointing in that direction, of course I would. I mean, uh, I can't, uh, can't deny the truth."[10]

Four years later, this investigation came as close to the truth as we were going to get.

In 2015, Brian and his father, Dwayne (then forty-four and sixty-three, respectively) sat down with reporter Jim Forbes and a cameraman in their hometown of Mena, Arkansas, for our History Channel documentary.

When the question came up about how his son discovered the money on the Columbia, the father took a big breath.

"I said, 'Let's build us a fire here and burn some logs.' [Brian] said, 'Yeah, okay Pappy!' So I grabbed up some driftwood, and I'm looking around and stuff, and he runs up and gets on his hands and knees. He says, 'Let me clear us a place, Daddy.' And I said, 'Not right there! Let's do it right over there. You see them two little sticks over there? Let's do it right there."

Why Dwayne thought the two sticks were an important detail for this thirty-five year-old retelling, we didn't know. But the instruction certainly raised Forbes's eyebrows.

The reporter followed up with a surprise. With their permission, he pulled out a laptop and played the footage of former runner Ron Carlson's 2011 interview—cued up to the part about the Ingrams' colluding with Dick Briggs on the Tina Bar money stunt.

The documentary cameraman zoomed in on Dwayne as he suddenly removed his glasses, closed his eyes, tightened his facial muscles, and grimaced. Then he turned away from the rolling allegation and wrung his hands, over and over. At the tape's end, Brian was silently side-glancing at his father.

Dwayne nodded toward the screen. "That guy was tweakin'. He's a drugster. He don't have no idea what he's talking about."

Forbes was ready for him. "I'm wondering why, years later, he would come out and, I'm presuming you would say, concoct this story?"

I don't know what to say," muttered Dwayne.[11]

Tom Fuentes, a former FBI assistant director hired by the History Channel, was brought in to the documentary production offices and asked to study the family's recorded interview. When he saw Dwayne's peculiar mannerisms while watching Carlson's accusation, the retired G-man smiled broadly. He then labeled the father's nervous actions to be common signs of someone lying.[12]

Truth be told, that wasn't a surprise.

Eleven days after Dick Briggs's river "prophecy" was right on the money, his drug-trafficking operation and his private life began to unravel.

What should have been a routine coke drop in Phoenix by Carlson ran headlong into an ambush by the Drug Enforcement Administration (DEA). The thirty-year-old runner lived up to his title, escaping in a car chase that hit speeds of ninety miles per hour.

Briggs would not be happy that his product, and the Phoenix buyer, had been intercepted, and Carlson was not looking forward to telling him. On top of that, both he and partner Vern Burke, who had been away with his woman at the time, decided they had stretched their luck to the limit. After making their amends with Briggs and Shell, both "retired" from the drug-trafficking business—by vanishing.[13]

The DEA in Phoenix quickly learned about the cocaine's Portland connection. In a final crusher, just a few months later, a detained Oregon cocaine client thought he might buy some leniency by telling an Internal Revenue Service (IRS) investigator virtually all of Briggs's drug-trade secrets. By the end of 1980, Briggs would be broke, miserable, and convinced that he was about to be killed. By whom, he would never say.[14]

Rackstraw disappeared from the public stage on August 19, 1980, when he was released from California's Folsom State Prison after having served a little more than a year behind bars. Officially cleared as a D. B. Cooper suspect, he was quietly paroled to supervision in Columbus, Ohio, where he had extended family on his mother's side.[15]

Briggs, meanwhile, had become increasingly depressed and fearful. His inner circle had been taking serious hits, contributing to his apprehension.

Middleman Shell was arrested by the DEA seven months following the bust that Carlson managed to escape in Phoenix. Shell received no time behind bars, however, but instead was wrist-slapped to the tune of five years' probation.[16]

It's understandable if Briggs wondered why the sentence was so light. The walls must have seemed to be closing in.

In the early hours of December 12, Dick Briggs, Oregon's self-proclaimed cocaine kingpin, died in a mysterious one-car accident on an isolated road.

Old friend and former classmate Jim Hollingsworth had remained with him until 4:30 that morning, specifically because Briggs was intensely afraid that he would be murdered.[17]

Briggs's former girlfriend, Bev Nevin, was blunt. "I believe he was killed."

She recalled he had ended their last telephone call that same evening with disturbing words: "Gotta run; they're after me."[18]

One of Briggs's high-school friends, Daryl Hedland, trying to make sense of what had happened, said an officer at the crash scene told him Briggs was crushed under his flipped car. Reports from the Portland Police Bureau and the coroner describe the incident as a speeding drunk-driver's crash.[19]

But much about the incident didn't make sense. More than thirty years later, the clear-eyed Pudgy Hunt remained puzzled about the high-speed, one-car accident theory.

"He was not a fast driver. That's what surprised me about this crash. He always had stuff that shouldn't be seen with him, so he obeyed the laws pretty well when he was driving."[20]

And yet somehow, after a night of fearing openly for his life, Dick Briggs drove fast enough to flip his car on a curve and be crushed to death. Was it simply the onset of an even more acute cocaine-fueled paranoia? Or, perhaps more logically, was it because someone in another vehicle was following him? The official logs only revealed that the drunk lost control, skidded ninety-nine feet, went airborne over a ditch, and then smashed into a parked car on a driveway. He was found beneath the wreck, impaled on a jagged door mirror.[21]

Others, including Briggs's oldest son, John Jr., insisted that the crash was not an accident at all but a covered-up murder.[22]

Hunt added, "The thing I heard was that [Dick Briggs] got a call, and that he thought somebody was after him."[23]

Support for this position comes from surprising sources. The day after Briggs died, an IRS investigator who had been building a case against him called Portland police for details about his death.[24] If, in fact, the flamboyant trafficker was murdered because he knew too much—as family members and friends suggested—the forthcoming IRS and DEA indictments could well have provided the killer or killers with plenty of motive to silence him.

For instance, if Briggs were to spill the truth about D. B. Cooper, he might very well have a clear pathway to immunity from prosecution. The nervous, real D. B. Cooper, well aware that the claimant to his nom de hijack knew enough to bring him down, might have found that kind of vulnerability unacceptable—and grounds for doing something that would permanently remove the threat.

Briggs's memorial service was a mélange of the all-American values of his adoptive family and the thuggish sensibilities of desperado friends and associates straight out of the meanest streets imaginable. Mom and Pop came face to face with drug traffickers, dopers, pimps, prostitutes, and just plain guys with bent noses. All had come to pay their respects, sharing their sense of loss and sadness.[25]

There is no evidence that his seven-year coworker, friend, and crime partner, Rackstraw, was among them—perhaps conspicuously absent.

Briggs's old middleman and college frat brother, Jim T. Shell, also weighed in. But he did it with a personal letter written directly to the dead man, the day after Briggs died, which he shared for the first time in 2015.

"My Friend: We have been like brothers these last several years. I hope you end your suffering and torment—your rage of temper—and discover the peace of mind you so richly search for. Find true happiness in your next life and appreciate all those wild and crazy days ahead. I could hate and love you at the same time, my friend. God rest your wicked soul.

"Remember me because I'll always be on your side. Cheers Dickie . . . Love, James T."[26]

Briggs's adoptive parents, John and Ruth—along with his sister, Phyllis, his two young sons, and his former wife, Stella—buried him in a private ceremony on a hillside overlooking the Columbia.[27]

The perfect sentinel for a river of secrets.

CHAPTER 17

From Takeoff to Tailspin

1981–2010

Sixteen months after Rackstraw was paroled in Ohio, the ex-con married his next wife, Dorothy L. "Dottie" Busch-Klayer, a wealthy thirty-three-year-old divorcee. It was the third round of nuptials for both, and it took place in nearby Kenton, Kentucky. Ohioan Dottie took her new husband's last name, as did her five-year-old son, Walter. Everything looked rosy.[1]

First wife Gail Marks said Bob called her after the December 26, 1981, wedding and excitedly said, "I've finally married someone rich."[2]

The thirty-eight-year-old Rackstraw soon moved his new bride and stepson back to California, this time settling in the southern half of the state. On August 3, 1982, he created a company called California Aviation Transportation Systems, or CATS, in Santa Monica.[3]

Dottie soon began training to become a state-certified masonry inspector—masonry being one of her husband's numerous construction trades.[4] Was her move to join the workforce based on forward thinking or an intuition about her new man?

Either way, the training would come into play for the family two years later when Rackstraw's latest business, CATS, had its articles of incorporation suspended by the state for back taxes.[5] As Linda Lee had come to realize years before, her brother was once again better at coming up with a new idea than following through.

One thing he excelled at, however, was getting involved in legal actions. On April 20, 1983, Rackstraw became embroiled in a series of suits in Rancho Cucamonga, a city where, years later, he would work at an arbitration firm. It all started when he crashed his '79 Chevy Malibu into the left-hand-turning '73 Olds Delta 88 of Pat "Patsy" Lamberson, a forty-seven-year-old mother of four. Now eighty, Lamberson admitted she was at fault in a recent phone interview. Reviewing her copy of the thirty-three-year-old collision report and accident photos of both cars, she vividly recollected what happened before and after the accident.

"I was driving home from my Bank of America job, and it was pouring rain and dark as I approached. I was making a left with another car facing me, its headlights on," Lamberson said. "I couldn't see [Rackstraw] coming toward me in the other lane. Then I blanked out. I still don't remember the crash or rescue. I woke up in the hospital."

According to the deputy's narrative, the impact from Rackstraw's smaller Malibu, traveling at approximately thirty-five miles per hour, spun her four-door sedan around and left it straddling on the southwest corner sidewalk, seventeen feet away. But because the Olds was built like a tank, Lamberson suffered only a cracked rib, a few broken teeth and bruises.

When paramedics pulled the bleeding Rackstraw out of his car, with "its whole front end caved in," they immediately noticed his severely broken leg.

One other person came out on the losing end in Rancho Cucamonga that evening: Rackstraw's new bride. Lamberson remembered that when Dottie arrived in the emergency room, her greatest issue was the destroyed vehicle. It was hers, and Rackstraw had apparently taken it without permission.

"She came in all loud and huffy, angry at [Rackstraw]. She bummed a cigarette from [Lamberson's husband] Harold, then blamed me for the accident. My husband told her to take it easy."

Lamberson's insurance policy gave Rackstraw the maximum $50,000 payout. A year later, he sued the emergency room doctors and the San Antonio Community Hospital where he had been treated. Then on July 14, 1986, Rackstraw took the city to court, seeking a million dollars for medical expenses, loss of earnings, and damages. County records in both cases don't indicate that he received any cash settlements.

He had, however, one small victory—a left-hand lane was put in at the intersection, something Rackstraw had argued for in his original July 21, 1983, "Claim for Damage or Injury" paperwork.

Rackstraw today walks with a prominent limp; one could imagine it was a result of the accident.

One more odd fact about the incident: Lamberson's collision report shows Bob Rackstraw gave the address of a home in Rancho Cucamonga, while Dottie, in only the sixteenth month of their marriage, listed her residence as an apartment near Ontario International Airport, seven miles away.[6]

Five years after Rackstraw's 1978 acquittal of the charges in the murder of stepdad Philip, Calaveras County officials ordered all case transcripts, evidence, and exhibits used in the trial to be destroyed. Any DNA evidence on the never-tested bloody pair of pants would be lost also. However, more than three hundred pages of pretrial transcripts, motions by the district attorney's office, Bell Helicopter letters dealing with Rackstraw's surrender in Iran, and more than sixty newspaper clippings covering all the drama survived for the history books.[7]

In May 1984, Bob and Dottie Rackstraw, with Walter now seven, quietly moved into an exclusive gated community at Canyon Lake Golf Course in Riverside County, California.[8]

In 1991, twenty years after the army forced him to resign for reasons including his faking attendance at two California colleges, Rackstraw earned a bachelor of science in applied economics from the University of San Francisco.[9] Even though it took eight years, he had achieved a long-sought goal. Perhaps it erased—in his own mind, at least—a glaring weakness: the inability to see something through to the end.

Bob Rackstraw was forty-seven years old and had no doubt decided it was time to take his future seriously. The year before, he had begun to teach contract law and mediation—both in classrooms and later in online courses—for the University of California, Riverside (UCR). Even he must have marveled at his profound change in status. He continued as a UCR staff instructor for a decade, becoming director of law and public policy at the school from 1990 to 1992.[10]

Being an academic, however, did not stop Rackstraw from being Rackstraw.

Apparently in a mood to clear up as many loose ends as possible, he petitioned the court in Santa Cruz County on December 9, 1991, to change his child-support agreement with Gail Marks, who had remarried, since their three kids were now legally adults over the age of twenty-one. The court-ordered support was officially ended a year and a half later.[11]

Marks maintains Rackstraw had never written a personal check to support his children in those two decades. She also revealed that after Rackstraw's petitioning, she explored the possibility of suing him. That's when a lawyer told her that Rackstraw had quietly sold off or "gifted" all his real estate properties.[12]

Less than three months before that county hearing, Bob and Dottie Rackstraw were granted a formal separation in Riverside County Superior Court. They told the judge they had actually parted ways on January 1, 1988, "separated all assets," and divided their real properties in a private "written settlement agreement."[13] That private agreement is the only missing document in the now twenty-four-year-old court file.

The year 1991 also saw Marks host the civil wedding between her twenty-one-year-old son, Robby W. Rackstraw II, and Kristen, the mother of his year-and-a-half-old baby boy, Robert W. Rackstraw III. According to an anonymous guest who attended, everyone in Marks's Grass Valley, California, home was cordial,

Freed and flourishing, Bob Rackstraw and family at son Robby's wedding in 1991.

including the beaming patriarch, Bob. He was photographed there with his arm around Dottie—both looking surprisingly chummy after their three years of separation.[14]

To add to the event's simmering tension, Bob's estranged sister, Linda Lee, also came. "I bit the bullet 'cause I knew Bob was going to be there. But I wanted to go," she said, for her nephew's sake.[15]

It was the last time the two siblings would ever see each other in the flesh.

Continuing his quest for "legitimacy," Rackstraw soon enrolled in the Northwestern California University School of Law, the first online college in the state. He earned a juris doctorate in 1993, followed by an LLM (master of laws) in the field of international law and economics.[16] Bob no doubt hoped the new qualifications would help him land consulting opportunities with private law firms, as well as arbitration and mediation work through the state court system.

Another product of the California State Court system—the nightly news melodrama that was the 1995 trial of O. J. Simpson—would also have an indirect effect on the personal life of the man who many believe is D. B. Cooper. But it had nothing to do with whether or not Rackstraw was the famous skyjacker and getaway artist. It had far more to do with the 1977 murder of his stepfather, Philip, and what his sister would come to understand about it.

"All these years, you go over the facts so many times," Linda Lee said in reflection, fighting her tears. "And I always tried to keep a higher percentage that Bob did not do it in my mind. You know, like, okay, 70 percent he didn't do it; 30 percent he could have done it. And over the years, I realized, who else did it? Who else would have killed Dad?

"If it had been a passerby, they wouldn't have buried the body . . . Somebody had to have killed him and didn't want the body to be found. Who else? Who else was there? And so I was starting to let go"—she began crying once more—"of the idea that he was innocent.

"I remember in the nineties when I was watching the O. J. Simpson trial and everything that had gone on. You know, the chase in the Bronco

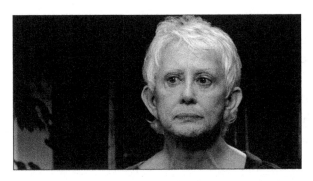

Linda Lee Loduca, conscience of the Rackstraw family.

and the way that O. J. acted, and when he was saying, 'I'm going to catch the murderer. I'll catch Nicole's murderer.' And just things he said and did. I pretty well figured out the man was guilty. And I thought, that's a guilty man. And he sounds exactly like Bob sounded during the trial."[17]

Rackstraw, you may recall, swore to his jury in 1978 that he was not the murderer and that he would find his father's killer and "bring him here to justice."[18]

"One time I remember saying something [to Bob] about going up to Calaveras and looking into something. And he goes, 'No, don't do that, 'cause it's too dangerous for you, you know, once you're up there.' And I said, 'Well, I have to make plans to have a grave marker.' You can't put grave markers on the graves for a year because they have to settle. And I said, 'I need to go back and do that.' And he goes, 'I'll take care of that. I'll take care of all that.' He didn't want me up there asking questions in Calaveras County."

After watching the Simpson trial and reaching her conclusions about the similarity between Simpson's comments and Rackstraw's words and actions, Linda Lee never spoke to her brother again.[19]

Eighteen years after the Simpson verdict, in San Luis Obispo, California, surrounded by her daughter's loving family, she succumbed to reoccurring cancer—just four weeks after giving that final interview.[20]

From 1997 through much of 2000, Bob Rackstraw suffered a series of reversals both personal and legal. An astrologer might have told him to lie low and not try to do too much. But then, Rackstraw wasn't the kind of fellow who asked astrologers for advice—he was always inclined to try to shape the future himself.

On October 19, 1997, three days after his fifty-fourth birthday, the college instructor was pulled over by a peace officer for suspicion of driving under the influence of alcohol and, possibly, drugs. Never one to pass up the opportunity to make a bad situation worse, he resisted arrest and gave a fake name. Because of the phony ID faux pas, a Riverside County judge revoked Rackstraw's driver's license on December 15.[21]

As bad as things had been for Rackstraw up until this time, he managed to interrupt his string of setbacks the following year. But even that victory looked like a loss, following an apparently sham six-month battle in Riverside divorce court with wife number three, Dottie. On May 28, 1998, their marriage of seventeen years was officially dissolved.[22]

So how was that a win for Rackstraw? Ex-wife number one, Gail Marks, who was still owed the lion's share of two decades worth of child support, claimed the couple's entire proceeding, starting with their official estrangement in 1991, was a staged scam to prevent her from getting any of her former husband's possessions.[23]

Court divorce files show Rackstraw's cherished twelve-acre home in Wildomar, California, was turned over—home, keys, and baggage—to Dottie, with her ex stating in writing he "does not have ownership of any real property." A half year later, she pocketed $279,000 for its sale.[24]

In reality, records and surveillance have shown that Bob and Dottie never separated. They carried on with everything in Dottie's name, as they have ever since.[25]

On June 23, 1999, the FAA caught up with Rackstraw's extracurricular activities. It suspended his medical certificate and flying license because he had failed to report—as is clearly required—his guilty plea for driving under the influence in 1997 and the subsequent suspension of his driver's license. According to FAA rules, if a pilot is involved in a "vehicle action," he or she has sixty days to report it to the agency.[26]

Rackstraw may not have believed it, but the rule also applied to him.

A month later, the Contractors State License Board revoked Rackstraw's permit for his latest California business, First Team Construction. He apparently had "misrepresented facts" in the application: the questionnaire asked, "Ever been convicted of a crime or found in violation of any professional standards or regulations?" The answer typed into the felon's paperwork was "No."[27]

On December 9, 1999, the grounded Airborne Bob filed a "petition for extraordinary relief" with the Veterans Administration (VA) after "disputed disabilities" came up following a VA hearing examination. The medical diagnosis was left unchanged, three months later, when the US Court of Appeals for Veterans Claims rejected his argument.[28]

In the midst of this pitched battle against federal authorities that would deny him the necessary credentials—and therefore the right—to fly, Rackstraw severed his ties with UCR. He was fifty-six years old and had been teaching college economics, mediation, and international contract law there for ten years.[29]

On May 9, 2000, Rackstraw's skydiving uncle, John "Ed" Cooper—whose name, we believe, was the inspiration for Rackstraw's alias on Northwest Airlines flight 305 out of Portland International Airport in 1971—died at the age of eighty-seven in Arizona.

Rackstraw now turned his attention to bettering his living conditions, moving in 2003 from Riverside to the far tonier and opportunity-rich climes in San Diego and nearby Coronado Bay, California.[30] Coronado was the home of the famed Hotel del Coronado, and was also the place where much of the most intense Navy SEALs training took place. The upscale neighborhood was situated just across a long, graceful bridge from San Diego.

On August 1, 2003, Rackstraw made an attempt to lift the 1999 suspension of his pilot's license. Two months before his sixtieth birthday, he took another medical examination for FAA certification. The gamble did not pay off. His license was revoked permanently.[31]

Rackstraw would take one more run at squeezing money out of the VA, attempting in March 2006 to claim eligibility for posttraumatic stress disorder (PTSD) compensation due to pain and suffering related to his Vietnam War experiences. But the facts of his exposure to that combat did little to support his assertion. In truth, the closest he *officially* got to Charlie was during his six weeks flying Huey slicks for Operation Left Bank, a top-secret intelligence-gathering program that routinely stayed hundreds to thousands of feet above the jungle fray. He was essentially a hovering observer, reporting the location of enemy troops or hardware to his superiors so aerial forces could respond with machine guns, bombs, and rockets.[32]

Unofficially, however, he in fact did participate in a lot of face-to-face combat, with the Special Forces and CIA. But as veteran eyewitnesses and his former commander noted earlier, it was all off the books and without the army's permission.[33]

Tied to the 1999 rejection by the US Court of Appeals for Veterans Claims, even Bob Rackstraw recognized that his hope of monetary rescue from the military—in any form—was rapidly sinking. Consequently, he decided the way to stay afloat was to buy a boat. And hanging around Coronado Island in San Diego, cultivating his new beach boy lifestyle, he knew it wasn't going to be just any boat.

With an $86,000 bank loan, he became the sixth owner of the 1983 luxury cruiser *Poverty Sucks*. The forty-five footer was moved to a private slip at Coronado's Navy Yacht Club, which he and Dottie joined. They have remained members.[34]

Ten years after Dottie pocketed a quarter-million dollars after selling Bob's "gifted" twelve-acre home in that suspicious divorce settlement, she bought a plush condo on Bankers Hill in San Diego for a similar amount. And when she moved in on September 5, 2008, she had no problem finding a roommate.[35]

Brian Ingram was eight when he was credited with finding the rubber-banded ransom money in the Columbia River sand at Tina Bar. Thirty-six in June 2008, the father of three decided to auction fifteen of the Cooper twenty-dollar bills he had been allowed to keep. He received $37,000 for his crumbling dead presidents with a total face value of $300. Such was—and still is—the lure of anything related to the legend.[36]

It is not an exaggeration to say that without FBI Special Agent Larry Carr literally applying in 2007 for the job that nobody wanted—running the Cooper case out of the Seattle office—discussions about the forty-five-year-old evidence would still be in the Dark Ages. This mystery required someone willing to come at matters from a fresh direction, employing DNA evidence, sophisticated laboratory techniques, and that most essential of investigative tools, an open mind.

Carr, originally from Minnesota, had spent most of his FBI career handling bank robberies—the one area in which the normally secretive bureau has historically sought the cooperation of the public. For him, putting information out there seemed like the most natural and logical way to proceed.

One of the first steps the new case agent took was take his message to the web, inviting the maelstrom of opinions and ideas raging over what really happened to D. B. Cooper, as posited by the Cooper faithful who lived and breathed the legend. On a skydiving blog site that had become the gathering point for "Cooperites," appropriately known as the *Drop Zone* or simply DZ, Carr did the unheard of: under the tongue-in-cheek nickname of Ckret (as in "secret"), he posted dusty details on numerous subjects that before would have warranted a "no comment."

He then generously took on all comers in an effort to demystify as much as possible and even offered his own theories—in the hope, inadvertently or otherwise, of picking up a clue or two along the way.

Here are a few choice postings from Agent Carr, AKA Ckret:

- "There are 1057 sub files in the DB Cooper case, each representing a subject that has been investigated. To my knowledge, there is not one piece of verifiable information or evidence linking a subject to the case. This is one of the reasons for going public."
- "Cooper had A.D.[H.]D., his attention to detail was poor. He got the big picture, but missed the brush strokes. He was also a 'know-it-all.' One of those people who has just enough knowledge to be dangerous."
- "There were many [Ingram] family members at the beach the day the money was found, and some said Brian's cousin [Denise, 5] helped find and had a claim to it."
- "Why would Cooper bury the money? Some have said to throw the investigation off. If you were going to throw the investigation, why would you do it with buried money that may never be discovered?

For the answer to that last question, see chapters 14 and 16.[37]

The rapid exchange of information from multiple sources soon proved Carr's approach to be sound and quickly gave rise to several forensic questions—including whether or not anyone had scientifically examined the Cooper money from Tina Bar. The case agent assured the inquirers that no one ever had, and the bureau wanted someone to perform exactly that kind of analysis.

The forensic examination began in 2009 with Carr overseeing the creation of a three-member team of volunteer scientists, or "Citizen Sleuths."

Led by Tom Kaye, the esteemed group was given unparalleled access to a variety of unreleased materials and information, with testing results later published. In the view of this investigation, nothing was more significant than defining what actually happened along the river in 1980.[38]

It is true that while in charge of the D. B. Cooper files from 2007 to 2010, Special Agent Carr had his detractors and ultimately didn't crack the case. But it is equally true that without his courageous altering of the rules of the access game, this new look at Robert W. Rackstraw would never, ever have been possible.

Thank you, Larry Carr, for your passionate service and foresight.

CHAPTER 18

Day 1: Suddenly, a Sit-Down

NOVEMBER 6, 2012–MAY 20, 2013

With the help of an independent cold case team made up of private investigators and law enforcement consultants (including twenty-three former feds—twelve being retired FBI agents), Tom Colbert and his crew of journalists have chronicled an astonishing ninety-five pieces of physical, forensic, direct, testimonial, foundational, hearsay, and documentary evidence allegedly linking Robert W. Rackstraw back to the 1971 hijacking.[1]

At the end of the project's second year, it was time to lay out the case to the subject himself.

Jim Forbes, the team's documentary reporter, was the first to converse with Rackstraw. The process started in November 2012 with an e-mail to Rackstraw requesting an interview for a documentary covering the "folklore" surrounding the hijacking of the Northwest flight in 1971, along with a look at some of the suspects wrongly "maligned" during all the hysteria.

His response, exactly twenty-four hours later, showed a sixty-nine-year-old mind that, when unleashed, requires a seat belt. The italics in some noted passages were inserted by the authors:

Hello Jim,

I just read your e-mail and found it very interesting. *The particular episode of my life was certainly an eye opener* which prompted me to pursue a few college degrees including economics and a Doctorate in Law, and other ancillary credentials [to] teach it, such that I could better understand the graft, corruption, politics, deception and outright lawlessness that exists in our legal/political system. I became a professional legal expert and some say a scholar in mediation and arbitration, to help people resolve issues to preclude being judged by someone they don't even know, or worse, being prosecuted by someone who's only driving force is to "win."

There is an historical parallel there with the courts of the Third Reich.

The Cooper incident was, as I suspected, in-fact initiated internally by individuals in DC (the little 5'7" culprit) [a slight directed at the FBI's then director, J. Edgar Hoover] that desperately wanted to know everything about everyone in the US and, at that time, to be able to search everyone, preferably without a court order or warrant and most especially those that traveled internationally (which they now have today). Therein, *a mission was set up that was very similar to the 'Fast and Furious' of today* [the 2010 ATF 'gunwalking' sting], but similarly did not go as planned. *They needed someone to track down their key player* [Cooper]—that's what I was hired to do. I was unsuccessful as the intel I was given was not truthful (duh), so I dropped the pursuit and was recruited *to go the Middle East for the State Department (Iran)* where I found that someday that debacle would turn on us.

So Jim, I can give you an earful which I will reserve some rights over, *and there will be a compensatory discussion.*[2]

Wow. And like the Beatles' *White Album*, if you read his bluster, conspiracies, insults, and lies backward, you'll learn who really shot JFK.

His e-mail screeds evolved into cordial phone calls, but the pleasant conversations, lousy jokes, and meeting offers and counteroffers went on for more than six months.

Forbes knew he was stringing his quarry along but later reflected, "We needed to play it out, as a sit-down interview was by far our preference."[3]

The reporter had initially contacted Rackstraw with "an open mind," prepared to accept plausible denials of the circumstantial evidence Colbert's team had collected. Rackstraw was cagey about answering questions directly, but the more he talked, the more he unwittingly swayed the reporter that he could indeed be Cooper.

Asked if he thought Cooper had survived his jump, Rackstraw answered, "Oh yeah!" He then proceeded to list, *in the first person*, all the relevant military training he had received himself. When Forbes later observed that he thought Cooper would want to come out of the shadows and tell all, Rackstraw answered by noting there was a sealed indictment against the hijacker, with a death penalty attached.[4]

In another telephone joust, Rackstraw inadvertently revealed to Forbes his deep knowledge of the case development in 1980: "That kid found some [Cooper cash] in the river up there . . . their official thought being that, well, he drowned and the dollars were still with him, lost in the river." Even when reminded that recent FBI-sponsored forensic tests had concluded that the river cash could not have washed down and was therefore quite possibly planted, the veteran didn't miss a beat: "Yeah, I heard that too," he said, adding that he thought it was "to get them off-track."[5]

These were details, you might argue, only a very interested party would have uppermost in his thoughts.

As for the hijacker's motive, he ascribed an antiauthoritarian, antigovernment bent to Cooper that was in keeping with the profile the team had compiled on Rackstraw. He also dished up a string of diversions and blatant deceit. Rackstraw maintained during that first conversation that the FBI brought a Northwest stewardess to the Stockton jail, but she had failed to identify him as Cooper. He also denied that he owned a boat.[6] The lies were compounded in the months that followed.

After backing out of one interview, he continued to string Forbes and Colbert along. The only choice left was to get in Rackstraw's face.

Colbert sent three armed private investigators, two of them former FBI agents, to conduct a week of surveillance around San Diego's Coronado Bay neighborhood on May 11, 2013. They staked out Rackstraw's condo on Bankers Hill, his post office box, and his ocean-cruising boat, the *Poverty Sucks*, docked at the Navy Yacht Club.[7] If Rackstraw had any idea he was being watched, it had no apparent effect on him.

He then went about business as usual at his boat shop, Coronado Precision Marine, coming and going throughout the day. He clearly ran the place, hands-on to the smallest detail. The three investigators advised Colbert that the maritime business would be the best place to confront Rackstraw.

Hoping that when he saw his predicament, Rackstraw would face reality and take the opportunity to confess, Colbert decided to get things started

Rackstraw's philosophically named yacht, Poverty Sucks, *docked near Bob and Dottie's Coronado Island luxury condo in San Diego.*

with a softball approach. On May 20, he pulled his Jaguar into a parking space in front of Rackstraw's shop. Strolling forward, he was as friendly as could be, introducing himself as the "Hollywood producer behind the "*Expendables*-style television series" they had discussed on the phone. His long campaign to get Rackstraw to consider a consulting position on that show had been a setup for this very moment.

Rackstraw tried, with limited success, to appear pleased and relaxed as they shook hands.

"Oh for Christ's sake, Tom, uh, yeah, how are you?"

Ken Dirk, the lead investigator and an eleven-year FBI veteran, was present for this introduction, having approached Rackstraw earlier that morning under the pretense of buying a yacht. Pointing to Dirk, Rackstraw asked Colbert if he could wait a moment to talk.

"Let me take care of this gentleman here."

"That's okay," said Dirk in a professional tone. "We're together." Rackstraw could manage only, "All right, and . . ."

Dirk smiled. "So have a seat with him."

"Oh really?"

Rackstraw became a bit more open about his confusion. "And what's your name?"

"It doesn't really matter," Colbert recalled Dirk saying. "I answer to anything." Rackstraw laughed nervously. "What is it?"

To which Dirk replied, "It's Greg."

"Okay. Greg what?"

"Greg White," said Dirk.

Colbert began his matter-of-fact explanation of what this meeting was really about. Rackstraw was busy casing everything around him during this exchange. Colbert remembered the description he'd heard from Dick Briggs's right-hand man, Jim Shell, about Rackstraw having "a linebacker's eyes."

The linebacker was on full alert now.

Derek—Rackstraw's surly and much younger employee and a former navy military policeman—suggested that Colbert and Rackstraw sit in the patio chairs on the walkway in front of Coronado Precision Marine. That's where they moved.

"Well look," said Colbert, "it's so great to meet the real guy."

"Yeah."

Colbert noted the nervousness in Rackstraw's laugh. He seemed to be adjusting to the unfamiliar playing field he was on, wondering what happened to his home-field advantage. But before Colbert could ask a question, Rackstraw got his thoughts together enough to turn back to investigator Dirk, who was standing nearby.

"Were you in law enforcement or what?"

"I've been around," replied Dirk.

"Huh?"

"I'm retired."

"Yeah," said Rackstraw, pointing to his ponytailed coworker, Derek, "so is he," presumably referring to his MP background.

Colbert remembered the unflappable quality of Dirk's answer. "Yeah, and so are you, kind of."

Moving to stem what might turn into a testy moment, Colbert opened a folder and showed Rackstraw a blown-up copy of a crime-link chart he'd brought along. It showed Rackstraw at the center of a decades-long swirl of misdeeds, with lines and arrows to the names of all the other people who were involved in his capers.

"First, I kind of want to ask you why you're in the middle of this."

Handing the chart over so the ex-con could take a look, he pointed to Rackstraw's never-released 1970 army ID photo.

"There's an old picture you haven't seen in a while."

On the left side of the chart were the two widely circulated FBI renderings of D. B. Cooper. The similarities shared by all three images were impossible to miss.

"Yeah," said Rackstraw.

From his vantage point, Dirk noted that Rackstraw was suddenly very thoughtful.

Colbert pointed at the military headshot, noting, "That was [taken] fourteen months before the big day."

"Yeah, yeah," said Rackstraw.

Dirk realized he hadn't denied "the big day" in 1971 as a concept.

Colbert thought his confirmation meant more: "There's only one man who'd have those two calendar dates tucked away in his brain."

Rackstraw continued to scan the chart as Colbert explained that he was working with Jim Forbes, helping fund the documentary he was doing.

"Jim has told me he has found fifty-four of your old friends, from San Francisco to traffickers up in Portland to Astoria."

The silent Rackstraw showed no reaction, continuing to examine the chart.

"We're in essence here to tell you that we've got ten hours of tape on these folks, and they have told us a very intriguing story about you. And we're here to—"

Rackstraw interrupted him as he reacted to something he saw on the chart. "Hey, there's Dick Briggs," he laughed.

"Yeah, your old buddy," said Colbert.

The producer grinned—with that chuckle, his naive subject had confirmed the central premise to the two-and-a-half-year investigation: Rackstraw was linked to Briggs, the man behind the so-called Cooper money plant in 1980.

Assuming a hopeful expression, the felon looked up for a moment from the chart. "He's still alive, huh?"

Colbert realized what was going on: army PSYOP training had come to the fore. He was getting a dose of the Rackstraw shuffle, but the difference was, he knew it.

"Oh no," he shot back. "You know he's dead."

"No. I didn't know that," feigned Rackstraw, adding that he hadn't seen Briggs since the 1970s. "He was a teacher up in Oregon."

There you go again, thought Colbert.

"Well, yeah, until he got into other things," said the producer.

Rackstraw looked back at the laminated panorama of criminal activity laid out before him. Colbert sensed that it was time to advance the conversation. He referred to the many witnesses lined up and willing to talk, saying, "We're about to go forward with the documentary and a book."

But while the project had been underway for more than two years, he had come to offer Rackstraw "good news" along with the bad. He then revealed two $10,000 cashier's checks, with Rackstraw's name on them, and said they could be his if he signed over his story rights. That would push the other witnesses and sources to the back of the tale to be told. All this then "becomes your book, it becomes your documentary and your movie," Colbert said.

"Okay," was all Rackstraw, nodding and absorbing the offer, could muster.

In phone conversations in the past, Forbes had told Rackstraw that journalistic ethics prevented him from paying for an interview. But Colbert clarified that, as a film producer, he absolutely could option Rackstraw's story about his Cooper exploits. He would hand over the checks right after he sat down and gave Forbes his interview. The recorded history, it was explained, would become the backbone of the documentary, book, and later, a film.

The producer then shared what a Hollywood agent had told him: if he was indeed Cooper, Rackstraw could easily recoup a quarter- to half-million dollar rights fee, plus another high-six to low-seven-figure check once the book and movie came out.

"Okay," Rackstraw responded again.

Colbert's multilayered offer was not unique. He had observed horse-trading like this at the television networks for years, where news and entertainment divisions would discreetly collaborate to pay for the rights to a dramatic news story breaking in the headlines.

What *was* unique was the last part of the proposal: if Rackstraw came clean and turned himself in to the FBI, the producer said he would use some of the projected movie-rights fee to pay back the $200,000 in ransom money he had taken. This restitution would be split between two charities—half to the veterans-support group Wounded Warriors and the other half to an FBI fund that covered college tuition for children of agents killed in the line of duty.

Rackstraw switched tracks, pointing out that paying $200,000 dollars to any organization would be "an admission of guilt."

Colbert reminded him all these plans rested on his confessing to being D. B. Cooper.

"I told everybody I was," admitted Rackstraw. But he described it all as an elaborate identity stunt.

Nice try, thought the producer.

Colbert moved on to his prosecution, telling Rackstraw he personally felt it would be in both sides' interests to make a plea deal—considering Rackstraw's age, his health issues, and the challenge of getting a verdict on a forty-year-old case. The producer then shared what one well-informed attorney (Galen Cook), who had been in touch with several of the retired Cooper case agents over the years, had recently told him: there was major doubt any jury would convict a legend who had pulled a stunt where nobody got hurt.[8]

Colbert leaned back and pulled out a background folder, which included a letter that outlined his just-discussed offer, so Rackstraw could scrutinize it all later.

"My point is," said Colbert, "this is going to happen. We've set all this up so that you and Dottie can join the process. And we're going to keep your families from [your] two previous wives, the grandchildren, all of them, anonymous. No one is going to have their names, location [exposed]. It'll just be focused on you."

Rackstraw's immediate response was "That gives me a thumbnail sketch," followed by an extensive explanation of his side of the story. Colbert perceived a shield materializing in Rackstraw's voice as he offered a combination of weak denials and claims of innocence, along with statements that, profilers later maintained, were the type a guilty man would make.

For instance, twice Rackstraw said, "I want to see that [story rights] check." He couldn't resist taking a good, long look and making sure his name really was on both of them, after which he seemed to relax a bit more.

Out of the shadows, Forbes suddenly walked up to join them. As planned, he took over, ready to assume a harder tone. The reporter had been assured that investigator Dirk would be right there to protect him against any sudden outburst or action by Rackstraw. He was covered from the parking lot, too. Cocked and ready, two more private investigators sat in separate, darkly windowed vans, keeping a close eye on the conversation in front of Coronado Precision Marine.

More than once during the tense back and forth, they later reported, their fingers had inched closer to gun triggers—such as when Rackstraw again claimed the FBI flew in one of the hijacking's original stewardesses to his Stockton jail for a viewing.

"You're saying that they brought the stewardess to look at you?" repeated Forbes, knowing Rackstraw had made the same assertion during their first phone conversation.

"The FBI brought her in."

"I'm telling you they're saying no one ever did [that]. You think we're new at this?"

Rackstraw leaned back. "You know what, I'm thinking about backing off and watching and seeing what you put together, and see how it comes out without me!"

"Well, that's what we're gonna do."

Derek, lurking nearby, wasn't happy.

"I don't want him to have a damn stroke," Dirk recollected Derek muttering. "He's not healthy. He's got seriously high blood pressure. So just take it easy, all right?"

Derek had shown himself ready to give Rackstraw any kind of assistance he might need—right down to fetching a bottle of water. The boss later excused himself to take a business call on his cell phone; then he made a restroom run. While he was away, with Derek busy inside the office, Colbert suddenly heard both Forbes and Dirk "pssst-ing" at him. Forbes had grabbed Rackstraw's now-empty and abandoned water bottle, complete with fingerprints and, more importantly, a probable DNA sample. He handed it to Colbert, who casually strolled to his Jag and put the bottle inside, returning before Rackstraw or Derek was any the wiser.

Colbert's mind raced with the possibilities: this fresh forensic sample should, of course, be more reliable than the DNA left on Rackstraw's two 1979 Stockton jail letters mailed to KNBC's Noyes.[9] Could it help connect him to the stamps on Norman de Winter's 1971 pen-pal envelopes to Jim Mott?[10] What about the four anonymous Cooper letters that the FBI is believed to have genetically profiled— will the bottle link him to the first and last envelopes, dropped into mailboxes near his remote family home?[11] And finally, just maybe, the sample could help place Rackstraw on the plane where partial DNA was recovered on the abandoned tie and in hairs from the headrest. If so, an undeniable association would be forged between Rackstraw and D. B. Cooper. Once DNA tests on the 1971 letters and bottle were completed, Colbert planned to give the bureau an opportunity to compare the forensics.

After Rackstraw returned to his chair, Forbes started up again. As Colbert recalled it:

"Why would you call up NBC News and say, 'I'm D. B. Cooper'?"

"I didn't."

"You did."

"I did not."

"Your call went to Peter Noyes. He's a good friend of mine." The con man was cold-cocked, but he swung back.

"Peter Noyes came and interviewed me after it hit that paper. Ask him."

"I did."

"I didn't call him. How can I call him?"

"From jail. You did two interviews with him," said Forbes.

Indeed, this investigation found the 1979 jail phone log, documenting his outbound calls. When Rackstraw learned the team also had access to his thirty-four year-old television news footage, his combative temperament cooled.

"On the phone you were playing so coy with me," said Forbes, "with [KNBC reporter Warren] Olney, too."

Rackstraw shook his head. "Coy, wrong word."

"Well, he said to you on camera, 'Bob, are you D. B. Cooper?' And you looked at him, smiled, and said, 'I'm afraid of heights.'"

The ex-con grinned. "Yeah, that probably would be true, that would be coy."

Colbert next probed Rackstraw about the four so-called D. B. Cooper letters. "What're the odds those letters are gonna come back to your neighborhood?"

Once again, Rackstraw feigned surprise. "That is interesting, yeah."

Forbes's next question, rehearsed for the closer, made Rackstraw lock on him like a laser beam.

"Your disaffection with government," said Forbes, "your disaffection with law enforcement . . . all of that said to me: 'You know what? I believe I could see a motive here where somebody decided, in a turbulent time in his life . . . to pull this off.' So does D. B. Cooper want to go down as a petty hijacker, or does he want to make a statement as to the conditions that led him to do it. And have this opportunity to come off as a good guy and make restitution?"

Rackstraw's gaze, which had been as shifty as his responses, remained fixed on Forbes for a long silence as he seemed to weigh his options. He had repeatedly denied being D. B. Cooper during the ebb and flow of the conversation but finally, perhaps not realizing the contradiction, he divulged a stunning concern.

"The problem," he said, "is I don't remember a lot of it."

The reporter did not let a moment go by. "We'll help you," he said, his words locking around Rackstraw's admission like handcuffs.

The conversation had lasted an hour and a half. Colbert and Forbes's good-cop, bad-cop routine was finished, and they stood up to depart. Forbes firmly grabbed Rackstraw's hand and looked him squarely in the eyes.

"Do the right thing," he repeated. "Do the right thing."

Rackstraw said he'd call that night.

"No, you won't," replied Forbes, reading his body language and knowing his history.

Rackstraw showed he was still curious, though, as he eyed the link chart in Colbert's hands. Earlier he had asked if he could get a copy. The producer knew the analytical map of Rackstraw's adventures, crimes, and associates—created by Lockheed Martin—would come as a shock to the perpetrator of all that mayhem.[12] It was with a sense of satisfaction that he assured Rackstraw, "You'll get a copy as soon as you sign on to work with us."

As the three said their goodbyes, Rackstraw agreed to Colbert's deadline of 9:00 a.m. to sign the deal to collaborate on the project.

"Otherwise," Forbes injected, using the no-nonsense tone he had employed moments before, "the cameras are coming."

Both Forbes and Colbert knew Rackstraw was never interested in talking when he didn't control the conversation, and he most certainly had not controlled this one. The moment when Rackstraw confessed that he had forgotten a great deal of what had happened was a huge breakthrough. But this was also the man who had "admitted" in a Stockton court that he was absolutely not D. B. Cooper and then, a day later, reverted to playing verbal games when he sensed KNBC reporter Olney knew nothing of that assertion. Who knew what he'd claim after a few hours of reflection?

Even when it was pointed out a second time that his participation would "change everything" by giving him ample opportunity to tell his side of the story, Rackstraw was noncommittal.

"I said it was a chance for him to clear the record," Forbes remembered. "But he was keeping us at arm's length."

What followed confirmed Colbert's and Forbes's suspicions that Rackstraw was not buying into the proposal.

Whether he was immobilized by uncertainty, furious at having been cornered by the producer and reporter, or heeding advice he got from his divorced housemate, Dottie, Rackstraw blew off the phone call that night as well as the 9:00 a.m. deadline he had set to announce his decision the next morning. As he had proven so adept at doing in the past, he seemed to disappear. And so, too, did any pretense of truthfully telling his story.

CHAPTER 19

Day 2: Confronting His Past

MAY 21–OCTOBER 16, 2013

A s Forbes had promised would happen the day before, the cameras came to Coronado Island with the intent of putting to the test Rackstraw's 1979 KNBC interview rumination about letting the people decide if his story was fiction or fact.

Colbert's Hollywood pitch was done, so he felt ethics dictated he should stay away. Forbes was geared for investigative hardball, with Dirk and his two fellow private eyes, along with veteran cameramen Richard Kashanski and Barry Conrad, joining the team. This time there could be no mistake about what Forbes and his crew were looking for as they staked out the office of Coronado Precision Marine. As Forbes had directly told Rackstraw the day before, "We believe you are Cooper and that's why we are here."

Eventually a white truck pulled up towing a boat. As Rackstraw, the driver, remained in the cab with another man in the backseat, the ponytailed Derek got out and headed to the office to retrieve the keys to open the gate to the storage yard. He saw the reporter and the two cameramen.

"Still?" said Derek, agitated.

"Still," replied Forbes.

"Jesus, fuck, man. I got work to do."

"So do we," said the reporter.

After Derek retrieved the keys and opened the gate, he walked up to the open window on the driver's side of the truck, evidently telling his boss that Forbes had returned. Rackstraw then pulled the truck and boat into the middle of the yard and then backed it up to the fence.

The crew, respectful of the private property, stayed back about fifty yards outside the lot.

"I don't want to spook them," Forbes told Conrad. "Ponytail's not happy."

"No, he's not," Conrad agreed.

Although two cameras were following the action from a distance, Rackstraw managed to disappear. Derek, meanwhile, took the cover off the twin engines of the boat and began to work on one. After waiting at the gate for about twenty minutes, Forbes spotted something behind another boat toward the back of the yard.

"I saw his feet under there, between that boat and the trailer," Forbes said. "But I don't see him now."

He began calling Rackstraw's name, but no response.

"Really, Bob? Is this how it's going to be?" Forbes said loudly. "Come on. Come out and talk. Tried to do it the right way. . . ."

There was no response. The reporter peered in through the fence, pacing on the sidewalk, dialing up the pressure as he tried to make contact with Rackstraw.

"Stay out," Derek said as he approached the front gate. "This is private." Soon after, Forbes turned to the camera.

"If you're an innocent man, why don't you just come out and say you're an innocent man?" he asked.

A few minutes later, one of the investigators spotted someone hiding in a shipping container in the back of the yard.

"Back there, inside that storage bin," one of the men said. "I saw him in there."

Rack in the box. Bob hides out in a storage shed at his marine repair business to avoid cameras, microphones, and his past.

A look through the zoom lens on both cameras confirmed it was Rack-straw. All eyes trained on the slit in the big blue box.

"He's right there. He's going to sit it out. We got all day, Bob," said Forbes, who wasn't about to let his quarry pull some sort of Mayday trick after six months of trying to arrange a one-on-one interview with him. He walked around the yard's fenced perimeter, trying to get closer to the container.

"This is the way he's done it," Forbes said to cameraman Conrad as they walked, referring to his experience with Rackstraw since November in numerous phone conversations. "Absolute falsehoods, absolute lies, and now he's hiding in a storage bin to not talk to me? What does that mean? Why would you do that? Why wouldn't you just come out and say, 'I am not D. B. Cooper. I don't know why you keep thinking I am. You're crazy'?"

When they arrived behind the bin, he thought for a moment before speaking loudly and clearly so that Rackstraw, who was on the other side of the metal wall, could hear him.

"Bob, it's Jim Forbes. Come on, Bob, let's do this the right way. Come out and talk to me. Why are you hiding in a storage bin? Innocent men don't hide in storage bins, Bob. You said you could answer all the questions; you had reasonable answers. I have reasonable questions. Come on out and answer them. I told you yesterday I came into this with an open mind, but our conversations and your actions yesterday, your actions today, just lead to suspicion, and I can't imagine why an innocent man would be hiding in a storage container afraid to talk to me."

He let that resonate.

"Simple words, Bob. Represent your position. I've got all day. I can wait, Bob, and I will. And if not today, another day. So let's talk."

Rackstraw remained silent. Forbes took a different tack.

"Just imagine the visuals of this, Bob. I've got some easy questions, and you're hiding in a storage bin to avoid them. We have no interest whatso-ever in prosecuting, no interest whatsoever in anything in terms of the legal system. Our only interest is to get to the truth. And it's as I described to you yesterday and you didn't answer me. Do you want to go down as a petty hijacker, or do you want to tell the real story as to why you did it? Why you were compelled to do it?"

Again, the words hung in the air.

"And the full life story you've built since then. Everybody knows about the jump. That's not news. What people want to know about is who did it and why and what are their reasons—and we're giving that forum to do it, Bob. Because if we go out this way, you can imagine how many people are going to be sitting outside this fence over the coming months, years, from all over the world. So do the simple thing and come out and talk and we're done. Or pick up the phone and call Tom, tell him you signed the deal. I'll photograph it, and we come back and do a sit-down interview the right way, the way I've been trying to do it for the last six months. Choice is yours, Bob. I'll wait. I'll be out front by the gate."

The reporter started walking back toward the front of the yard, approaching Kashanski.

"When I was talking to him, did you see any movement in there? Could you hear me?"

"I could hear you," said Kashanski.

"Okay. Cool. Cool. I wanted to make sure it was loud enough that he could hear me," said Forbes, noticing Derek was working on an engine nearby. "I've never seen anybody that was an innocent man hiding in a storage bin."

"What did he say? Did he talk to you at all?" asked Investigator Trent Johnson, another former FBI agent.

"No response. I said I'm here all day. I'm not going."

Soon after, the reporter gave a phone briefing to Colbert, who had been waiting anxiously at their hotel in nearby Mission Bay. It was agreed that the producer would call Rackstraw. Shortly after, Rackstraw emerged from the storage bin and took a circuitous route across the yard toward Derek, who was still working on the boat motor. For a moment, it almost felt too easy. The charging Forbes, surrounded by cameramen and his security team, had no trouble hailing Rackstraw, now just across the fence. The reporter asked if he'd spoken to Colbert.

"That I did, yeah. But see, he's talking to the attorney right now, I guess."

Forbes knew the attorney game could mean endless delays, so he tried to sound as agreeable as he could.

"So why don't we do this the right way?"

"Okay, yeah, well, you have your way. I have my way." He remained impenetrable.

"Well, I've been trying to do it your way for the last six months," Forbes said.

"And I've also turned it onto the attorney, and he said don't talk to Jim. He's one of those—he'll make up stories and do things all sideways," Rackstraw continued. "And I said, okay, I won't."[1]

Rackstraw seemed to be ready for anything the reporter might say.

"Okay, so without making you make up stories, let me ask you a simple question," Forbes shot back.

"You're not going to ask me any questions. I just told you."

"Oh, I'm going to ask you lots of questions."

Rackstraw gave him a 'these are the rules' look, saying, "I won't ask any questions and I won't answer any questions. Okay?"

"That's okay. That's okay. That's your prerogative."

"That a boy," Rackstraw nodded.

"Are you the person who boarded a flight on November 24th, 1971—"

"What did I just tell you, Jim?"

"Identifying yourself as Dan Cooper?"

Rackstraw made a weary face and then smiled toward the cameras. "Maybe I didn't—"

Rackstraw verbally spars with reporter Jim Forbes through the chain-link perimeter of his boat repair yard on Coronado Island.

"Did you hijack the plane? When it was coming out of Seattle toward Reno, did you jump out with—"

"Maybe I wasn't clear, Jim." Impatience and annoyance were creeping in. "Maybe I wasn't clear. Don't try and play junior Dan Rather!"

"Are you that person?" Forbes pressed. "Are you D. B. Cooper?"

Derek, who had never been far away, interrupted.

"Bob, do me a favor."

"Yeah?" said Rackstraw.

"Come on in the shop and just lock the door."

"Yeah."

"Do that for me," said Derek.

"Yeah."

The reporter lobbed the question again. "Are you D. B. Cooper? Yes or no."

"I answered your question, Jim," waving him off.

"Bob, we have eyewitnesses that have you in Astoria and Corvallis, Oregon, from the time of your discharge in 1971 to the time of the hijacking. Were you there?"

"Talk to Tom Colbert," Rackstraw replied.

"Bob—"

"Your buddy," said Rackstraw.

Instead of following Derek's request to retreat to the office, Rackstraw walked back toward the container. Forbes's questions got louder the farther away he went, as he again shifted gears.

"Your license plate and sticker say that you have Purple Hearts. The Department of Defense says you have none. Is that true?"[2]

Rackstraw, walking away, seemed to tighten at the question. "Talk to Tom Colbert."

Forbes then cited Department of Defense records, showing several other medals and citations were not "as you described. Is that true?"

Rackstraw stopped and turned back, for the first time looking genuinely angry at any question the reporter had asked.

"Who did I describe that to?"

"You described it in court when you were standing trial for the murder of your stepfather, Bob."[3]

After letting that one hang for a moment, Forbes continued as Rackstraw turned around and continued to walk away.

"Bob, after your acquittal for murder, why did you steal a plane? Why did you run, Bob, if you're not guilty?"

Getting no response, Forbes charged ahead. "Bob, it wasn't insufficient funds, it was theft of an airplane. It was grand theft. It was check kiting. It was explosives. Why did you run five days before that trial and steal a plane?"[4]

Rackstraw was now back at the far end of the yard.

"Bob, why don't you just come out and say that you are not D. B. Cooper?" The reporter looked over to Conrad, the nearest cameraman.

"We'll wait for him."

"Where did he go, back [in the container]?" wondered Conrad.

"The Purple Heart [question] got him," said Forbes.

The wait was an exercise in hand-wringing and pent-up energy. The reporter and his crew kept up a running chatter of opinion about how it was going, what Rackstraw might do next, and strategy. Forbes called Colbert to find out whether Rackstraw's attorney had called. The answer was no. The reporter was not surprised.

Then Rackstraw reappeared to tinker with his company truck, and Forbes moved near the fence to engage him again.

"Bob, I just called Tom."

Rackstraw wasn't interested in responding to the reporter's next line of inquiry. He was busying himself, moving about the storage yard performing various tasks. While he did, Forbes and the crew took the opportunity to get some footage of the area, making sure Rackstraw could see what they were doing outside the fence. Finally, as the target came closer, the reporter spoke up loudly.

"Tom hasn't heard from the attorney yet, Bob."

Rackstraw again showed no reaction. He was close enough for Forbes to speak to him in almost a normal tone of voice. "You understand it'd be much better for us to just sit down and do the interview, don't you?"

"You lied to me from the get-go," said Rackstraw.

"No, Bob. I haven't lied on anything."

"Oh, come on, Jimmy."

"Bob, there hasn't been a single lie out of my mouth."

"Oh, there hasn't, huh?" Rackstraw's said with a smug smile.

"No, no. But there's been many out of yours."

"You and Tom and the other guy [investigator Ken Dirk] who tells me 'Oh, I'm interested in a seventy-six-foot boat.'"

The reporter spread his arms, as if to say there had been no choice but to confront him. "Yeah, well, you know what his story is. We came down here eventually because you wouldn't talk to us, Bob."

Rackstraw laughed. "Uh, yeah. I don't want to talk to you."

The limping Rackstraw suddenly left the private yard and headed into the public parking lot, heading for his store. The team quickly caught up with him.

"Simple question," Forbes tried again. "Did you board a Northwest flight on November 24th, 1971, as Dan Cooper?"

"What difference does it make?" said Rackstraw, his voice rising in frustration. He put his arm around the reporter's shoulders for a few seconds.

"Because if you're D. B. Cooper, the world would want to know your story."

"Yeah, sure they would. So would the FBI, the secret indictment, and Washington, DC."

"Bob, you're a folk hero. You're a folk hero. Nobody cares. Everybody wants to know the story."

"Oh, no. Come on."

Rackstraw then went into self-diminishing mode. "The only thing I have is a Silver Star, a couple DFCs. Means nothing, okay? I helped a lot of guys in combat. That's it."

"I have no doubt about it, but why would you say in your first trial that you had forty-plus commendations and five Purple Hearts?"

"I have thirty-seven air medals alone," insisted Rackstraw.

"Do you have five Purple Hearts?"

"Purple Hearts mean nothing anymore," retorted the veteran. "If something goes wrong, shrapnel goes off in your face and they—"

"Are you a lieutenant commander, or what?" Forbes stated, referring to the inappropriate command sticker on his car window. "Why do you have a Purple Heart plate?"

"Silver Stars, which are saving guys' lives," Rackstraw's voice was getting louder.

"Why do you have a Purple Heart plate?"

Rackstraw couldn't keep the sarcasm out of his voice. "Why do we have Silver Stars? Why do we have Distinguished Flying Crosses?"

"But if you're not telling the truth on something that simple, where does the truth begin?"

"You haven't told me the truth from the get-go, Jim."

"I'm not the subject of the story. And I've told you the truth from the beginning," insisted Forbes.

"I don't even know that you're Jim Colbert!" the red-faced Rackstraw blurted.

"I'm not Jim Colbert." The reporter seized the chance to smile. "I'm Jim Forbes."

"Mmhmmm. I mean, excuse me." Even Rackstraw had to laugh. "Jim Forbes."

"See?" Forbes had his gentle "gotcha" moment.

"I'm getting old," Rackstraw shook his head. "Yeah, I'm getting old. I don't remember anything."

He stepped into his office at Coronado Precision Marine and closed the door.

"That's good, guys," said Forbes, ordering the team to stand down. "Just going to get my water. I'll be right back."

The reporter quickly encountered the dour Derek, just outside Rackstraw's office. "You know," Forbes told him, "I know we're driving you crazy, and I don't mean to—"

"Yeah, you do." Derek shot him a particularly hard, fed-up look.

"No, I don't."

"Give him some space or my fangs are going to come out. And I'll tell all four of you that," said the former MP.

They weren't going anywhere, however. The time passed slowly. Plans were reviewed, and phone conversations went back and forth; Forbes to Colbert, Colbert to Forbes. At one point, the team speculated about what Rackstraw could be doing inside. Johnson, who'd been watching him through binoculars, said, "I notice he's not calling the police."

Forbes laughed as cameraman Conrad responded, "Yeah, that's a good point."

A pair of women wearing colorful, big hats strolled by, wondering what all this was about. "Actually, I'd rather not say at the moment, if you don't mind," Forbes smiled.

"Oh," came the answer.

"Thank you. We're working on a documentary. Are you here with the marina management? Or—?"

The woman in a yellow hat said that they were simply curious.

"Okay," said Forbes. "We have some questions for the gentleman who owns the marine shop, and—"

"Yeah. Oh, okay, it's the owner," said the second woman, in a blue hat, who seemed to know who that was.

The reporter offered up a little more information. "We just have some questions for him based on his past history and the possibility—"

"He's obviously not going to answer them," said the blue-hatted woman. "I don't think he's coming out," she added.

"He'll come out eventually," said the reporter.

"Midnight?" cracked the woman in the yellow hat.

"I mean," said Forbes, "we've talked to him a couple of times and already—oh, we've gotten him a couple times already."

The woman in the blue hat didn't attempt to hide how funny she thought that answer was. So Forbes decided, what the hell, drop it on them and see what they say.

"Yeah, actually we think he may be D. B. Cooper."

The women stopped cold. "Oh, you're kidding," said blue hat.

"No."

"Seriously." Blue hat was taken with the idea. "Oh my gosh, that would be quite something."

"It would be. And so we, we don't understand why he wouldn't want to answer questions," said Forbes.

"Oh my God," said blue hat.

"Maybe 'cause he is," said yellow hat.

As the woman in the blue hat laughed again, the reporter said, "That could be it."

"Pick up a piece of DNA," said the woman in the blue hat.

"Uh, we have. Thank you." Forbes smiled.

This got both women giggling. "Good luck with your story," said yellow hat.

"Thank you," the reporter laughed.

When Rackstraw finally emerged from the office seventeen minutes later, he was giving Derek some business instructions before leaving, ostensibly for "the hospital." He didn't say why. He did, however, tell Forbes that port security had called to ask what he and the cameras were doing in the parking lot all day.

As the old con man climbed into his SUV, Forbes brought up his medals again. Rackstraw just looked at him from behind the wheel.

"It's all past, Jim. I don't remember any of it. You know, I'm so old."

Not believing him for a moment, Forbes nodded. "But that's why we should sit and talk, Bob."

"The problem is, I don't remember a lot of it." Bob Rackstraw in his car, about to drive away from confrontation yet again.

"Old and feeble," the old man added.

"One last question. Did you board that Northwest flight and hijack it for $200,000?"

Shaking his head, avoiding Forbes's gaze, Rackstraw said, "I don't think I've ever been on a Northwest flight."

"Why are you so evasive about what should be a simple thing to say?"

"Because you guys'd make such a big deal out of it."

His frustration clear, his limit nearly reached, the man who was so often in control of his every gesture, expression and tone of voice sounded more genuine in that moment than he had over the last two days.

Moments later, after one or two quick questions were deflected as the car was put into gear, Rackstraw drove away from Forbes and the cameras, no doubt relieved to the core.

"The attorney will be calling you," he said. And he was gone.

On the team's drive back to the Mission Bay hotel, Conrad looked at Forbes and realized he had one more job to do: He zoomed his camera in on the man who had been trying to arrange this face-off for six months and asked for his closing thoughts. The veteran newsman contemplated for a moment as they crossed over the Coronado Bay Bridge; then he turned back.

"You would think an innocent man would say, 'Jim, you're crazy! I'm not D. B. Cooper! The FBI was wrong then; you're wrong now. Throw all the evidence you have at me and I'll give you any explanation.' In thirty-four years as a journalist, this is the first time I've ever encountered anybody like this in a situation like this. And it's mind-boggling."

Conrad asked one more question, eye still glued to the lens: "Summing up in one word, how would you describe Bob Rackstraw today?"

"Yesterday I described him as cagey," said the reporter, staring out at the bay. "Today—cornered."

It may have been a reflection of how seriously threatened Rackstraw felt by the two days of grilling by Colbert and Forbes, but when the attorney did, in fact, call Colbert, it wasn't just any lawyer. It was Dennis

Roberts, the man who had represented Rackstraw when he stood trial for the murder of his stepfather, Philip, in 1978.

His involvement dates to May 23, 2013, one day after Colbert made a last effort to impress the gravity of the situation on Rackstraw, via the following e-mail:

Airborne Bob:

Sorry to hear about your rough day on Tuesday. Now you know why I drove all the way down there to give you another option. By ignoring it, you left Jim's team only one choice. Now, if you multiply that ordeal by 50, you have an idea what the size of the national media response will be in Coronado when the documentary comes out—trust me, I've seen it happen before. Hundreds of reporters from around the globe will also phone and write. If you don't respond, they'll go hunt down your relatives. I'm afraid this will be the Rackstraw clan's new life.

But it doesn't have to be. I've again attached my contracts to this e-mail. It's not too late to put an umbrella of privacy around your extended family, receive my hefty option fee, and tell us the truth about Nov. 24th, 1971—one time, in a private, controlled setting. Then by next year, you'll be sharing the profits (6–7 figures) from my best-selling book and hit movie. And we'll work to keep your neighborhood media-free and peaceful.

Sign away and I'll make it all happen.

My Best, Tom

Two days later, Roberts sent Colbert an e-mail. In it, he explained that he now represented Robert Rackstraw in all matters and requested that Colbert not contact Rackstraw again but "direct all inquiries to my attention." He promised that he would be discussing the offer with his client soon and asked if his message could please be passed on to Jim Forbes.

Colbert, following the polite tone of Roberts's e-mail, sent him the original May 20, 2013, proposal pitch and follow-up e-mail from May 22. He urged Roberts to call him if there were any questions but said that for any matters regarding Forbes and the ongoing documentary, he should contact attorney Mark Zaid, in Washington, DC.

Less than one-half hour later, Roberts e-mailed Colbert again, with copies to Zaid and Rackstraw, stating that before he could recommend a course of action to his client, he needed to know all about Colbert's prior experience and, in an interesting conversational detour, included a "what if" about his client.

> Assuming for this discussion that he is in fact D. B. Cooper, or falsely claims to be Cooper, I don't know if indictments were returned or what charges were brought back in the day, but that certainly has to be re-searched before I would suggest he enter into negotiations and depend-ing on varied factors whether he would still expose himself to a federal prosecution today either for overt criminal acts or some sort of false personation charge. I have not had a moment to look into these ques-tions and will need a bit of time before I can satisfy myself that I should recommend we proceed.

Really? Colbert thought. *Exactly what kind of tap dance was that? Did Roberts not completely trust the story he was hearing from his own client?* The last paragraph of Roberts's e-mail was less cryptic about his intentions but delved much too deeply into the process of Colbert's investigation.

> Another threshold question is how you learned about Mr. Rackstraw and what information you were given, and by whom, to lead you to be-lieve he is in fact the elusive Mr. Cooper. This is another issue, and a very important one, which needs to be resolved prior to my giving him any advice about pursuing this matter. So please let me have an answer to this question immediately.

Colbert obliged on May 24, 2013, providing a litany of facts and anony-mous quotes, before concluding with the suggestion that if Roberts needed more, "I'm afraid you'll have to ask your client."

Roberts e-mailed his thanks for the information on the same day, most of which he claimed not to have known. He concluded his response with "I will be in touch with Airborne Bob (why does this sound like some cold remedy that never works for me) and get back to you."

With the exception of five e-mails between Colbert and Roberts, in which the lawyer displayed an ability for changing the subject to unre-lated matters that nearly rivaled that of his client, Roberts's next significant communication came on May 31, 2013. It consisted entirely of the following:

> Here is my client's response to your offer.
>
> *Now, we will consider a real offer if they provide virtually every piece of data and information that they have acquired in the past years (as they claim) subject to our review of same.*

Less than twenty minutes later, Colbert sent the entire e-mail stream between himself and Roberts to Zaid, whom Colbert had been willing to recommend to Rackstraw before the old ex-con decided to take evasive action. Zaid had been familiar with the investigation for some time; his style was direct and to the point in his first e-mail to attorney Roberts on June 2, 2013.

> With all due respect, Mr. Colbert and his team have already made your client quite a significant "real offer." There will be nothing further forthcoming and we will not be providing your client with "every piece of data and information" concerning the evidence that he is D. B. Cooper. Your client does not need our sources, witnesses or documents to tell him whether he is or is not D. B. Cooper. He already knows full well what the truth is.

Zaid added that if Rackstraw chose not to cooperate and reap his share of the benefits, he would be left

> watching on the sidelines as Mr. Colbert and his colleagues broadcast to the world that Bob Rackstraw is D. B. Cooper. He will be able to watch the television documentary, see the follow-up news programs, and read the forthcoming book—along with millions of other people—as to the facts that have been accumulated and which implicate him in the hijacking. Unfortunately, he will gain nothing from that. . . . But respectfully, we will not play games with your client any longer. My client has nearly five-dozen independent sources from Mr. Rackstraw's past and more than enough information to proceed and he will do so regardless of your client's decision. The simple question is whether Mr. Rackstraw wants to be a part of that process or not. Therefore, the very generous offer my client made to Mr. Rackstraw will remain open until Friday, June 7, 2013. At that time our communications will cease and the documentary and book will move forward.

June 7 came and went without response from Rackstraw, or Roberts on his behalf. It was not until much later—October 11, 2013—that Roberts e-mailed Zaid again.

Dear Mr. Zaid:

My client, Mr. Bob Rackstraw, has brought to my attention the fact that your clients plan to go through with this false and defamatory presentation wherein they accuse my client of being the infamous D. B. Cooper. For the record, Mr. Rackstraw is NOT D. B. Cooper, and has never claimed to be. I believe the FBI dropped their inquiry regarding this fact many years ago.

I think you owe it to whoever plans to broadcast this false and defamatory accusation that they will be party to this litigation and they will be advised that your clients have also exposed, for liability purposes, anyone who broadcasts this material.

So let me assure you that you will have your opportunity to depose Mr. Rackstraw in the litigation which will flow from your broadcast of this "documentary." This letter is simply to again advise you that your clients will be sued for defamation should they go forward.

After a series of cordial exchanges over six days, a friendlier Roberts let his guard down on October 17, 2013, making a thought-provoking admission to Zaid.

Between us Bobby always enjoyed letting people think he is D. B. Cooper (can you imagine how much pussy D. B. would get) but from everything I know it is an act that got out of hand. Well, anyway you'll find out soon enough. I'll look forward to the depo.

Dennis

The next day, Zaid wrote back a short answer, without crassness.

"I have no doubt Bobby's depo will be quite enjoyable, and I do look forward to handling it!

Mark

In Conclusion

Thomas J. Colbert

At the end of this five-year quest, Robert W. Rackstraw and the FBI revealed they had one thing in common: when asked if they'd like to participate in the 2016 multihour History Channel program on D. B. Cooper, both had the same question: "Is Tom Colbert involved in this?"

I can understand Rackstraw's anxiety, considering the less-than-stellar performance he gave my camera crew during their unscheduled visit on May 21, 2013. But a special agent's surreptitious inquiry—which, of course, was really about my subject—truly was a surprise.[1]

My wife and I have been upfront with the bureau since the beginning, consulting and sharing some of our earliest new evidence on Rackstraw, a man we believe was wrongly cleared. Cordial thank-you e-mails came after each offering, and on August 15, 2012, a note from DC headquarters encouraged us to press on: "The FBI welcomes any further information you uncover, and you can provide that to Special Agent [Curtis] Eng."[2]

As noted earlier, that's when Dawna and I made the decision to organize and fund our own cold case team, a huge task force with skill sets and forensic knowledge to dig deep.

Several former agents warned me how our Rackstraw effort would translate to those on the inside: A "Cooperite" amateur, seeking fame and fortune, was strongly challenging the FBI's decision-making process.

Others shared an old office adage that would soon seem prophetic: "The Number One Rule is you don't do anything to embarrass the bureau."[3]

After six months of negotiations, LMNO Productions, the company shooting for the History Channel, was invited to come up to the Seattle Division with a crew to review the Cooper case. In April 2016, file summaries were shared on almost a dozen former suspects—including Rackstraw (the only one living). Curtis Eng and two senior agents would not reveal what cleared our man in 1979, but an anonymous insider gave a hint: "Prove he was at Portland Airport that day."

As cold case members explained, that meant an alibi. By the way, this would have been his *third* alibi—we discovered two others he gave in the same time period.[4] I guess the third was the charm?

In a planned approach, a senior member of our documentary crew mentioned to the three feds that I had "a cold case team" now working on Rackstraw's trail, and there was "new evidence" to share. But Eng ended the topic with a bombshell: the FBI had decided it was "no longer accepting circumstantial evidence." While the forty-five-year-old case wasn't "unsolvable," the bureau now feared it was "unprosecutable" based on just circumstantial evidence.

That was followed by a letter from the Seattle special agent in charge, Frank Montoya Jr., which was read in front of the crew's camera: the Cooper case was officially closed, and the redacted files were being packed for a move to a Washington, DC, archive. The case would now only be opened for two types of physical evidence: the discovery of more ransom cash or the actual parachute.[5]

Two gut punches—the same day we were to schedule our delivery of the team's ninety-five pieces of physical, forensic, testimonial, direct, documentary, foundational, and hearsay evidence? This smacked of a preemptive strike on behalf of the FBI's Number One Rule. All on the fear-filled, ill-informed assumption our circumstantial case was a loser.

Like the rest of America, the Seattle agents were at home on July 10, 2016, the premiere night of the four-part series. I could imagine their red faces when my team, filled with their bureau brethren and mentors, revealed much of the new evidence on Rackstraw—featuring numerous credible witnesses and a half-dozen former crime partners, now cooperating.

The hard facts in our rejected ninety-three-page investigative report (IR) now fill the airwaves, newspapers, the web, and these pages as history. But the hunt's ultimate legacy, no doubt, are the awkward details on how this master outlaw outwitted the bureau six times:

1. He made his unfettered, night escape from the '71 hijack crime scene by small plane, eleven hours before the morning's ground search had begun (chapter 6).
2. After his '73 Iowa chopper crash, he convinced oblivious FBI agents there that he wasn't the droid they were looking for (chapter 7).
3. In '78 recapture, he lawyered up, then "jabberwocked" his way out of FBI Cooper custody in New York City (chapter 12).
4. Eight months later, he ditched an FBI interrogation by faking a Mayday ocean plane crash (chapter 13).
5. The FBI cleared him as the hijacker in '79 because investigators couldn't find his prints on the plane; a former agent, however, had claimed Cooper's drink glass and the rear stairway revealed no prints (chapter 15).
6. In '80, he devised a scheme to plant Cooper cash along the Columbia River, which left the FBI believing the jumper had drowned; that allowed Rackstraw to walk away and live under his own name (chapters 14 and 16).

The results from our final research inquiries put more fuel to the bureau's fire.

Forensic tests on Rackstraw's 2013 recovered water bottle and a 1971 lick stamp on one of con-artist Norman de Winter's letters (chapter 18) came back with "significant results," said attorney Jeffrey T. Renz—a clinical professor of law, Fulbright Scholar, forensic DNA expert, and cold case consultant at the University of Montana.

The two items were among five objects shipped to Sorenson Forensics, a Salt Lake City lab that has collaborated in the past with the

FBI. When the company's fifty-nine-page case report was released on December 2, 2014, a copy was forwarded to Renz for his analysis.

He began by stating that, although there was "no conclusive match between the '71 letter" and the bottle, "the analyst found a mixture. This means there are potentially 2–4 alleles for each [item's] locus. In other words, the DNA does not prove that Rackstraw is or is not de Winter, but the matches at three alleles are significant." The professor added, "I have seen murder convictions based on the same quality of DNA evidence."[6]

"I agree with Jeff [Renz]," said Sorenson Forensics technician and company spokesperson Cami Green. She added, "From an investigative standpoint, this is usable data. The subject [Rackstraw] cannot be excluded."[7]

Professor Renz then brought it home: "No exclusion and the probability of a match across three alleles," plus having multiple credible eyewitnesses, means there is "particularized suspicion that Robert W. Rackstraw is Norman de Winter. There's enough there to go forward with a new investigation."[8]

One wonders how these "three alleles" might have compared to, say, the FBI's partial DNA strands found on the Cooper tie or the two genetically profiled "D. B. Cooper" letters, sent to the Reno paper and both mailed from mailboxes within fifty miles of Rackstraw's former mountain home in Valley Springs—both letters still in the discreet custody of the FBI.

Where were you, forty-four years ago today? And who was with you? If you're struggling for an answer, imagine the dilemma of the four former key witnesses who were asked by the FBI to avoid media and hold on to their memories of that fateful 1971 day, just in case a credible suspect came forward. Between the four—stewardesses Tina Mucklow, Florence Schaffner, and Alice Hancock, along with college student Bill Mitchell—they have been shown hundreds of photos, but that flow pretty much ended by the mid-1970s. And ever since, the media has been after them.

Bill Mitchell (chapter 6), now sixty-five, sat down in September 2015 for the History Channel, his first American television interview, and agreed to participate in a photo test. It's important to remember that he was the only one of these four who was unaware of the ongoing hijacking (passengers were kept in the dark until after their departure), so his critical observations, from the same row as Cooper, came without any duress or anxiety.

Mitchell viewed six old black-and-white photos in a "six-pack" Cooper identity test that was prepared by former Detective Sergeant John Bocciolatt, a cold case team member who had conducted hundreds of such tests while at the Portland Police Bureau. Warning "it's been forty-four years," Mitchell started scanning—then pointed at Rackstraw. But he identified him as Richard McCoy, another cleared hijack suspect.

When told that was not McCoy, Mitchell's eyes became very big and he stared back at our man for a few minutes—then shook his head. The former passenger said in all honesty, he couldn't declare Rackstraw the hijacker. "After all these years, all I can remember is the face on the FBI sketch," referring to the more accurate second drawing that he helped create.[9]

When my longtime collaborator, state investigator Jay C. Todd (chapter 6), heard a retelling of Mitchell's closing statement, Todd offered to help connect the dots: "If you compare the sketch to Rackstraw's 1970 army picture, there are nine absolute points of match—in the brown eyes, ears, noses, short mouths, frown lines, chins, brows, odd head shapes, and male-pattern baldness." Todd added, "Frankly, it looks like Mitchell's sketch was traced from his photo."[10]

FBI number two sketch, courtesy of the alert college student Bill Mitchell.

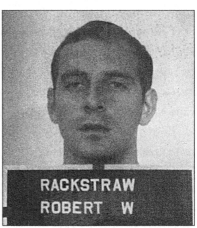

Rackstraw's Army ID in 1970, taken fourteen months before the hijacking.

A forensic psychologist had another intriguing take. After viewing Mitchell's photo-test video, Kris Mohandie, PhD, commented, "I believe it is no coincidence that the witness mistakenly identified this man as another hijacker who had been captured and shown to the media, when in fact he had pointed to the picture of [Rackstraw]. It seems likely the current prime suspect was encoded in the witness's memory accurately as the hijacker during events so many years before, and he subconsciously made his choice upon that basis. He reacted as if he had seen him before, and with the accompanying label of hijacker."[11]

Tina Mucklow, the twenty-two-year-old stewardess who sat next to Cooper for hours, became the FBI primary witness. Now in her mid-sixties, she also agreed to sit down for the program, her first television interview since the 1971 Reno press conference (chapter 6). She likewise warned it had been forty-five years—then failed to recognize any of the six pictures. She was then shown one of Rackstraw's KNBC television news clips, recorded seven years after the hijacking, with him bearded and balding.

Mucklow shook her head. "I don't think so."[12]

There have been serious allegations for decades, however, about Mucklow's ability to recall anything significant on the plane—and they come from two respected former FBI agents.

Five years ago, the *Washington State Mountain News* reported the two retired lawmen—Salt Lake City special agent in charge Russ Calame and field agent Richard Tosaw—had secured interviews with Mucklow in the 1980s for their separate books on the Cooper case. For most of that decade, she was a nun at the Carmelite Monastery in Eugene, Oregon.

Both authors felt she was suffering severe memory loss. Calame "came to realize that Tina would never be a credible witness in any Cooper trial because her memory of the skyjacking had become too fuzzy."[13]

In the 1991 book he coauthored, *D. B. Cooper: The Real McCoy*, Calame added, "She tried to cooperate but could remember very little about the skyjacking of Flight 305. She agreed to look through photographs" later, but "I knew as we talked that it wouldn't be necessary."[14]

After Tosaw interviewed Mucklow, he described her "mental state" similarly. She answered most of his questions "with the same response, 'I can't remember.'"[15]

Not only is Mucklow the former primary witness, but she is part of the bureau's extended family—her recently deceased brother-in-law, Lee E. Dormuth, was a thirty-two-year FBI agent. So these revelations have left a troubling question: if she was no longer a "credible witness," she "can't remember" anything significant, and her recollection is "fuzzy," why did the bureau assist in setting up this poor woman to judge Rackstraw?

FBI Rule Number One be damned.

I followed up this controversy by calling on one of the sharpest Cooper citizen sleuths, Vicki Wilson, to help track down the remaining two stewardesses. The senior attendant, Florence "Flo" Schaffner, now sixty-eight, was located in South Carolina. The final approach was former first-class attendant Alice Hancock—ironically, living in Wilson's home state of Minnesota. Both, like Mucklow, had memory issues.[16]

For a professional understanding of these mental-health developments, I sought the guidance of cold case team member Thomas P. Mauriello. Once a former special agent and chief of police with the US Department of Defense, he is now a professor of criminal investigation and forensic sciences at the University of Maryland, where he was recently ranked as one of the "Top 15" CSI professors in the nation.

Professor Mauriello addressed the outcomes with eyewitnesses Mitchell, Mucklow, Schaffner, and Hancock:

"A crime victim or a witness facing a traumatic event can sometimes experience a 'memory block' that results in a loss of information at a conscious level. It has nothing to do with the time span between the event and the request for recall, but rather the state of mind of the subject at the time of the event. Research indicates that there is more opportunity for a witness experiencing anxiety or trauma at the time of an event to have a lack of recall or sometimes a total loss of memory, than with a witness at the same time, place, and event who was not experiencing the same anxiety or trauma. This certainly would explain the lack of memory by the three stewardesses with that of Bill Mitchell, the college student."[17]

Along this journey, I've had many pose the question, do you regret pursuing this long investigation? My wife and I asked each other that every few months, and the answer always remained the same: absolutely not. We both were raised to use our talents, seek the truth, and help others. This episode filled all three of those marching orders.

Speaking of the truth: I end the book with an extract from the brilliant master criminal theory mentioned earlier by Jay C. Todd (chapter 6), which has always bucked me up during this quest's toughest moments. I hope you find that same clarity in all of your pursuits.

"It's statistically impossible for three master criminals—Rackstraw, Norman de Winter and D. B. Cooper—to be operating within a hundred miles of each other, let alone three that look alike, have the same flying skills, and their arrivals and departures are synchronized like whack-a-mole."[18]

Amen.

Acknowledgments

We are forever indebted to the cold case team who assisted us in tracking the misdeeds of Robert W. Rackstraw, the professionals who assisted us in crafting our story, and the dozens of sources who talked to us about their dealings with our subject during his forty-five year trail of crime, connivance, and denial. These former coworkers, neighbors, friends, victims, veterans, lawmen, classmates, and business associates—along with relatives, ex-mates, and former desperados—put aside their fears and reservations to help us tell the full tale of the man we believe is "D. B. Cooper," America's most mysterious and elusive outlaw legend. We are forever grateful for their trust, courage, and candor.

The Cold Case Team (Service Providers and Consultants)

Kevin Adley, private investigator, former FBI agent
William M. Baker, former FBI assistant director
Jack Ballentine, former homicide detective, Phoenix Police Department
Emil "Bud" Bladow, former detective, Portland Police Bureau
John Bocciolatt, private investigator, former detective sergeant, Portland Police Bureau
Robert C. Bonner, attorney, former US attorney and federal judge
Johnny "Mack" Brown, former US marshal (South Carolina)
Geoff Bruton, senior scientist, Forensic Services, Ventura County Sheriff's Department
Stockton Buck, former FBI special agent

Jon Campbell, special agent, South Carolina Law Enforcement Division

Frank Cowan, former instructor, California Specialized Training Institute/State Office of Emergency Services

David D'Alessio, course manager, Lockheed Martin Center of Security Analysis

Daniel Dewell, executive public affairs officer, US Coast Guard, 11th District

Frank Doyle Jr., former FBI agent

Doug Fogg, chief operations officer, Sorenson Forensics

Christopher Freeze, aviation investigator, Check-Six.com

Jamie Graham, former chief superintendent, Royal Canadian Mounted Police

Robert J. Graham, retired US Army Special Forces, staff sergeant/Canada

Ron Hilley, private investigator, polygrapher, and former FBI agent

Dan Horan, former detective sergeant, Major Crimes, Los Angeles Police Department

Jack Immendorf, private investigator

Thomas R. Kinberg, former FBI special agent

Erik A. Kleinsmith, Associate Vice President, American Military University

Daniel D. Kunkel, former senior intelligence officer, US Customs and Border Protection

Mark M. Lowenthal, former CIA assistant director

Thomas P. Mauriello, University of Maryland adjunct lecturer and president, ForensIQ

Linton Mohammed, PhD, forensic document examiner

Kris Mohandie, PhD, forensic, police, and clinical psychologist

Donald "Max" Noel, former FBI special agent

Kenneth L. Overturf, retired US Army lieutenant colonel

James T. Reese, PhD, former FBI profiler and behavioral science unit supervisor

William "Willie" Reagan, former FBI undercover special agent

Jeffrey T. Renz, attorney; clinical professor, University of Montana

Shannen L. Rossmiller, Montana state investigator, former judge, and FBI cyber-counterintelligence asset

Joseph P. Russoniello, former US attorney (two tenures) and FBI agent

Richard W. Smith, private investigator, former FBI intelligence agent

Ron Sterrett, former detective, Phoenix Police Department

F. Clark Sueyres, former judge and deputy district attorney, San Joaquin County

Jack Trimarco, PhD, polygrapher and profiler, former FBI agent

Bill Tyler, intelligence officer, Denver Police Department
Shannon Van Zant, archivist, Calaveras County
Richard F. Vigna, former Pacific Coast director, US Customs and Border Protection
Patrick J. Webb, former FBI special agent
Mark S. Zaid, attorney, national security and Freedom of Information Act expert
James Zimmerman, former sergeant, Niles Police Department

Story Development Associates

Lori Ansaldi, senior vice president, LMNO Productions
Bruce Bivens, data-mining consultant
Steve and Whitney Boe, interview transcribers
David Brand, photo editor
Barry Conrad, cameraman
Kevin Cooper, Creative Artists Agency
James J. Forbes, documentary correspondent
Thom Forbes, book editor
Stephanie Gans, PowerPoint editor
Sharon Goldinger, book copyeditor
William P. Jacobson, entertainment law attorney
Richard Kashanski, cameraman
Michael B. London, entertainment law attorney/manager
Michael McGarry, cover artist
Don Ray, investigative journalist and producer
Eric Schotz, executive producer, LMNO Productions
Ted Skillman, documentary director, LMNO Productions/History Channel
Jay Snyder, documentary video "sizzle reel" editor
Lynn Wood, accountant

Story Sources

Carol A. Abraczinskas	Dick Clever
Charles R. Allen	Kelly D. Cline
Terry W. Baker	Diana L. Cline
Eric Best	Galen C. Cook
John A. Briggs Jr.	Betty Dagget
Verlan C. "Vern" Burke	Gayle Downing
Marc A. Caporrimo	Willis L. Van Dusen
Ron L. Carlson	Ellyn R. Error

Gary Fasnacht
Greg Fasnacht
Joyce Fasnacht
Mike Fasnacht
Joy Fasnacht
Mark J. Fick
Daniel R. Finkle
Heidi J. Finkle
Sonia Finkle
Pat Forman
Ron Forman
Michael Forrester
William H. "Ben" Gay
Geoffrey Gray
John E. Hannay
Gary R. Hartman
Daryl Hedland
Ralph P. Himmelsbach
Paul "P. K." Hoffman
Jim C. Hollingsworth
Daniel F. Hunt
Robert "Pudgy" Hunt
Connie Hunt
Brian Ingram
Fred Jaross
Roxanne Jaross
Tom Kaye
Mike Kerley
Thomas R. Kinberg
Doug Kriegel
Philip R. LaCross
Patty Lamberson
Harold Lamberson
Delailah Little
Linda Lee Loduca
Clarence Manley Jr.
John E. Mattingly
Linda S. McGarity
Tim R. McCormick

Thomas R. McWilliams
Joaquin "Mike" Menezes
Charles E. Merritt
Bill M. Mitchell
Greg D. Mobley
James C. Mott
Patty Mott
Bev L. Nevin
Marilyn Newton
Larry E. North
Peter Noyes
G. Wayne Olmstead
Warren Olney
David E. Palmberg
Frank Peters
Peggy E. Potwin
Pete Roscoe
Jeff A. Salo
Michelle N. Sass
Richard G. Schlies
Kevin Seaman
James T. Shell
Richard A. Sherwood
Robert M. Shoemaker
Alfred A. Silva
Bruce Smith
Marian K. Soderberg
David B. Sweeney
Jim L. Sweeney
Gary E. Tallis
Jerald W. Thomas
Carol Turner-Mohr
Willis L. Van Dusen
Wayne Walker
Evilyn "Vicki" Wilson
Herb Woods
Steve Woods
Wilfred "Willy" Wyffels

Notes

Documenting the last forty-five years of a seventy-two-year-old man's life was a monumental task that needed every day of five years to complete. In the field, it required the hiring of researchers, multiple camera operators, surveillance teams, and armed guards, along with an award-winning investigative television journalist—James J. Forbes—to get all the right answers. Behind the scenes, a platoon of archivists, forensic document examiners, and librarians were enlisted to find crumbling documents and articles from the pre-Internet 1970s. All were hellbent on hunting down vanishing history.

The result was two giant file drawers of court records, photos, and forgotten journalism accounts of Robert W. Rackstraw, as well as notebooks and video- and audiotapes full of countless hours of personal testimonials, gathered along his alleged trail through five countries, all subdivided into unofficial folders involving a lifetime of alleged crime partners and collaborators (Perps), victims and witnesses (Non-Perps) family, and ex-lovers.

The following terms were used to describe the various documents and sources used in research:

Article written from screen: An article from a website that was unretrievable but typed by hand into a Word document

Clipping copy: An article cut out from a newspaper that no longer exists

Phone photo: An article or photo that was unretrievable but captured by a cell-phone camera

Scanned article: A digitally copied or forwarded article

Scanned   An article cut out from an old newspaper and digitally
clipping: copied

Scanned   A digitally copied court or government document
document:

Scanned photo   A digitally copied photo from a newspaper that no
with paragraph: longer exists

In citing works in the notes, short titles have generally been used. Entities and terms frequently used have been identified by the following abbreviations:

ACT	American Construction Team
AP	Associated Press
BHI	Bell Helicopter International
CCSC	Calaveras County Superior Court
DA	district attorney
DBC	D. B. Cooper
DOB	date of birth
FAA	Federal Aviation Administration
FOIA	Freedom of Information Act
HALO	high-altitude, low-opening
HC-LMNO	History Channel / LMNO Productions
IR	Investigative Report
JJF	James J. Forbes
LC	Larry Carr
MP	military police
NdW	Norman de Winter
PI	private investigator
PLB	Project Left Bank
PSYOP	Psychological Operations
RWR	Robert W. Rackstraw
SJC	San Joaquin County
SJCS	San Joaquin County Sheriff

TJC	Thomas J. Colbert
TJCC	TJC Consulting, LLC, Productions
UPI	United Press International
USC	University of Southern California

Preface

1. Tom Fuentes (former FBI assistant director and principal History Channel documentary liaison between the bureau and the network), on-camera interview by TJC, October 17, 2015. (LMNO Productions partner/executive producer Eric Schotz provided TJC with the full transcript.)

2. *Wikipedia*, s.v. "D. B. Cooper," last modified April 8, 2016, https://en.wikipedia .org/wiki/D._B._Cooper.

3. Walter Cronkite (anchor), CBS Evening News, November 25, 1971, https://www .youtube.com/watch?v=mxtgibncQlQ.

4. *FindingDulcinea*, s.v. "D. B. Cooper," by Denis Cummings, posted November 24, 2011, http://www.findingdulcinea.com/news/on-this-day/November /DB-Cooper-Hijacks-Plane.html; "The Bandit Who Went Out into the Cold," *Time*, December 6, 1971, http://content.time.com/time/magazine/article/0,9171,877495-1,00 .html. ("By week's end officers were scratching their heads and wondering where to look next for the dapper, audacious fellow with $200,000 to spend.") UPI, "Skyjacker Eludes FBI," Nevada State Journal, November 26, 1971, front page.

5. "Skyjacker Note Words Clipped from Newspaper," *Reno Evening Gazette*, November 30, 1971, 1–2, scanned article. (Dr. Otto Larsen, University of Washington, called DBC "kind of a curious Robin Hood.")

6. Rich Kashanski (Cooper-story tipster and cameraman), phone interview by TJC, February 2, 2011, Notebook #1, signed rights agreement.

7. TJC was an associate producer in film, 2012. IMDb listing: http://www.imdb.com /name/nm0170309/.

8. Brendan I. Korerner, "How Hijackers Commandeered Over 130 Amercan Planes—in 5 Years," *Wired*, June 18, 2013, http://www.wired.com/2013/06 /love-and-terror-in-the-golden-age-of-hijacking/.

9. Ron Carlson (drug runner), interview by Rich Kashanski (cameraman), February 2, 2011, TJCC DVD #7, transcript p. 3, timecode 00.05.38, signed rights agreement.

10. New York Times wire service, "Muddy Clue to D. B. Cooper," *New York Times*, February 17, 1980, scanned clipping; Tomas Alex Tizon, "D. B. Cooper: the Search for Skyjacker Missing Since 1971," *Los Angeles Times* (printed in the *San Francisco Chronicle*), September 4, 2005, http://www.sfgate.com/crime/article /D-B-Cooper-the-search-for-skyjacker-missing-2611758.php.

11. Leverett Richards, "Part of Cooper Cash Uncovered," *Oregonian*, February 13, 1980, front page, scanned article. (The quote is from Portland FBI Special Agent in Charge Ralph P. Himmelsbach.)

12. Jerome M. "Jerry" Jacobs (professor), California State University, Northridge, 1972–92. (TJC graduated in 1981; a photo of TJC and Jacobs in class and at reunions is available); Jacobs, obituary, http://www.legacy.com/obituaries/montereyherald /obituary.aspx?pid=158012918. (The obituary was originally printed in the *Monterey Herald*, June 13, 2012.)

13. Carlson, TJCC DVD #7, transcript p. 3, timecode 00.05.38.

14. "Auto Accident Kills Portlander," *Oregonian*, December 13, 1980, F3, scanned article; John Richard "Dick" Briggs (trafficker), obituary, *Oregonian*, D6, December 14, 1980, scanned article; Robert C. "Pudgy" Hunt (bartender and frat brother), interview by TJC, November 25, 2011, TJCC DVD #2, transcript p. 7, timecode 00.13.21, signed rights agreement. ("The thing I heard was that he got a call, and he thought somebody was after him.") Bev Nevin (Dick Briggs's former girlfriend), phone interview by TJC, July 18, 2013, Notebook #2, signed rights agreement. ("I think he was killed.") Daniel F. "Dan" Hunt (Pudgy's brother and RWR's coworker), interview by TJC, November 25, 2011, TJCC DVD #1, transcript p. 14, timecode 00.27.12, signed rights agreement. ("I heard it was an accident, but I don't believe that's what happened.")

15. "Rackstraw Gets 3-Year Term," *Stockton Record*, July 26, 1979, scanned clipping. (*Record* papers from the 1970s are gone; only a bag of fifty-four clippings on RWR was recovered.) UPI, "D. B. Cooper Case May Have a Suspect," *San Jose Mercury News*, February 3, 1979, 4B, phone photo. (TJC has a total of ten FBI leaks to papers about RWR possibly being DBC.) Richard Zahler, "California Suspect Apparently Ruled Out," *Seattle Times*, February 3, 1979, scanned clipping.

16. Times Wire Services, "Suspect in Family-Slaying May Be Famed D. B. Cooper," *Los Angeles Times*, June 30, 1989, http://articles.latimes.com/1989-06-30/news /mn-3121_1_ralph-himmelsbach-hijacking-robert-p-clark. (The discovery of ransom money on the banks of the river led to "speculation that Cooper landed in the river and drowned.") Richard Zahler and Steve Johnston, "More D.B. Cooper Cash Sought," *Seattle Times*, February 13, 1980, front page, scanned article. ("Dorwyn Schreuder, an FBI agent in charge of the beach search, said Cooper is probably not alive today.")

17. Delailah Little (librarian at the *Stockton Record* library), e-mail to TJC, October 31, 2011, email.pdf and clipping copies retained for records. (The e-mail lists all fifty-four article clippings on RWR, February 22, 1987 to November 13, 1980.)

18. TJC, e-mail to Shannon Van Zant (archivist at Calaveras County Archives), December 10, 2012, email.pdf and copies retained for records. (The e-mail is regarding paying a fee for access to public documents [court documents, articles, jail letters, photos, etc.] available from RWR's murder trial period [July 11, 1978 to July 28, 1978]); RWR's San Joaquin County Court Appeal Letter, undated, scanned document. (RWR's appeal letter is a six-page rant against his deputy DA, Clark Sueyres, written after RWR's May 19, 1979, conviction for grand theft–check kiting.)

19. A. J. Maloney (BHI security chief), BHI Security Letter Synopsis, February 20, 1978, from Calaveras County Archives, scanned document. (The FBI's first felony fugitive warrant for unlawful flight to Iran is noted by Maloney on page 6 of the synopsis.) Calaveras County Bail Reduction Petition Denial, May 4, 1978, scanned CCSC document. (Superior Court Judge Joseph S. Huberty noted that the "defendant fled the United States to Iran, which has no treaty of extradition . . . in anticipation of criminal prosecution against him.") Ben Remington and Helen Flynn, "How 2 First Suggested Rackstraw-Cooper Link," *Stockton Record*, February 3, 1979, front page, scanned article. (Investigators Buck and Murray state in the article that earlier in 1978, they "gave Rackstraw's name to FBI Agent Warren Little.") "Valley Springs Contractor Facing a Murder Charge," *Stockton Record*, March 1, 1978, scanned clipping. ("A federal fugitive warrant was issued for his arrest.") "FBI Joins the Hunt for Missing Fugitive," *Stockton Record*, January 23, 1979, scanned clipping. (The article mentions the FBI's second felony fugitive warrant for unlawful flight.)

20. Linda Lee Loduca (RWR's sister), interview by JJF, July 13, 2013, TJCC DVD #16, transcript p. 66, timecode 12.44.48, signed rights agreement. (Loduca said her brother used a provided volunteer deputy badge to claim he was a sheriff.) Pudgy Hunt, interview by TJC, November 25, 2011, TJCC DVD #1, transcript pp. 28–29, timecode 00.56.27. (RWR faked being Governor Ronald Reagan's pilot.) Betty Daggett (stewardess), phone interview by TJC, October 22, 2015, notes in Non-Perps folder. (RWR told Daggett on January 16, 1975, that "he was CIA." This is one of the sixteen identities, fake names, false professions, and false government positions that RWR used; the full list of sixteen is available in TJC's records.)

21. "Is Rackstraw D. B. Cooper?" *Stockton Record*, February 2, 1979, front page, scanned article; James T. Shell (former drug middleman), phone interview by TJC, January 22, 2015, Notebook #2, signed rights agreement. (In July 1974 RWR visited Shell's home roommate, trafficker Dick Briggs, in Portland.) Daggett, phone interview by TJC. (RWR was traveling from Seattle to Portland on January 16, 1975, when they carpooled from a fogged-in airport.) Steve Woods (floor company owner), phone interview by TJC, October 29, 2014, Notebook #2. (RWR traveled to Portland for a dozen jobs with Woods for five months, starting October 1976.) Pudgy Hunt, phone interview by TJC, April 24, 2012, Notebook #1. (RWR visited Pudgy Hunt's Portland bar in March 1977; he was in state for alleged revenge on RWR's business partners, the Woods family.) John A. Briggs Jr. (son of drug trafficker Dick Briggs), phone interview by TJC, April 13, 2013, Notebook #2, signed rights agreement. (As a thirteen-year-old, Briggs Jr. saw his father meet RWR on their home driveway in December 1978. Briggs Jr. was forty-eight years old at the time of the interview.)

22. Pete Noyes (former KNBC news editor), interview by Don Ray, April 13, 2012, TJCC DVD #8, transcript p. 6, timecode 00.09.54, signed rights agreement. (On March 9, 1979, Los Angeles FBI agent Roger "Frenchy" LaJeunesse told Noyes that RWR is a phony.) Richard Zahler, "California Suspect Apparently Ruled Out."

23. Richard Zahler and Richard Johnston, "More D. B. Cooper Cash Sought"; Leverett Richards, "Part of Cooper Cash Uncovered."

24. "Convictions Upheld," *Stockton Record*, November 13, 1980, scanned clipping.

25. Pudgy Hunt, interview by TJC, TJCC DVD #1, transcript p. 28, timecode 00.55.06. (Pudgy revealed how he introduced Dick Briggs to RWR in 1973.) Dan Hunt, interview by TJC, TJCC DVD #1, transcript pp. 5–9, timecode 00.06.06. (Dan revealed that his veteran partner, RWR, used violence, stole, and used fake names during their two and a half years on the road together.) Brian "River Money Boy" Ingram (forty years old at the time of the interview), interview by TJC, November 26, 2011, TJCC DVD #3, transcript pp. 9–11, timecode 00.29.50, signed rights agreement. (At the fortieth DBC anniversary symposium in Portland, Ingram revealed that he believes the money was planted; he also asked if his parents could be lying.) Gary E. Tallis (the first Seattle FBI officer at the hijack scene), interview by TJC, November 26, 2011, DVD #3A, transcript pp. 1–10, twenty-three-minute tape, signed rights agreement. (At the fortieth DBC anniversary symposium in Portland, Tallis revealed that he was the first agent to arrive at the Seattle hijack landing, and he discussed his later aerial search and the many theories on what happened to the jumper.) Tom Kaye (senior forensic volunteer), interview by TJC, November 26, 2011, TJCC DVD #4, transcript pp. 1–11, timecode 00.01.30, signed rights agreement. (At the fortieth symposium in Portland, Kaye revealed recent forensic results on the money; it appears that the money couldn't have arrived on shore and buried

itself there "without mechanical or human intervention.") Pete Roscoe (Astoria resident), phone interview by TJC, December 22, 2011, Notebook #1. (Roscoe identified a photo and video of RWR as the "Swiss Baron Norman," a visitor in a small town before the hijacking; Roscoe then spent months tracking down and locating eleven other local con victims for investigation.)

26. Susan McKee (FBI unit chief at the Investigative Publicity and Public Affairs Unit, Office of Public Affairs), e-mail to TJC, August 27, 2012.

27. Full Evidence List from TJC. (This is a summary, in bullet form, of the Cold Case Team's ninety-five pieces of physical, forensic, testimonial, direct, documentary, foundational, and hearsay evidence that point back at RWR.)

28. RWR, e-mail to TJC, March 29, 2013. ("I am not interested in notoriety or recognition, filmed interviews, or anything of that sort.")

29. TJC, e-mail to Ken Dirk (undercover PI and former FBI agent), May 9, 2013. (TJC provided locations and instructions to a PI company, "Alternative Solutions Offered," for a three-man team.)

30. RWR's party photo postings on social media, accessed April 11, 2016, https://www.facebook.com/airborne.bob.7?fref=ts, https://www.facebook.com/dorothy.rackstraw, https://www.facebook.com/photo.php?fbid=546170675542192&set=ecnf.100004477920456&type=3&theater.

31. Calaveras County Bail Reduction Petition Denial. (Superior Court Judge Joseph S. Huberty notes that RWR was discharged "under honorable"—meaning less than honorable—conditions, and he lied twice in court about "voluntarily" returning to the United States.) San Joaquin County DA Petition for Writ of Habeas Corpus, April 12, 1978, scanned document. (Sueyres said FBI agent Warren Little told him that fourteen of RWR's medals and awards were phony.) "Rackstraw, Plane Are Still Missing," *Stockton Record*, October 13, 1978, front page, scanned clipping. (Sueyres tells the reporter that RWR was discharged from the army over "'chronic intentional omissions for misrepresenting' his education record—at two colleges—which the military called 'conduct unbecoming an officer.'"); California Contractors State License Board Violation Disclosure, Case # N 1997 000357, July 13, 1999, Business and Professional Code 7112, scanned article. (When RWR applied to be a court mediator in 1997 for "engineering and design disputes," he lied about having four felonies, and his business license was revoked.)

32. National Personnel Records Center FOIA, response letter, July 29, 2013, scanned document. (RWR's seven-page military records show explosives, advanced weapons, and special forces survival training.) Steve Woods, phone interview by TJC. (After a business dispute in Hawaii, RWR took revenge by traveling to Woods's company in Oregon, smashing his car through closed gates, and stealing valuable equipment.) Dan Hunt, interview by TJC, TJCC DVD #1, transcript pp. 23 and 9, timecodes 00.47.16 and 00.15.57. (When a union picketer showed up at Hunt and RWR's floor job, RWR put a gun to the man's head and said, "'If you ever come back on this fuckin' job again, I'll blow your head off!' . . . After that I knew that, if he had to, he'd kill somebody without even thinkin' about it. Wouldn't bother him a bit.")

33. Robert D. Hare, PhD (psychologist), http://www.hare.org/scales/pclr.html, last updated March 8, 2016.

34. Loduca, interview by JJF, July 13, 2013, TJCC DVD #16, transcript p. 14, timecode 11.51.45. (Loduca admitted that as a teen, RWR was a liar and "a person with no moral compass.") Gail Marks (pseudonym, RWR's first wife), phone interview by

TJC, August 8, 2013, Notebook #2. (Regarding his failed business schemes and company start-ups, Marks said "Bob was a jack of all trades but didn't stay a master of anything.") Pudgy Hunt, interview by JJF for an LMNO/History documentary, September 18, 2015, transcript page 15, timecode 12:25:37. (Schotz provided TJC with the full transcript. Hunt described the details that Briggs relayed about the gun-store robbery he conducted with RWR, including RWR's preplanning: "Bob says, 'I've been following [the cops] for the last three nights. Every night between eleven and eleven-thirty, they're at this diner.'") Jack Trimarco, PhD (former FBI polygrapher), interview by JJF, September 19, 2013, TJC DVD #18–19, transcript pp. 15–35, timecode 01.31.39, signed rights agreement. (After viewing the San Diego confrontations, Trimarco said, "This man is probably a sociopath, more recently known as a psychopath or an antisocial personality, clinically.") Clark Sueyres, e-mail to TJC, October 12, 2012. ("I have dealt with a number of clever sociopaths in court, but he has more smarts and nerve than the rest put together.") Pudgy Hunt, interview by JJF, HC-LMNO transcript page 5, timecode 11:57:16. ("Rackstraw waves to the audience, big grin. I mean he was like a sociopath," said Hunt.)

35. National Personnel Records Center FOIA. (RWR's military records show training in demolition and underwater explosives; paratrooper, HALO-jumper, advanced weapons, and Special Forces survival training; PSYOP classes, land navigation courses; both fixed wing and rotary pilot training; and that he earned fifty air medals.) Full Evidence List from TJC.

36. Pudgy Hunt, interview by JJF, HC-LMNO transcript p. 15, timecode 12:25:37; Trimarco, interview by JJF, TJCC DVD #18 and #19, transcript pp. 15–35, timecode 01.31.39; Clark Sueyres, e-mail to TJC, October 12, 2012; Pudgy Hunt, interview by JJF, HC-LMNO transcript p. 5, timecode 11:57:16; "Is Rackstraw D. B. Cooper?" (The article mentions the November 24, 1971 hijack flight.) "Fugitive Believed in Iran," *Stockton Record*, February 10, 1978. (The article mentions the December 1978 Iran Fugitive Flight.) Peggy Townsend, "Airplane Crash Could Be a Hoax," *Santa Cruz Sentinel*, October 16, 1978, front page, scanned article. (The article mentions the October 11, 1978 Mayday escape flight.) Briggs Jr., interview, Notebook #2. (As a thirteen-year-old, Briggs Jr. saw his father meet RWR, a fugitive, on their home driveway in December of 1978; TJC believes this is where RWR turned over the $5,800 of Cooper money to Briggs for the river stunt, which was more than a year away.)

37. Dirk, interview by JJF, May 21, 2013, TJCC DVD #12, transcript p. 7, timecode 02:28:56. (After a week of surveillance and eyewitness of RWR's verbal confrontation, Dirk said, "I feel certain he was hiding the truth.") Trimarco, interview by JJF, June 3, 2012, TJCC DVD #18, interview transcript p. 24, timecode 01.48.13. (After viewing the San Diego video confrontation, Trimarco said, "I think that Mr. Rackstraw is D. B. Cooper. I think it's time for him to take credit for what he did.") James Reese, PhD (former FBI pioneer profiler), phone interview by TJC, September 8, 2013, Notebook #2. (After reviewing the ninety-two-page investigative report, Reese said, "I usually study reports three times, but my first read says yes, he's the guy.") Joseph P. Russoniello (former two-time US attorney and dean of San Francisco School of Law), four-page legal opinion, March 5, 2014. ("My review leads me to the conclusion that Robert W. 'Bob' Rackstraw, DOB 10-16-43, is D. B. Cooper and subject to federal prosecution for the crimes of airline hijacking, extortion and kidnapping.")

Authors' Note

1. RWR, interview by Warren Olney (KNBC reporter), KNBC News, July 26, 1979. (RWR: "I coulda' been [Cooper] . . . coulda' been." Olney: "You don't want to commit yourself one way or the other?" RWR: "No . . . You say with a story like that, should it be fiction or should it be fact? It's primarily up to the American people someday, how that comes out.") "Not D. B. Cooper, Rackstraw Insists," *Stockton Record*, July 25, 1979, front page, scanned clipping. ("Rackstraw said he decided to go along with the idea he might be Cooper because he said, 'I knew it would trigger press reaction.'") RWR, in-person interview by TJC, San Diego, California, May 20, 3013. ("I told everybody I was" Cooper, admitted Rackstraw. But he described it all as an elaborate identity stunt. "Nice try," thought the producer.) RWR, e-mail to TJC (forwarded by attorney Dennis Roberts), May 31, 2013. ("Now, we will consider a real offer [for RWR's Cooper story rights] if they provide virtually every piece of data and information that they have acquired in the past years subject to our review of same.") Dennis Roberts, e-mail to Mark Zaid (TJC's attorney) on October 17, 2013. ("Between us Bobby always enjoyed letting people think he is D. B. Cooper—can you imagine how much pussy D. B. would get—but from everything I know it is an act that got out of hand.")

Chapter One

1. George Hoeper, "War Hero Says Criminal Charges Part of Campaign to 'Get Him,'" *Stockton Record*, July 6, 1978, front page, scanned article. (The article features a photo of RWR chained to a wheelchair.)

2. Calaveras County Bail Reduction Petition Denial. (Superior Court Judge Joseph S. Huberty notes that the fugitive RWR lied twice in court about "voluntarily" returning to the United States and, on return from Iran, was "denied means of deplaning" at the stop in Paris, France.)

3. "Suspect Arraigned on Murder, Theft Charges," *Calaveras Enterprise*, March 15, 1978, scanned article. (The article's photo shows RWR being carried up steps in a wheelchair for his murder arraignment); "$350,000 Bail Continued," *Stockton Record*, March 7, 1978, clipping copy. (Regarding the wheelchair, Sueyres told the paper, "Doctors say they can't find anything wrong with him, and we suspect that he wants to go to the hospital from the jail in an attempt to escape.") Loduca, interview by JJF, TJCC DVD #16, transcript pp. 92–93, timecode 14:27:36. ("That's the way Bob is. He would do that to, you know, make everybody else's life miserable. He would, you know, [to get] sympathy.")

4. Carol Deck, "Jury Says Rackstraw Not Guilty of Murder," *Calaveras Prospect*, August 3, 1978, front page, vol. 97, no. 31, scanned article. (Attorney Dennis Roberts told the jury that his client RWR was "a tough guy, a little conceited, a war hero, a big shot—but not a stupid man.") "Medals 'Influence' Judge," *Stockton Record*, April 5, 1978, clipping copy. (After hearing that RWR is "a decorated war hero," Judge William H. Woodward was stunned. "This simply can't be true. If this is true, his record will bear weight with this court.")

5. "Medals 'Influence' Judge," *Stockton Record*. (The article references the judge's shock at RWR's large number of medals and his declaration that RWR's record "will bear weight.")

6. "Medals 'Influence' Judge," *Stockton Record*. (The article references Sueyres's derogatory reaction and the judge's warning.)

7. Calaveras County DA Military Records Waiver documents, April 12, 1987, scanned document. (In an exchange of court documents, Deputy DA Sueyres and defense attorney Roberts argued over how much RWR is cooperating in turning over his military records.)

8. Kelly D. Cline, phone interview by TJC, January 17, 2013, notes in Non-Perps folder. (Cline provided graphic details about the body recovery.) "Testimony of Witnesses in Murder Trial Continues," Calaveras Prospect, July 20, 1978, front page, scanned article; "Fraud Suspect's Stepfather was Slain, Buried," Stockton Record, July 22, 1978, scanned clipping.

9. Kelly D. Cline, phone interview by TJC.

10. Ibid.

11. "Blood-Stained Jeans Introduced at Trial," Stockton Record, July 26, 1978, scanned clipping. (RWR was also put on the stand in his own defense.)

12. "Rackstraw Acquitted of Slaying in Lode," Stockton Record, July 28, 1978, front page, scanned clipping.

13. Vivian Jones (pseudonym, former movie producer and cocaine trafficker), phone interview by TJC, March 20, 2014, Notebook #2. (Jones said her attorney referral to RWR, Dennis Roberts, agreed to take his murder case "for $10,000 and his Corvette.") Mary Yontel (pseudonym, former girlfriend), phone interview by JJF, October 1, 2015, HC-LMNO audio, transcript p. 26, timecode 01:46:03. (Schotz provided TJC with the full transcript. In the interview, Yontel confirmed the Corvette-and-cash deal.)

14. "Rackstraw War Record Doubted," Stockton Record, August 3, 1978, scanned clipping. (The article mentions RWR's facing charges of "bad check operation and for alleged illegal possession of explosives" and also that he is "now free on $60,000 bail.") "Judge Thinks Rackstraw Still Alive—Somewhere," Stockton Record, October 31, 1978, scanned clipping. ("Rackstraw posted the bail with the help of friends in Sacramento.") Jones, phone interview by TJC. ("I personally signed and guaranteed" the $60,000 bail bond.)

15. "Rackstraw's Military Record Ordered," Stockton Record, September 16, 1978, scanned clipping. ("He appeared in the courtroom without his crutches or wheelchair.")

16. Dirk, interview by JJF, TJCC DVD #12, transcript p. 7, timecode 02:28:56. (After a week of surveillance: "I feel certain he was hiding the truth.") Loduca, interview by JJF, DVD #16, transcript p. 15, timecode 11.23.28. ("I started to really see the difference in him, more pronounced habits that he had developed in lying, deceiving . . . a person who has no moral compass.") Dan Hunt, interview by TJC, TJCC DVD #1, transcript p. 7, timecode 00.09.23. ("If he was renting an airplane, he'd put down wrong names.")

17. Remington and Flynn, "How 2 First Suggested Rackstraw-Cooper Link." (Investigators Buck and Murray state that earlier in 1978 they "gave Rackstraw's name to FBI Agent Warren Little.")

18. AP, "Rule Out Hijacking Suspect," January 22, 1979, scanned article. (RWR "was sought for questioning in the Cooper case last year," FBI agent Pete Norregard confirmed. "But Rackstraw disappeared" in the sudden Mayday escape.)

19. San Joaquin County DA Petition for Writ of Habeas Corpus. (Sueyres writes that FBI agent Warren Little told him that fourteen of RWR's medals and awards were "missing" and later proved to be phony.)

20. Townsend, "Airplane Crash Could Be a Hoax." ("He had apparently called his ex-wife in Santa Cruz County and asked him to meet him at the Skypark Airport.") Marks, phone interview by TJC, August 8, 2013, Notebook #2.

21. Ken Bunting, "Defendant Vanishes; Police Doubt 'Mayday,'" *Sacramento Bee*, October 13, 1978, B1, scanned article.

22. "Rackstraw on 'Lost' Plane; Possible Hoax," *Stockton Record*, October 12, 1978, front page, scanned clipping. ("Five Navy, Coast Guard and Air Force planes, as well as three Coast Guard cutters.")

23. Tim Reiterman, "D. B. Cooper Suspect Is, in Any Case, a Lot of Trouble," *San Francisco Examiner and Chronicle*, February 4, 1979, front page, scanned article. ("Using a map drawn by Rackstraw, investigators went to Meadowlark Airport in Huntington Beach and located the Cessna. Its green stripe and numbers had been painted over brown.") Yontel, phone interview by JJF, HC-LMNO transcript pp. 17–18, timecode 01:15:58. ("The plane was . . . hidden after the flight.")

24. Yontel, phone interview by JJF, HC-LMNO transcript p. 25, timecode 01:43:05. (RWR "found the place in Laguna. And his friend Pat Ebert, the three of us lived together.")

25. *Wikipedia*, s.v. "D. B. Cooper." (Two reporters are credited for the "D. B. Cooper" name: UPI reporter Clyde Jabin by most accounts, AP reporter Joe Frazier by others.)

26. Jack Immendorf (PI), "D. B. or Not D. B.?" *Private Journal*, April 16, 1997, scanned article. (The article contains a narrative on the RWR investigative assignment, September 1977 through February 1978.) Calaveras County Probate of Murder Victim Philip Rackstraw, filed July 10, 1978. (Page 5 of the probate contains Immendorf's July 3, 1978, invoice for six months of work.)

Chapter Two

1. Loduca, interview by JJF, TJCC DVD #16, transcript p. 2, timecode 11.00.23. (Loduca discussed the young, blended family moving to Santa Cruz, California.) *Archives*, s.v. "Robert W. Rackstraw," accessed April 29, 2012, http://www.archives.com. (This database documents RWR's family tree, including his parents, his roots in Ohio and England, and his aunts, uncles, nieces, and nephews.)

2. Loduca, interview by JJF, TJCC DVD #16, transcript pp. 3–8, timecode 11.01.23.

3. Ibid., transcript pp. 115–117, timecode 15.04.46. (Loduca talked about her uncle Ed Cooper and his love of skydiving that he passed on to RWR.)

4. National Personnel Records Center FOIA. (RWR's military records show he was a paratrooper.) Remington and Flynn, "How 2 First Suggested Rackstraw-Cooper Link." (The Stockton police department and fire investigators said they discovered that RWR was a highly trained HALO jumper.)

5. Don Ray (former KNBC researcher), interview by TJC, April 13, 2012, TJCC DVD #9, transcript p. 5, timecode 00:06:30, signed rights agreement. (Ray claimed former KNBC editor Pete Noyes told him in 1979 that "a guy up north in jail who [called] says he's D. B. Cooper, and to prove it, he says, he has an uncle named Ed Cooper who lives in Arizona.")

6. Loduca, interview by JJF, TJCC DVD #16, transcript pp. 8–11, timecode 11.10.24. (Loduca said that RWR was known as the mischief-maker and discussed his first lies and lust for money.)

7. RWR's original Santa Cruz High School sophomore year report card, 1958–59. (This report card, along with dozens of family photos, were licensed from Loduca, who inherited them from her mother's estate.)

8. Loduca, interview by JJF, TJCC DVD #16, transcript p. 19, timecode 11.30.33. (Loduca discussed the first time RWR impregnated somebody and the adoption arranged by his father as well as social media links for and photos of RWR.) Marks, phone interview by TJC, August 12, 2013, Notebook #2. (Marks learned that RWR had a second child needing support when the California Department of Child Services knocked on her door after her wedding to RWR. Marks provided the names in both of these teen pregnancies: the first mother was Cindy S. Robinson, and the son was Chris Mason; the second mother was Jackie Miller, and the daughter was Kim A. Carlton-Houch [DOB March 23, 1963—she's connected through social media links and photos to "dad" RWR.])

9. Loduca, interview by JJF, TJCC DVD #16, transcript p. 11, timecode 11.15.28. (Loduca discussed RWR's fake licenses.) "Youth Has Hot Time in Jail," *Santa Cruz Sentinel*, October 23, 1963, scanned article. (Loduca mentioned twenty-year-old RWR's roadside arrest for "false identification.")

10. Marks, phone interview by TJC, August 12, 2013, Notebook #2. (Marks named RWR's truck-driving job as a sixteen-year-old: Graham & Son Concrete Company.) Ed Hill (former cement-truck driver), interview by TJC, October 21, 2015, notes in Perps folder. (Hill confirmed that he drove a cement truck with Bob in 1961.)

11. "Obituary," *Santa Cruz Sentinel*, May 20, 2003, scanned article. (The obituary includes the life story of Bill D. Graham, former mayor and owner of Graham & Son Concrete Company.)

12. Loduca, interview by JJF, TJCC DVD #16, transcript p. 15, timecode 11.23.28.

13. Marks, phone interview by TJC, August 12, 2013, Notebook #2. (Marks discussed RWR's band, the Insanos, later known as the Stormtroupers.) Donna (widow of Insanos/Stormtrouper member Dick Tranchina), interview by TJC, September 17, 2015, Notebook #2. (Donna discussed the band's background.) Helene (sister of late Insanos/Stormtrouper member Earl Latham), interview by TJC, September 17, 2015, Notebook #2. (Helene discussed the band's background.) "Talent Contest, Show Set at Cabrillo Theater Saturday," *Santa Cruz Sentinel*, March 18, 1964. (The article names RWR and other members in the Stormtroupers talent show.) Advertisement for talent contest and show set at Cabrillo Theater, *Santa Cruz Sentinel*, March 3, 1964.

14. "Eisele-Webb Vows Recited," March 21, 1962, scanned article. (RWR is named in the newspaper wedding article as the best man of former Santa Cruz high school classmate Bill H. Eisele); Bill H. Eisele, phone interview by TJC, April 19, 2015, notes in Perps folder.

15. Loduca, interview by JJF, TJCC DVD #16, transcript pp. 15 and 154, timecodes 11.23.28 and 16.04.47. Marks, phone interview by TJC, August 12, 2013, Notebook #2. (Marks said RWR's lying was so bad, he had earned the nickname Bullshit Bob.) Linda S. McGarity (RWR's second wife), phone interview by JJF, October 6, 2015, HC-LMNO audio, transcript p. 6, timecode 15:44:35. (Schotz provided TJC with the full transcript; McGarity signed rights agreement and licensed photos. McGarity said, "There was two letters [from separate mistresses]. I freaked out . . . tears are flowing everywhere.") "Rackstraw, Plane Are Still Missing." (RWR "highly exaggerated" his army rank and medals and was dismissed from military for "chronic intentional omissions for misrepresenting his education record" at two colleges.) Riverside County, California, Superior Court Criminal Records, December 15, 1997, obtained through the service Instantcheckmate. com. (RWR was convicted for resisting arrest, driving under the influence of drugs, and providing a false ID to a peace officer.)

16. "To Be Sentenced," *Stockton Record*, April 18, 1961, scanned article; "Jobless Benefits Prove Expensive," *Stockton Record*, April 21, 1961, scanned article; "Correction," *Stockton Record*, April 26, 1961, scanned article. (Lucille L. Rackstraw's wrote a correction to readers and friends: "This involves a misunderstanding . . . I have paid my fine plus a suspended jail sentence and paid back . . . the employment department.")

17. Loduca, interview by JJF, TJCC DVD #16, transcript pp. 19–21, timecode 11.30.33.

18. "Youth Has Hot Time in Jail," *Santa Cruz Sentinel*; Loduca, interview by JJF, TJCC DVD #16, transcript pp. 10 and 154, timecodes 11.13.10 and 16.04.47. (RWR "had been drinking" at the time of his arrest; Loduca told the rest of the story.)

Chapter Three

1. "Six SC Youth Join National Guard Battalion," *Santa Cruz Sentinel*, March 25, 1964, scanned article.

2. Loduca, interview by JJF, TJCC DVD #16, transcript p. 27, timecode 11.47.01; Loduca, phone interview by TJC, July 5, 2013, Notebook #2.

3. Donna, interview by TJC, September 17, 2015, Notebook #2; Helene, interview by TJC, September 17, 2015, Notebook #2; "Talent Contest, Show Set at Cabrillo Theater Saturday," *Santa Cruz Sentinel*, March 18, 1964; Advertisement for talent contest and show set at Cabrillo Theater, *Santa Cruz Sentinel*, March 3, 1964.

4. Loduca, TJCC DVD #16, transcript p. 29, timecode 11.50.02.

5. RWR, phone interview by TJC, March 12, 2013, Notebook #1. (RWR described the horrible ordeal of the Watts Riots.) Loduca, phone interview by TJC, July 5, 2013, Notebook #2. (Loduca confirmed RWR's Watts Riot story.)

6. Marks, phone interview by TJC, August 12, 2013, Notebook #2.

7. Ibid.

8. National Personnel Records Center FOIA, responce letter. (RWR's military records show he was a paratrooper and demolition expert and trained to become sergeant.) Remington and Flynn, "How 2 First Suggested Rackstraw-Cooper Link"; Pete Noyes (former KNBC news editor), interview by Don Ray, April 13, 2012, TJCC DVD #8, transcript p. 7, timecode 00:12:00. ("My interest solely involved the fact that he was a HALO [jumper] in Vietnam.")

9. "Theft of Musical Gear Investigated," *Santa Cruz Sentinel*, January 27, 1967, scanned article.

10. National Personnel Records Center FOIA, response letter. (RWR's military records show he was training at Cabrillo College and the Presidio of Monterey with the US Navy Reserve.)

11. John Bocciolatt (Cold Case PI, Portland, OR), investigative database search, May 7, 2013. (In a background search, PI Bocciolatt found that RWR had three social security numbers.)

12. Gail Marks, phone interview by TJC, August 12, 2013, Notebook #2. (In 1966, Rulon and Donald King came to talk to RWR about abuse.) "Divorces Filed," *Santa Cruz Sentinel*, April 3, 1968, scanned article. (According to paper, Marks filed for divorce under "extreme cruelty"; then shortly after, the court documents were withdrawn.)

13. Loduca, interview by JJF, TJCC DVD #16, transcript p. 16, timecode 11.25.48. (Regarding RWR's wives, Loduca said she'd heard from her mother that he "slapped a couple of them around.")

14. National Personnel Records Center FOIA. (RWR's military records show he returned to Fort Bragg, North Carolina, for ten weeks of classes at the Special Warfare School. His courses include 140 hours on conducting special forces operations and survival skills; 140 hours in internal defense and development [ID&D]; and 130 hours in PSYOP [training in deception, propaganda, interrogation and mind-control.]); Herb Friedman (sergeant major and PSYOP Expert), http://www.psywarrior.com. (140 articles are posted, from World War I to the present.) Loduca, phone interview by TJC, June 25, 2013, Notebook #2. ("The army only sharpened his [lying] skills.") Trimarco, interview TJCC DVD #18, transcript pp. 15–35, timecode 01.31.39.

15. National Personnel Records Center FOIA, responce letter. (RWR's military records show, while at Fort Bragg, he applied to join the regular army so he could train to be a full-time helicopter pilot.)

16. Marks, phone interview by TJC, August 12, 2013, Notebook #2. (Marks said she has a photo of RWR at home, wearing a Green Beret uniform, from 1968.)

17. National Personnel Records Center FOIA, responce letter. (RWR's military records show training at Primary Helicopter School in Fort Wolters, Texas, and advanced flight training and graduation at Fort Rucker, Alabama. The Primary Helicopter School photo is military public record, and the Fort Rucker graduation and base photos were licensed from Loduca.)

18. Loduca, interview by JJF, TJCC DVD #16, transcript p. 16, timecode 11.26.01. ("They had a very volatile relationship. They wouldn't talk, they screamed at each other. She would get mad and pick up something of his and destroy it. He'd pull the phone out of the wall, and he took some stuff of hers and destroyed it.")

19. Loduca, interview by JJF, July 13, 2013, TJCC DVD #16, transcript p. 14, timecode 11.51.45; RWR's original Santa Cruz High School sophomore year report card, 1958–59, licensed from Loduca. (The report card was from his dropout year; he had four Fs, three Ds, and forty-four class cuts.) "Youth Has Hot Time in Jail," *Santa Cruz Sentinel*; Loduca, interview by JJF, TJCC DVD #16, transcript p. 10 and 154, timecodes 11.13.10 and 16.04.47; Ibid., transcript p. 10, timecode 11.12.41. ("Bob was driving and he was pretty smashed. And he ran into the side of the people's house and did some damage.") Noyes, interview by Don Ray, April 13, 2012, TJCC DVD #8, transcript p. 6, timecode 00.09.54. (Noyes said FBI Agent Roger "Frenchy" LaJeunesse told him in 1979 that RWR was "a con man.") Sueyres, e-mail to TJC, October 12, 2012; Pudgy Hunt, interview by JJF, HC-LMNO transcript p. 5, timecode 11:57:16; Marks, interview by TJC, August 8, 2013, Notebook #2. (She said when Fort Rucker army officials arrived during the domestic attack, they found RWR "choking me over the sink.")

Chapter Four

1. Rick A. Sherwood (retired noncommissioned officer, CommCenter, Phuoc Vinh Airfield, Vietnam) phone interviews by TJC, April 30 to July 22, 2015, Notebook #2. (Sherwood provided a verbal portrait of Vietnam life.)

2. Loduca, interview by JJF, TJCC DVD #16, transcript pp. 3–8, timecode 11.01.23.

3. "Grant Shaw" (blogging veteran), November 6, 2014, 7:27 a.m., https://usastruck.com/2009/09/24/phuoc-vinh-airfield.

4. "Dave" (blogging veteran), comment on "Phuoc Vinh Airfield," August 16, 2011, 6:59 p.m., https://usastruck.com /2009/09/24/phuoc-vinh-airfield.

5. Roland Hayes (blogging veteran and retired sergeant first class), comment on "Phuoc Vinh Airfield," July 6, 2010, 5:12 p.m., https://usastruck.com/2009/09/24 /phuoc-vinh-airfield, personal website: http://www.kneesinthebreeze.com.

6. Officers Roster, Department of the Army, Eleventh Aviation Company (General Support), First Cavalry Division (Airmobile), APO 96490, March, 1970. (RWR is sixteenth of twenty listed Vietnam pilots.)

7. "Completes Training," *Corpus Christi Caller*, August 26, 1968. (The article includes Joe C. Schlein's chopper school graduation notice.) G. Wayne Olmstead (retired captain, RWR's army bunkmate and copilot), e-mails to TJC from May 25, 2015, to May 28, 2015. (Olmstead provided details on RWR's life in Vietnam, both his heroics and his trouble-making.)

8. Yontel, phone interview by JJF, HC-LMNO transcript p. 19, timecode 01:19:47. (Yontel said that in 1977, "We flew down to see his friend, Joe [Schlein]. His old Vietnam buddy.")

9. *Wikipedia*, s.v. "Aircraft Losses of the Vietnam War," last updated March 8, 2016, https://en.wikipedia.org/wiki/Aircraft_losses_of_the_Vietnam_War. (The entry includes statistics on the largest troop transport, Chinook choppers, and how many aircraft were lost in the war.)

10. Ronald "Ron" Ferrizzi (blogging veteran), "Dear John Letters," November 22, 2012, 7:00 p.m., https://usastruck.com/tag/c-troop-19th-blues/.

11. Olmstead, e-mail to TJC, May 27, 2015. (Olmstead provided details on Vietnam, RWR, and using RWR's stolen Jeep.) Ken L. Overturf (retired lieutenant colonel and RWR's former Project Left Bank [PLB] commander), e-mails to TJC from May 12, 2015, to July 2, 2015. (Overturf provided details on Vietnam, RWR, and seeing RWR in a stolen Jeep with a CIA man.) Clarence Manley Jr. (retired pilot), phone interview by TJC, June 11, 2015, Notebook #2. (Manley Jr. provided details on Vietnam, RWR, and seeing RWR in a stolen Jeep with Special Forces.) Richard G. "Dick" Schlies (former PLB intercept operator), phone interview by TJC, June 15, 2015, Notebook #2. (Schlies said RWR was a "great pilot," but he had also heard that RWR had "stolen a commander's Jeep.")

12. Overturf, e-mails to TJC, May 12, 2015, to July 2, 2015.

13. Lonnie M. Long and Gary B. Blackburn, *Unlikely Warriors: The Army Security Agency's Secret War in Vietnam 1961–1973* (iUniverse, 2013): 315–328, 336. (These pages discuss PLB.) Selected chapters and pictures from Long and Blackburn's *Unlikely Warriors* are also posted at facebook.com/UnlikelyWarriors/posts/682442755186750.

14. Sherwood, phone interviews by TJC.

15. Long and Blackburn, *Unlikely Warriors*.

16. Ibid.; "The 45th Anniversary of the Shoot-Down of 'Jaguar Yellow,' November 29, 1969" (iUniverse, 2013), chapter 23.

17. Olmstead, e-mail to TJC, May 22, 2015. (Olmstead provided details on the death of Jack D. Knepp, who flew the first PLB chopper to be shot down.)

18. Larry E. North (blogging PLB veteran), "Helecopter UH-1H 68-15246," March 1997, https://www.vhpa.org/KIA/incident/69112929KIA.HTM. (North was a signal maintenance soldier for PLB in 1969–70.) North, e-mail to TJC, April 29, 2015. (North provided more details on the death of Jack D. Knepp.) Vietnam Helicopter Pilots Association, https://www.vhpa.org/KIA/incident/69112929KIA.HTM, last updated March 30, 2014. (The website provides statistics and a history of actions and shoot-downs, including Knepp's.)

19. Overturf, e-mails to TJC, May 12, 2015, to July 2, 2015; Manley Jr., phone interview, Notebook #2.

20. Overturf, e-mails to TJC. (Overturf gave temporary permission to RWR to fly for PLB.) Olmstead, e-mail to TJC, May 27, 2015. (Olmstead called RWR "pleasant, personable, very capable, fearless, and a natural leader.") Dick Schlies, phone interview by TJC, June 15, 2015, Notebook #2.

21. Ken Overturf, e-mail to TJC, May 14, 2015. (The e-mail contained an eleven-year-old letter: "Statement of Mission Requirements & Performance in Vietnam, March 1969–March 1970." The letter says that aerial surveillance duties for intelligence gathering in PLB required "nap-of-the-earth reconnaissance flights.")

22. Sherwood, phone interviews by TJC. (Sherwood talked about high- versus low-altitude flying.)

23. Tom R. McWilliams (former Green Beret and PLB pilot), e-mail to TJC, April 10, 2016. (McWilliams discussed the dangers of flying low.)

24. Overturf, e-mails TJC. (Overturf discussed hand grenades and claymore mines placed in trees to take down PLB choppers; he knew of the damaged chopper count.)

25. Tim R. McCormick (former PLB pilot), copy of e-mail to TJC, July 1, 2015. (McCormick sent details on his chopper fire with copilot McWilliams.)

26. Overturf, e-mails to TJC.

27. Olmstead, e-mail to TJC, May 22, 2015.

28. Overturf, e-mails to TJC. (Overturf discussed RWR's illegal parachute jump.)

29. Ibid. (Overturf discussed RWR's involvement with the CIA.) Olmstead, e-mail to TJC, May 27, 2015. (Olmstead provided stories about RWR and the CIA.)

30. Olmstead, e-mail to TJC, May 27, 2015.

31. National Personnel Records Center FOIA, response letter. (RWR's seven-page military records show he received a Silver Star and Distinguished Flying Cross and include a description of his actions.)

32. Olmstead, e-mail to TJC, May 25, 2015; Marks, phone interview, August 8, 2013, Notebook #2. (Gail shared a memory of her Hawaii dinner with RWR, General Shoemaker, and Shoemaker's wife.)

33. Overturf, e-mails to TJC. (Overturf discussed RWR's arrival at the command-and-control chopper.)

34. *Wikipedia*, s.v. "Cambodian Campaign," last updated April 12, 2016, https://en.wikipedia.org/wiki/Cambodian_Campaign.

35. Jacob Brooks, "Task Force Shoemaker: A Bold, Risky Attack," *Fort Hood Herald*, June 17, 2015. (General Shoemaker "went from unit to unit in his helicopter, encouraging the troops.")

36. Olmstead, e-mail to TJC, May 23, 2015. (Olmstead discussed PLB's involvement in Cambodia.)

37. McWilliams, e-mail to TJC, April 10, 2016.

38. Olmstead, e-mail to TJC, May 27, 2015.

39. Ibid., May 28, 2015.

40. RWR, phone interview by TJC, February 28, 2013, Notebook #1. (RWR discussed his Hawaii dinner with General Shoemaker, Shoemaker's wife, and Gail Marks.) Marks, phone interview, August 8, 2013, Notebook #2. (Marks recalled her and RWR's dinner in Hawaii with the Shoemakers.) Eric Best and Dick Clever, "Rackstraw Talks from County Jail," *Stockton Record*, February 6, 1979, front page, scanned clipping. (The article mentions RWR's dinner with Marks and the Shoemakers.)

41. "Army Airman from SC Wins Distinguished Flying Cross," *Santa Cruz Sentinel*, May 17, 1970, front page, scanned article. (This controversial article was allegedly planted by RWR.)

42. Overturf, e-mail to TJC, May 12, 2015.

43. National Personnel Records Center FOIA, response letter.

44. Sherwood, phone interview by TJC, May 11, 2015.

45. RWR's original Santa Cruz High School Sophomore Year Report Card, 1958–59; Loduca, interview by JJF, TJCC DVD #16, transcript pp. 19–21, timecode 11.30.33; "Youth Has Hot Time in Jail," *Santa Cruz Sentinel*; Loduca, interview by JJF, TJCC DVD #16, transcript pp. 10 and 154, timecodes 11.13.10 and 16.04.47; Ibid., transcript p. 10, timecode 11.12.41.

46. Pudgy Hunt, interview by TJC, November 25, 2011, TJCC DVD #1, transcript p. 26, timecode 00.51.58. (In a 1973 meeting at a Denny's in San Jose, RWR showed Pudgy the "treasonous" 1970 *Santa Cruz Sentinel* story he planted.)

47. National Personnel Records Center FOIA, response letter.

48. Ibid.

49. Marks, phone interview, August 8, 2013, Notebook #2. (Marks discussed her ordeal and her departure from Fort Rucker, Alabama.)

50. Don Ray (former KNBC researcher), e-mail to TJC, May 11, 2012. (Ray forwarded three pages of RWR's FAA records. The records reveal that right after RWR's domestic abuse assault in February, 1971, he signed up for a four-month FAA course to receive a commercial chopper license and a fixed-wing instruction license; the timing suggests he was aware he may lose his military career, so just in case, he trained for the future as a civilian pilot.)

51. Best and Clever, "Rackstraw Talks from County Jail." (RWR told the reporter about his scuba instruction job in Pensacola, Florida, in early 1971.) Marks, phone interview, August 8, 2013, Notebook #2. (Marks discussed RWR's scuba instruction in Pensacola and has pictures of him training others in a pool.)

52. Marks, phone interview, August 12, 2013, Notebook #2.

53. Loduca, interview by JJF, TJCC DVD #16, transcript p. 16, timecode 11.26.01. ("They had a very volatile relationship. They wouldn't talk; they screamed at each other. He'd pull the phone out of the wall, and he took some stuff of hers and destroyed it.") Marks, phone interview, August 12, 2013, Notebook #2. ("Bob was threatening and beating me so many times—off the top of my head, I can't give a number. I was scared to death.")

54. Marks, phone interview, August 8, 2013, Notebook #2. ("He had physically choked me over the sink . . . the girls [two and a half and three and a half at the time] still can't forget it. After five days at the commander's house with his wife, I was advised to go home" to California and divorce him.) Clark Sueyres, email to TJC, January 28, 2013. ("My reading of [RWR's] service record was that he was the general's driver" during the four months leading up to RWR's dismissal.)

55. Marks, phone interview, August 8, 2013, Notebook #2.

56. Ibid.

57. Ray, e-mail to TJC, May 11, 2012. (The FAA documents say RWR's aviation licenses began on June 7, 1971, as did his divorce child-support order.)

58. National Personnel Records Center FOIA, response letter. (Under "Dates of Service," RWR's last date as a soldier is listed as June 21, 1971; in the "Civilian Education and Military Schooling" document page, both USC and San Jose State are crossed out.)

National Student Clearinghouse, search on April 18, 2012, http://studentclearinghouse .org. (Record checks cannot verify that RWR attended either USC or San Jose State.)

59. Loduca, interview by JJF, TJCC DVD #16, transcript p. 33, timecode 11.55.10. (Regarding RWR's phony college attendance, Loduca said, "It never occurred to me the army doesn't check those things out, at least back then. Somehow they did not check that out.")

60. Calaveras County Bail Reduction Petition Denial; "Rackstraw, Plane Are Still Missing."

61. Ryan Coward (attorney), Administrative Separation Attorney, Court Martial Law, http://courtmartiallaw.com /denver-colorado-springs-co-administrative-separations--lawyer_pa15399.htm. (The page includes details about Article 15 of the Uniform Code of Military Justice.)

62. "Rackstraw Gets 3-Year Term," *Stockton Record.*

63. Petition for Writ of Habeas Corpus for RWR, Superior Court of California, Calaveras County, April 6, 1978. (Sueyres reported that FBI agents had spoken to Houston County Alabama Sheriff, "and he states that he holds a warrant of arrest for RWR for criminal fraud.") AP, "Rule Out Hijacking Suspect." (Sueyres said, "I think that's how the speculation started.") Loduca, interview by JJF, TJCC DVD #16, transcript p. 31, timecode 11.52.06. (Loduca said that in 1971, "he did tell us about when he was flying that airplane for the, um, real estate guy up north.") Remington and Flynn, "How 2 First Suggested Rackstraw-Cooper Link." (Stockton investigators "Buck and Murray said . . . that [RWR] was known to be flying for a real estate development company in the Washington area about the time of the hijacking.")

64. Application for Habeas Corpus for RWR, Superior Court of California, Calaveras County, April 17, 1978. (Defense attorney Dennis Roberts said, "The FBI has allegedly spoken to the Sheriff of Houston County who advises an arrest warrant for petitioner is outstanding. My client advises me his is the result of a lease surrender on a leased automobile, which took place in about 1971.") "How 2 First Suggested Rackstraw-Cooper Link." (In 1979 article, Stockton investigators revealed RWR told FBI in 1978 he was "flying for a real estate development company in the Washington area about the time of the hijacking.")

65. "Rackstraw Gets 3-Year Term." (The article summarizes RWR's charges, cases, and convictions: three years for check fraud, two concurrent years for illegal possession of explosives, grand theft of airplane, and another bad check charge.) Maloney, BHI Security Letter Synopsis; "Valley Springs Contractor Facing a Murder Charge"; "FBI Joins the Hunt for Missing Fugitive."

Chapter Five

1. Patty Mott (widow of James C. "Jim" Mott), phone interview by TJC, September 9, 2014, Notebook #2, letters and photos licensed from Patty.

2. Alexandre Dumas, *The Three Musketeers,* http://www.online-literature.com /dumas/threemusketeers. ("First serialised [sic] between March and July of 1844." Dumas writes of Baron de Winter in chapter 59, http://www.online-literature.com/dumas /threemusketeers/59.)

3. Wilfred P. "Willy" Wyffels (former priest), phone interview by TJC, May 9, 2012, Notebook #1.

4. Paul "P. K." Hoffman (pottery sculptor) phone interview by TJC, May 19, 2015, Notebook #2.; Roscoe, phone interview by TJC, December 22, 2011, Notebook #1.

5. Ray, e-mail to TJC, May 11, 2012. (The FAA documents indicate that RWR's commercial aviation licenses for planes and choppers began on June 7, 1971. RWR was discharged from the army two weeks later.) Loduca, interview by JJF, TJCC DVD #16, transcript page 31, timecode 11.52.06. (Loduca said that in 1971, "[RWR] did tell us about when he was flying that airplane for the, um, real estate guy up north.") Roscoe, phone interview by TJC, December 22, 2011, Notebook #1; Marian K. Soderberg, phone interview by TJC, September 10, 2014, Notebook #2; Hoffman, phone interview by TJC, May 19, 2015, Notebook #2; John E. Mattingly, phone interview by TJC, September 19, 2015, Notebook #2. (In the preceding four phone interviews, the Astoria residents—Roscoe, Soderberg, Hoffman, and Mattingly—all claimed that between July and October 1971, "Norman de Winter" told them he had a small plane at their town's unsupervised landing strip.) Loduca, interview by JJF, TJCC DVD #16, transcript page 31, timecode 11.52.06; Remington and Flynn, "How 2 First Suggested Rackstraw-Cooper Link." (Stockton investigators Charles Buck and Michael Murray said that on November 24, 1971, "a small plane was heard in the area near where the FBI believes D. B. Cooper bailed out . . . and that [RWR] was known to be flying for a real estate development company in the Washington area about the time of the hijacking.") McGarity, phone interview by JJF, HC-LMNO transcript p. 1, timecode 15:26:00. (In 1973, McGarity asked RWR, "Oh, you have a plane?" He replied, "Yes, I have a small Cessna.") Christopher Freeze (aviation forensic researcher), e-mail to TJC, October 20, 2015. (Freeze forwarded four pages of RWR's FAA records from a database; the database showed no record of any ownership registrations under his name.) McGarity, phone interview by JJF, HC-LMNO transcript p. 2, timecode 15:24:23. ("I called my parents and said, 'You won't believe I'm dating this guy that has a plane, a helicopter [Hughes 500], all these things.'") McGarity, phone interview by JJF, HC-LMNO transcript p. 1, timecode 15:22:27. (McGarity said that RWR told her, "'Let's fly up there in my [Bell 47G Sheriff] helicopter and visit with them' [his parents]. And I thought, wow, that sounds pretty neat." A photo of her kids in the Bell chopper is available.) Jay C. Todd (pseudonym, state police undercover investigator), phone interview by TJC, May 15, 2014, Notebook #2. (Todd offered the Master Criminal Whack-a-Mole Theory.)

6. "FBI Enters Armory Bombing, Weapons Theft Case in SC," *Santa Cruz Sentinel*, July 27, 1971, scanned clipping; Pudgy Hunt, interview by JJF, HC-LMNO transcript p. 13, timecode 12:19:03. (In 1971, Jim Spitznas Jr. [RWR's boss] "told us that the FBI contacted him, regarding Rackstraw. The armory had been broken into. And then [RWR], I guess, was an explosive expert in the service, so he knew how to work with plastic explosives.")

7. Loduca, phone interviews by TJC, June 25, 2013, and July 7, 2013, Notebook #2; Loduca, interview by JJF, TJCC DVD #16, transcript p. 32, timecodes 11.53.22 and 11.54.01.

8. Hoffman, phone interview, Notebook #2.

9. Wyffels, phone interview by TJC.

10. Roscoe, phone interviews by TJC, December 22, 2011, and May 2, 2012, Notebook #1. (Roscoe, a former councilman, discussed the town history during the three-month NdW conference.)

11. Soderberg, phone interview by TJC, September 10, 2014, Notebook #2.

12. Wyffels, phone interview by TJC; Wyffels, interview by JJF for an LMNO-History documentary, September 19, 2015. (In both of the preceding phone interviews, Wyffels said that his parents were invited on NdW's Christmas trip and that they prepared their passports.) Willis L. Van Dusen (former mayor), interview by Ted Skillman

(director) for the LMNO-History documentary, September 19, 2015, on-scene production notes by TJC, Notebook #2.

13. Patty Mott, e-mail to TJC, September 10, 2014. (Mott emailed TJC two scanned letters she discovered from Norman de Winter, mailed to her husband during college, dated September 2, 1971, and September 17, 1971; the letters reveal the con man's thought process and corroborate several incidents already relayed by Astoria witnesses.)

14. Soderberg, phone interview by TJC, September 10, 2014, Notebook #2. (NdW's "thank you" note is available.) David Palmberg (Soderberg's ex-husband), phone interview by TJC, November 6, 2014, Notebook #2.

15. James Allen, *As a Man Thinketh* (Sublime Books, July 21, 2013).

16. Mark J. Fick, phone interview by TJC, December 1, 2015, Notebook #2.)

17. Mattingly, phone interview.

18. Jeff A. Salo, phone interview by TJC, December 1, 2015, Notebook #2.

19. Roscoe, phone interview by TJC, December 22, 2011, Notebook #1; Pudgy Hunt, phone interview by TJC, April 24, 2012, Notebook #1. (During dinner at Roscoe's restaurant, Hunt told a story of "Hollywood producer" TJC calling him recently about a DBC documentary; at the table, Roscoe revealed there was a con artist in town in '71 that he had always thought could have been DBC; Hunt then dialed TJC and introduced Roscoe.)

20. Roscoe, phone interview by TJC, December 22, 2011, Notebook #1; Van Dusen, phone interview by TJC, May 2, 2012, Notebook #2.

21. Soderberg, phone interview by TJC, February 10, 2015, Notebook #2.

22. Hoffman, phone interview by TJC, May 19, 2015, Notebook #2. (Hoffman claimed he went to the airport looking for NdW's plane.)

23. Willy Wyffels, e-mail to TJC, June 5, 2012. (After viewing RWR's photos and a *KNBC News* interview, Wyffels wrote, "Do I recognize his talking style and how that fit into the whole picture of what was happening? Yes! He was so good at his evasiveness and I wasn't doubting enough to pick up on it.") Pete Roscoe, interview by TJC at Pudgy Hunt's Portland, Oregon, house, June 21, 2012, notes in Astoria folder. (Roscoe pointed at the *KNBC News* video of RWR and said, "That's Norman de Winter!") Roscoe, phone interview by TJC, March 14, 2013, Notebook #1. (Roscoe reflected back to the 2012 viewing of RWR on the KNBC video at Hunt's house. He said RWR "had an unusual head, and I recognized his mannerisms.") Jim Mott, phone message to TJC, June 22, 2012, Notebook #1. (After viewing RWR's photos and the *KNBC News* interview, Mott said, "Wow! Oh yeah; sounds like him, and that's the way he looked. Could almost hear the Swiss Baron. The way he looked down, I remember that too.")

24. Loduca, interview by JJF, TJCC DVD #16, transcript p. 31, timecode 11.52.06; Ibid., transcript p. 35, timecode 11.57.27. ("He wasn't happy with the army. He didn't have good things to say about it.")

25. Marks, phone interview, August 8, 2013, Notebook #2; Loduca, interview by JJF, TJCC DVD #16, transcript p. 161, timecode 16.15.33. ("Well, business-wise, when the finances started collapsing and all of that, he just runs out on us. He's just like escaping the second time. He ran out on people.")

26. Loduca, TJCC DVD #16, transcript p. 37, timecode 11.59.22.

27. Ibid., transcript p. 108, timecode 14:44:49. (Loduca provided another example of RWR justifying his crimes: "He goes, 'The owners really were okay with the [stolen] airplane. They get to collect the insurance.'") Loduca, phone interview by TJC, July 1, 2013, Notebook #2. (Loduca said that after Disneyland, after RWR returned her to Stockton

and his kids to his ex-wife in Santa Cruz, Loduca heard from her parents that RWR was "suddenly gone" again.)

28. Loduca, interview by JJF, TJCC DVD #16, transcript page 31, timecode 11.52.06.

29. "Guilty Plea to an Old Drug Charge," *Stockton Record*, March 11, 1972, scanned article. (A gun middleman in the 1971 Santa Cruz armory robbery, a drug dealer, got ten years in prison but did not give up the mastermind. The FBI suspected that RWR conducted this crime.) Marks, phone interview, August 8, 2013, Notebook #2. (Marks said the FBI visited her after the 1978 Mayday escape and mentioned that they believed RWR was responsible for 1971 Santa Cruz armory theft.) Pudgy Hunt, interview by JJF, HC-LMNO transcript p. 13, timecode 12:19:03.

30. Jim Mott, phone interview by TJC, May 4, 2012, Notebook #1.

31. Fred Jaross, phone interview by TJC, May 15, 2014, Notebook #2.

32. Gayle Downing, phone interview by TJC, May 16, 2014, Notebook #2.

33. Jaross, phone interview.

34. Pete Roscoe, interview by Ted Skillman, September 19, 2015, HC-LMNO transcript p. 1, timecode 17:57:15; Ibid., transcript p. 2, timecode 18:04:30. "They would rather not talk about it.") Roscoe, phone interview by TJC, March 10, 2015, Notebook #2.

35. Casey McNerthney, "No Fingerprints Found on Item in D. B. Cooper Case," *Seattle Post-Intelligencer*, August 1, 2011. (The reporter and cameraman heard Case Agent Carr say, "This is where he signed it." While the gate attendant originally claimed he signed all of the boarding passes, he later admitted there were some he didn't—because of being short-staffed, workers sometimes asked passengers to sign their own.) Bruce Smith, "The Hunt for D. B. Cooper—Who Was Cooper?" *Mountain News*, February 6, 2013, https://themountainnewswa.net/2013/02/06 /the-hunt-for-db-cooper-who-was-cooper-what-is-known. (According to stewardess Tina Mucklow, Cooper "had a low voice with no accent.")

36. Patty Mott, e-mail to TJC, September 10, 2014.

Chapter Six

1. LC (FBI case agent), comment on "D B Cooper Unsolved Skyjacking," January 7, 2008, 6:44 p.m., http://www.dropzone.com /cgi-bin/forum/gforum.cgi?post=3073672#3073672. (LC, self-identified under the name "Ckret," revealed that Cooper brought a "small sized paper bag" on the plane.)

2. UPI, "Skyjacker Eludes FBI." (The FBI described the hijacker as having a "dark complexion with black hair.") Galen Cook (attorney and DBC researcher), phone interview by TJC, February 3, 2014. (Stewardess Florence "Flo" Schaffner told Cook that DBC appeared to be "wearing dark make-up.") *Coast to Coast Radio*, transcript, March 7, 2009, first hour. ("Schaffner also revealed to Cook that D. B. Cooper had been wearing makeup to darken his skin.")

3. Richard E. Meyer, "The Legend of a Jet Age Jesse James," *Los Angeles Times*, December 6, 1996, front page.

4. *This Day In Aviation*, s.v. "24 November, 1971," last modified November 24, 2015, http://www.thisdayinaviation.com/tag/boeing-727-51. (The Boeing jet in the hijacking was first known as the 727-051, later simply the 727-100.)

5. Geoffrey Gray, "Unmasking D. B. Cooper," *New York Magazine*, October 21, 2007. ("She looked at the man's eyes. When she got back, the man was wearing dark sunglasses.")

6. Tallis, TJCC DVD 3A, transcript pp. 1–12, timecode 00:24:05. (Tallis was the first special agent on the scene for the Seattle landing; he also flew the search in a chopper; four years later, he was interviewed in a chopper by LMNO/History Channel.)

7. Robert Stack, "D. B. Cooper Mystery," *Unsolved Mysteries*, July 30, 2014. http://unsolvedmysteries.us/db-cooper-mystery/. (The research website for the show reveals the details surrounding Cooper's money demand.)

8. Bruce Smith, "The Hunt for DB Cooper—the Resurgent Investigation," *Mountain News*, September 1, 2011, https://themountainnewswa.net/2011/09/01/the-hunt-for-db-cooper-the-resurgent-investigation-into-americas-only-unsolved-skyjacking-an-overview/. (The article includes the official details surrounding DBC's parachute demand.)

9. Geoffrey Gray, *Skyjack: The Hunt for D. B. Cooper* (New York: Crown Books, 2011). (Gray, given access to the FBI files, revealed exactly what DBC drank.)

10. "Dan (DB) Cooper and America's Only Unsolved Hijacking," *HubPages*, April 30, 2012, http://hubpages.com/entertainment/Mystery-Files-DBCooper-and-Americas-Only-Unsolved-Hijacking.

11. Stacks, "D. B. Cooper Mystery."

12. LC, comment on "The Two Chutes," February 28, 2012, 5:35 p.m., http://www.dropzone.com/forum/Skydiving_C1/Skydiving_History_%26_Trivia_F21/DB_Cooper_P3110098-1296. (According to LC, Cooper told Mucklow that "McChord is only twenty minutes from Tacoma.") *Wikipedia*, s.v. "D. B. Cooper." (Cooper recognized Tacoma from the air.)

13. Todd, phone interview by TJC, May 15, 2014, Notebook #2.

14. LC, comment on "Tina Bar Money Find," December 5, 2007, 3:25 p.m., *DB Cooper Forum*, http://www.thedbcooperforum.com/index.php?topic=4.1045;wap2. ("Georger," a former college professor and DBC sleuth with both familial and professional contacts at the FBI, revealed the exact words, timeline, and discussions from the FBI transcripts and testimony that occurred during the hijacking. He also repeated LC's postings for others. A copy of LC's blog post is available.) *Crime Museum*, s.v. "D. B. Cooper," last modified April 7, 2016, www.crimemuseum.org/crime-library/d-b-cooper. (The library provided details on Cooper's chute delivery and the ransom cash arrival.) LC, comment on "D B Cooper Unsolved Skyjacking," December 16, 2007, 1:52 p.m., http://www.dropzone.com/forum/Skydiving_C1/Skydiving_History_%26_Trivia_F21/D_B_Cooper_Unsolved_Skyjacking_P2540834-28. (LC writes that Cooper "stated several times, 'no funny stuff.'") Ibid., December 5, 2007, 3:25 p.m. (LC writes that Cooper became "child-like," showed both stewardesses the money, and joked with them.) Smith, "The Hunt for D. B. Cooper—Who Was Cooper?" (LC said, "Tina and Flo report that Cooper even jumped up and down.")

15. LC, comment on "D B Cooper," June 8, 2008, 11:04 a.m., http://www.dropzone.com/forum/Skydiving_C1/Skydiving_History_%26_Trivia_F21/DB_Cooper_P3110098-90. (LC writes that the released first-class stewardess, Alice Hancock, made a return for her purse and had an exchange with Cooper.) Gray, *Skyjack: The Hunt for D. B. Cooper.* (Gray, with access to the DBC FBI case files, found the response quote that Cooper gave to Hancock.) Georger, comment on "Did Cooper Inspect the Chutes???" April 22, 2014, 4:51 p.m., *DB Cooper Forum*, http://www.thedbcooperforum.com/index.php?topic=6.msg745#msg745. (Georger wrote a long summary about the parachute preps Cooper conducted, through Mucklow's and Hancock's FBI eyewitness testimonies.)

16. Bill Mitchell (former FBI key witness), phone interview by TJC, March 10, 2015, Notebook #2.

17. Stack, "D. B. Cooper Mystery." (Passengers were told there was a "minor mechanical difficulty.")

18. Mitchell, phone interview. (Mitchell talked about surviving the hijacking, his ironic future career at Boeing, and how his casual eyewitness helped the FBI draw the second sketch.)

19. LC, comment on "D B Cooper," January 12, 2008, 1:02 p.m., http://www.dropzone.com/forum/Skydiving_C1/Skydiving_History_%26_Trivia_F21/DB_Cooper_P3110098-224. (LC writes about the "I just got a grudge" exchange.)

20. LC, comment on "D B Cooper Unsolved Skyjacking," December 19, 2007, 4:35 a.m., http://www.dropzone.com/cgi-bin/forum/gforum.cgi?post=3053726;search_string=the%20captain%20can%20do%20after%20we%20take;guest=208166507&t=search_engine#3053726. (LC writes that Cooper wanted the stairs down on takeoff, and he thought the captain controlled them from the cockpit.) LC, comment on "D B Cooper Unsolved Skyjacking," January 1, 2008, 2:41 p.m., http://www.dropzone.com/forum/Skydiving_C1/Skydiving_History_%26_Trivia_F21/D_B_Cooper_Unsolved_Skyjacking_P2540834-33. (LC writes that Cooper was "wrong as to how [the stairs] opened and knew little to nothing of their operation.")

21. LC, comment on "D B Cooper Unsolved Skyjacking," January 22, 2008, 9:30 p.m., http://www.dropzone.com/cgi-bin/forum/gforum.cgi?post=3092261;search_string=It%20would%20be%20pure%20speculation%20that%20Cooper%20had%20an%20altimeter;guest=208166507&t=search_engine#3092261. (LC writes, "It would be pure speculation that Cooper had an altimeter.")

22. Bruce Smith, "The Hunt for DB Cooper—Chapter 1: An Introduction," *Mountain News*, December 9, 2012, https://themountainnewswa.net/2012/12/09/the-hunt-for-db-cooper-chapter-1-an-introduction-to-the-case-and-the-mystery/. (The copilot described DBC as a "smart guy," with "uncanny knowledge on covert specs.)

23. Manley Jr., phone interview by TJC, June 11, 2015, Notebook #2; Overturf, e-mails to TJC; Mike Machat (writer and artist), "Did He Get Away?" November 28, 2014, http://www.airlineratings.com/news.php?id=397. (The article documents the CIA's secret flight history at Thailand's Takhli Air Base during the Vietnam War.)

24. Smith, "The Hunt for D. B. Cooper—Who Was Cooper?" (The article documents the flight route of Victor-23 and the brilliance of how Cooper indirectly selected it.) LC, comment on "D B Cooper Unsolved Skyjacking," January 28, 2008, 11:13 a.m., http://www.dropzone.com/cgi-bin/forum/gforum.cgi?post=3100109;search_string=neither%20requested%20Victor%2023;guest=208166507&t=search_engine#3100109. (LC writes, "neither requested Victor 23.")

25. Gray, *Skyjack*, 78; Smith, "The Hunt for DB Cooper—the Resurgent Investigation." (Smith writes, "Tosaw also says Cooper waved goodbye.") Georger, comment on "Did Cooper Inspect the Chutes???" April 22, 2014, 4:51 p.m., *DB Cooper Forum*, http://www.thedbcooperforum.com/index.php?topic=6.msg745#msg745.

26. LC, comment on "D B Cooper," March 30, 2008, 2:13 p.m., http://www.dropzone.com/cgi-bin/forum/gforum.cgi?post=3168175;search_string=I%20think%20he%20is%20getting%20ready%20to%20jump;guest=208166507&t=search_engine#3168175. (LC writes that Tina entered the cockpit saying "I think he is getting ready to jump.") Georger, comment on "Did Cooper Inspect the Chutes???" April 22, 2014, 4:51 p.m., *DB Cooper Forum*, http://www.thedbcooperforum.com

/index.php?topic=6.msg745#msg745. (Georger provides more parachute and money-packing details from Tina.)

27. LC, comment on "D B Cooper Unsolved Skyjacking," December 19, 2007, 4:49 a.m., http://www.dropzone.com/cgi-bin/forum/gforum.cgi?post=3053737;search_string =The%20captain%20leveled%20and%20slowed;guest=208166507&t =search_engine#3053737. (LC writes that Cooper couldn't lower the steps, so he asked the crew to slow down and stabilize the jet, and then he jumped.) LC, comment on "D B Cooper Unsolved Skyjacking," January 9, 2008, 4:09 a.m., http://www.dropzone .com/cgi-bin/forum/gforum.cgi?post=3075528;search_string =found%20through%20testing%20the%20only%20way%20to%20cause%2 ;guest=208166507&t=search_engine#30755288. (LC writes, "It was found through testing the only way to cause this pressure bump was by the stairs hitting back against the aircraft when a weight was removed.") Georger, comment on "Did Cooper Inspect the Chutes???" April 22, 2014, 4:51 p.m., *DB Cooper Forum*, http://www.thedbcooperforum.com /index.php?topic=6.msg745#msg745. (Georger describes Cooper's last five minutes on the stairs, saying Cooper was "looking for an opportunity to jump.")

28. Remington and Flynn, "How 2 First Suggested Rackstraw-Cooper Link." (Stockton investigators Charles Buck and Michael Murray said that on November 24, 1971, "a small plane was heard in the area near where the FBI believes D. B. Cooper bailed out . . . and that [RWR] was known to be flying for a real estate development company in the Washington area about the time of the hijacking.")

29. Overturf, e-mail to TJC, May 12, 2015.

30. Marilyn Newton (photo librarian and photographer), phone call to TJC, July 9, 2014. (Newton's call was in response to an e-mail from TJC. She said she was the first still photographer at the landing; she shot the aircraft, the crew departing for the FBI meeting, and the dog going onboard.)

31. William Kroger, "Skyjack Beat: Rumors, Tension," *Nevada State Journal*, November 26, 1971, front page.

32. Phil Barber, "FBI Figures $200,000 Hijacker Bailed Out Before Reno Landing," *Reno Evening Gazette*, November 25, 1971, front page.

33. "FBI: Hot on the Trail of DB Cooper with Fresh Lead?"; *Sky Valley News*, August 8, 2011, front page, http://www.skyvalleychronicle.com/BREAKING-NEWS /FRESH-LEAD-IN-AMERICA-S-MOST-INFAMOUS-UNSOLVED-SKYJACKING -CASE-729895.

34. UPI, "Skyjacker Eludes FBI."

35. Downing, phone interview.

36. "Skyjacker Note Words Clipped from Newspaper."

37. Gray, *Skyjack*.

38. Bruce Smith, "DB Cooper—Top Ten Questions for the FBI," *Mountain News*, September 30, 2015, www.themountainnewswa.net/2015/09/30 /top-ten-db-cooper-questions-for-the-fbi/. ("No one went looking for him until the next day, giving Cooper an 11-hour headstart.")

39. Gray, *Skyjack*; http://huntfordbcooper.com/spy-plane-searches-for-cooper. (The author's book website, which is no longer available, included a photo and an article on the SR-71 Spy Plane's involvement in the search.)

40. Tallis, TJCC DVD #3A, transcript pp. 1–12, timecode 00:24:05.

41. Galen G. Cook, interview by George Noory, *Coast to Coast* AM Talk Radio, June 6, 2012, http://www.coasttocoastam.com/pages/the-d-b-cooper-letters; Bruce Smith, "The Hunt for DB Cooper—Letter Sent by 'DB Cooper' Is Now Causing a Flap," *Mountain News*, June 18, 2012, https://themountainnewswa.net/2012/06/18 /the-hunt-for-db-cooper-letter-sent-by-db-cooper-in-1971-is-now-causing-a-flap/.

42. Roscoe, phone interview by TJC, December 22, 2011, Notebook #1; Marian K. Soderberg, phone interview by TJC, September 10, 2014, Notebook #2; Hoffman, phone interview by TJC, May 19, 2015, Notebook #2; John E. Mattingly, phone interview by TJC, September 19, 2015, Notebook #2; Loduca, TJCC DVD #16, transcript page 31, timecode 11.52.06; Remington and Flynn, "How 2 First Suggested Rackstraw-Cooper Link."

43. Cook, interview by Noory. (In a radio transcript posted online, Cook revealed that the first two DBC letters end with the same close: "Thanks for Hospitality" in cut-and-pasted words and "Thanks for your hospitality" in handwriting.)

44. Linton A. Mohammed, "Document Examination Report, Re: DBC Investigation," November 17, 2014, scanned document. (Mohammed, a renowned forensic document examiner, compares writing samples between RWR, Norman de Winter, and Dan Cooper.) Casey McNerthney, "No Fingerprints Found on Item in D. B. Cooper Case," *Seattle Post-Intelligencer*, August 1, 2011.

45. Mark J. Fick, phone interview by TJC, May 16, 2014, Notebook #2. (Fick also scanned and e-mailed TJC his own pair of NdW letters, which arrived on December 9, 1971, and December 14, 1971.)

46. Downing, phone interview. (Downing said that Norman "said everything a brokenhearted woman would want to hear.") Dan Hunt, interview by TJC, TJCC DVD #1, transcript p. 6, timecode 00.08.55. ("If it came down to women, he'd tell 'em exactly what they wanted to hear. None of it would be the truth.") Pudgy Hunt, interview by JJF, HC-LMNO transcript p. 5, timecode 11:57:16; Bob Keefer, "Flyer Quizzed in 'D. B. Cooper' Probe." *Long Beach Independent Press Telegram*, February 3 1979, scanned article. (Sueyres said, "Rackstraw is "a helluva con man—you'd buy a used car from him every time.") Loduca, interview by JJF, TJCC DVD #16, transcript p. 14, timecode 11.21.26. (RWR "used his charm to manipulate; he grew a penchant for lying. Truth was definitely a casualty in that case, and he didn't seem concerned if it hurt somebody.")

47. Loduca, interview by JJF, TJCC DVD #16, transcript p. 32, timecode 11.53.38.

48. Cook, interview by Noory.

49. Todd, phone interview by TJC, May 15, 2014, Notebook #2.

50. Loduca, bulldozer photo, date-stamped June, 1972. (RWR's kids came to visit their divorced father in Valley Springs, California; their grandmother Lucille took a picture of two-year-old Robby Jr. riding on his grandfather Philip's lap while Philip was working a bulldozer; Loduca inherited the photo from her mother's estate.) "'Biggest Project' Means Trouble for Contractor," *Stockton Record*, December 22, 1977, scanned clipping. (Sergeant Marvin Krein said RWR had lived in Valley Springs for four or five years, meaning 1972–73.) Calaveras County Court, California Department of Fish and Game, Deer-Poaching Incident in Valley Springs, on or around November 4, 1972, scanned document. (Philip Rackstraw told the Calaveras County judge that RWR was in Laos, too "busy" to respond to his letter about RWR missing his court appearance for poaching a deer; according to court records, the poaching fine of $125 was paid on January 2, 1973, but it does not specify by whom.) "Body of Local Man Identified—Stepson Charged with

Murder," *Calaveras Enterprise*, March 1, 1978, front page, scanned article. (The article states that RWR's last-known address was in Rancho Calaveras in Valley Springs, where "he operated 3R Engineering Contractors . . . for about five years," meaning that he left in 1973.) UPI, "Two Hurt in Helicopter Crash," May 4, 1973, scanned article. (The Iowa-based article states that RWR said his home was Valley Springs, California.)

Chapter Seven

1. Calaveras County Bail Reduction Petition Denial; San Joaquin County DA Petition for Writ of Habeas Corpus; "Rackstraw, Plane Are Still Missing"; Loduca, interview by JJF, TJCC DVD #16, transcript pp. 152 and 35, timecodes 16.01.02 and 11.57.09. (An FBI agent at Loduca's house told her of her brother's "angry letter" to army brass. Loduca said, "Bob had been asked, or told to leave the army . . . He wasn't happy with the army. He didn't have good things to say about it." He described the military as "politics as usual, and I didn't fit in with that.")

2. Marks, phone interview, August 8, 2013, Notebook #2. (Marks said that years later RWR admitted, "alcohol destroyed my first marriage.") Ibid., (Marks discussed being choked over the sink; she also revealed that on her MP-escorted return to her mobile home to prepare for her California car trip home with her kids, she told the sulking RWR, "This is all your fault, Bob.")

3. Calaveras County Court, California Department of Fish and Game, Deer-Poaching Incident.

4. Loduca, phone interview by TJC, June 25, 2013, Notebook #2; Loduca interview by JJF, TJCC DVD #16, transcript p. 32, timecode 11.53.22. (RWR "had told Dad not to tell anyone he was there.") Ibid., transcript p. 19, timecode 11.30.33. ("Dad stuck up for him more times than he should.")

5. Loduca, wedding photo. (Loduca inherited the photo from her mother's estate.) Gail Marks' Child Support Petition, Santa Cruz County, October 27, 1975, scanned document. (The petition record states that RWR was $16,800 in arrears; Marks also claimed he had never written one child-support check in those first five years.) Marks, phone interview, August 12, 2013, Notebook #2; "Divorces Filed," *Santa Cruz Sentinel*; Loduca, interview by JJF, TJCC DVD #16, transcript p. 16, timecode 11.25.48.

6. Loduca, interview by JJF, TJCC DVD #16, transcript p. 44, timecode 12:09:47. ("He was definitely living in San Jose at that time. There was another girlfriend in between" RWR's failed marriage and mistress.) Ibid., transcript p. 37, timecode 12.00.05. ("He would say that he was up north, um, doing construction.") Steve Woods, phone interview by TJC; Loduca, interview by JJF, TJCC DVD #16, transcript page 31, timecode 11.52.06.

7. "Helicopter Drops on Sweeney Farm," *Altoona Herald*, May 10, 1973, front page, article written from screen, notes in Non-Perps folder. (Survivors said they made a "good landing, but the copter pitched over . . . breaking off the tail section.") AP, "Copter Crashes near Altoona," April 29, 1973, article written from screen, notes in Non-Perps folder. ("Polk County authorities called for State Bureau of Criminal Investigation and FBI agents to join in investigating the crash.") UPI, "Two Unhurt in Helicopter Crash." ("The men were identified as Robert Wesley Rackstraw, 29, of Valley Springs, Calif.") David B. Sweeney (farmer's son), phone interview by TJC, March 9, 2016, Notebook #2. ("They seemed suspicious. Where they smuggling drugs? Special agents, not regular deputies arrived.") National Transportation Safety Board Report Identification: MKC73FCD61,

File 3-1357, Investigation, Enstrom F-28A, May 4, 1973. (After "power-off autorotative landing, the chopper received 'substantial' damage.")

8. McGarity, phone interview by JJF, HC-LMNO transcript p. 1, timecode 15:22:27; Loduca, interview by JJF, TJCC DVD #16, transcript page 45, timecode 12:11:39. ("He had married Linda and she had a house from a previous marriage and it was a track, nice track house in Cupertino [California].") Pudgy Hunt, interview by TJC, TJCC DVD #1, transcript p. 26, timecode 00.51.58. ("I recall Rackstraw telling Mike Narro that he either owned or was running a Radio Shack in the area.")

9. Pudgy Hunt, interview by TJC, TJCC DVD #1, transcript page 26, timecode 00.51.58. (The floor company boss, Mike Narro, "saw Rackstraw in the restaurant. Recognized him. They kinda hugged each other. And they had, they had been in the paratroopers together.") Pudgy Hunt, interview by JJF, HC-LMNO transcript p. 3, timecode 11:49:57; Carol Mohr, phone interview by TJC, October 2, 2015, notes in Non-Perps folder. (Pudgy Hunt's former girlfriend, who was sitting with Hunt at Denny's, told the story of the Narro-Rackstraw reunion to TJC when he tracked her down. Mohr's adult daughter had posted her mother's story on Tumblr.com without her mother's knowledge.)

10. "Army Airman from SC Wins Distinguished Flying Cross."

11. Oregon Sports Hall of Fame and Museum, 2007, http://oregonsportshall. org/?page_id=171.

12. "Class of 1962 Graduates," *Oregonian*, June 4, 1962, 16. (The article includes a listing of Briggs's bachelor of education.) "University of Oregon at Eugene passed the 8000 mark of enrollment" (photo caption), *Oregonian*, October 1, 1961, 21. (Briggs is number 8000; the photo is of him paying tuition.)

13. Pudgy Hunt, interview by TJC, TJCC DVD #1, transcript p. 45, timecode 12:11:39. ("I went in the University of Oregon. And I pledged the ATO house. And Dick Briggs was one of the pledges. And we became pretty good friends right away.")

14. Connie Cunningham Hunt, interview by TJC, TJCC DVD #1, transcript p. 20, timecode 00.41.10. ("The first time I met Jon Briggs, I was, uh, dating my now husband of thirty-four years.")

15. McGarity, phone interview by JJF, HC-LMNO transcript p. 1, timecode 15:22:27. (RWR said, "'Let's fly up there in [my Bell 47G] helicopter and visit with them.' And I thought wow, that sounds pretty neat." A photo of her children in the chopper is available.)

16. Ibid., HC-LMNO transcript p. 2, timecode 15:26:34. ("He proceeded to surprise me with this big weekend trip; it was two days there in Lake Tahoe. He had a car waiting for us.")

17. Loduca, interview by JJF, TJCC DVD #16, transcript page 45, timecode 12:11:39.

18. Ibid., transcript p. 66, timecode 12:44:48. They let him go [because] he's part of the Sheriff's Department.")

19. McGarity, phone interview by JJF, HC-LMNO transcript p. 2, timecode 15:26:34. ("'I want you to go to a boutique,' he mentioned. I thought, boutique? If it's not Dillard's and Macy's, I didn't know what a boutique was at that time.")

20. Pudgy Hunt, interview by TJC, TJCC DVD #1, transcript p. 28, timecode 00.55.06. ("At Pepperdine University, we did a poured urethane basketball court. And Bob Rackstraw worked on that job with us.") Pudgy Hunt, interview by JJF, HC-LMNO transcript p. 2, timecode 11:49:16. ("Rackstraw was working on a [Pepperdine] job at the time so, you know, I just introduced [Briggs] and we were all working together.") Dan

Hunt, interview by TJC, TJCC DVD #1, transcript p. 3, timecode 00.03.55. ("I met Bob Rackstraw down at, in Malibu. We were doing the Pepperdine job.")

21. Pudgy Hunt, interview by TJC, TJCC DVD #1, transcript p. 28, timecode 00.55.06. ("We did tennis courts [near] the LA airport. And Bob Rackstraw worked on that job with us.") Ibid., transcript p. 1, timecode 00.01.11 (Pudgy Hunt showed a photo of Charlton Heston in a group with Dan Hunt, RWR, and two unnamed coworkers; the photo was licensed from owner Pudgy Hunt.) Dan Hunt, interview by JJF for an LMNO-History documentary, September 18, 2015, transcript p. 3, timecode 11:52:19. (At the Rod Laver Racket Club, "It was a party, [a] celebration that the job was complete, and we were playing, Rackstraw and myself and Brian, playing foosball with Charlton Heston.")

22. Pudgy Hunt, interview by JJF, HC-LMNO transcript p. 4, timecode 11:53:40; Pudgy Hunt, interview by TJC, TJCC DVD #1, transcript p. 28, timecode 00.56.27. ("Bob was a member of the Playboy Club. And he said, 'Come on, I'll take you guys")

23. Jan Cleveland, "New Ken Hubbs Gymnasium will be floored with durable polyurethane," *San Bernardino Sun-Telegram*, June 23, 1974, scanned article. (The article includes photos of Dan Hunt and RWR.) Marks, phone interview, August 12, 2013, Notebook #2; Loduca, interview by JJF, TJCC DVD #16, transcript p. 11, timecode 11.15.28. (Loduca discussed RWR's fake licenses for truck jobs.) Dan Hunt, interview by TJC, TJCC DVD #1, transcript p. 7, timecode 00.08.55. (Hunt said, "Bob wouldn't tell the truth because that was part of who he was. He would get to where he wanted to go by not telling the truth.")

24. McGarity, phone interview by JJF, HC-LMNO transcript p. 2, timecode 15:24:23; Freeze, e-mail to TJC.

25. McGarity, licensed photos, September 13, 2013, scanned copies. (McGarity provided photos of her wedding, honeymoon, Easter, the Pepperdine floor repair, and Christmas.)

26. McGarity, phone interview by JJF, HC-LMNO transcript pp. 3–4, timecodes 15:35:06 and 15:36:17. (McGarity said RWR "talked the guy into putting most of his retirement money into this print shop. I've never been to the print shop. . . . He went and signed my name on it as [a] mortgage, or owner of the print shop without me knowing about it," so McGarity had a lien against her house.) Loduca, interview by JJF, TJCC DVD #16, transcript pp. 46–47, timecode 12:13:13. ("I believe that was the business [McGarity] had put her house up to get financing for and they ended up losing it. There was also some good friends that lived a couple doors down. They had also put their house up and lost it.") Calaveras County Archives Search, County Recorder, January 15, 2013, scanned article. (There were two court judgments related to printing: Doc BK4206PG342, December 13, 1976, Dick A B Company; and Doc BK4318PG313, October 17, 1977, JC Paper Company Inc.)

27. McGarity, phone interview by TJC, August 19, 2013, Notebook #2. (McGarity said inside RWR's briefcase, she "found business paperwork, cards, and disguise—mustache and brown toupees.") McGarity, phone interview by JJF, HC-LMNO transcript p. 3, timecode 15:32:27.

Chapter Eight

1. Dan Hunt, interview by TJC, TJCC DVD #1, transcript p. 7, timecode 00.09.56. ("Here I was country boy. And he, you know, was accomplished. Vietnam vet. Medals. Helicopter pilot. I was of course, impressed.")

2. Dan Hunt, phone interview by TJC, August 19, 2013, Notebook #2. (Hunt was RWR's coworker for two and a half years; they spent time on the road together for floor company assignments); Dan Hunt, interview by TJC, TJCC DVD #1, transcript pp. 7–17, timecode 00.08.18; Dan Hunt, interview by JJF, HC-LMNO transcript p. 18, timecode 11:52:19; Ibid., transcript p. 18, timecode 12:33:10.

3. McGarity, phone interview by JJF, HC-LMNO transcript p. 9, timecode 15:59:10.

4. Dan Hunt, interview by JJF, HC-LMNO transcript p. 7, timecode 12:01:12. (RWR told the cop, "I don't have my license." The cop asked him, "What's your name?" to which he replied, "Pudgy Hunt.")

5. Dan Hunt, interview by TJC, TJCC DVD #1, transcript pp. 9–23, timecode 00.13.23.

6. Pudgy Hunt, phone interview by TJC, April 1, 2015, Notebook #2; Dan Hunt, phone interview by TJC, April 1, 2015, Notebook #2. (The floor company boss, Jim Spitznas Jr., called Pudgy, saying that the FBI was "looking at" RWR for explosives and a "hometown armory break-in." Spitznas also added that Rackstraw makes him nervous.) Pudgy Hunt, interview by JJF, HC-LMNO transcript p. 13, timecode 12:19:03. ("The FBI contacted him regarding Rackstraw. Rackstraw was working with us then. It had to do with explosives being stolen . . . [and] an armory.")

7. AP, "Dynamite Stolen at Felton," February 19, 1975, scanned article. (The FBI told RWR's coworkers and his sister that RWR was a suspect in this theft.) Tom Honig, "No Suspects in Dynamite Yet," *Santa Cruz Sentinel*, February 19, 1975, scanned article; AP, "Terrorist Bombings Will Likely Continue," May 24, 1976, scanned article; AP, "Stolen Felton Explosives: Bombers Plead Guilty," June 23, 1976, scanned article. (The explosives RWR was suspected of stealing that were found in the Richmond bomb factory came from the Felton Quarry.) Townsend, "Airplane Crash Could Be a Hoax." (Rackstraw was named as a 1975 quarry explosives theft suspect in this article.)

8. UPI, "California Bomb Blasts Occurring Once a Week," March 29, 1975, scanned article.

9. Bob Keefer, "Flyer Quizzed in D. B. Cooper Probe." (The county DA claimed he learned through the FBI that RWR "had been investigated for a possible role" in a 1975 PG&E power-line bombing.)

10. AP, "Predawn Raid by FBI Wins Judge's Okay," June 11, 1976, scanned article; AP, "Four Bombers Sentenced," August 10, 1976, scanned article.

11. Townsend, "Airplane Crash Could Be Hoax"; Marks, phone interview, August 8, 2013, Notebook #2. (Gail told TJC that the FBI visited her after the 1978 Mayday escape; the FBI mentioned they believed her ex, RWR, was responsible for the 1971 Santa Cruz armory theft.) Jones, phone interview by TJC.

12. AP, "Predawn Raid by FBI Wins Judge's Okay." "Police Believe Man in Custody Is Rackstraw," *Stockton Record*, January 27, 1979, front page, scanned article.

Chapter Nine

1. James T. Shell, interview by JJF for the HC-LMNO documentary, September 18, 2015, transcript p. 5, timecode 14:08:16. (Schotz provided TJC with the full transcript.) Ibid., transcript p. 6, timecode 14:10:13.

2. James T. Shell, phone interview by TJC, June 30, 2013, Notebook #2. (Shell heard Briggs occasionally say that RWR was DBC.) Shell, phone interview by TJC, January 22, 2015, Notebook #2. (Shell remembered Briggs telling drug runners in a Bentley in Febru-

ary 1979 that he was DBC; he also remembered hosting a party where Briggs bragged about a money plant; Shell was busy hosting the party and didn't catch the details, but he "sensed Briggs and Rackstraw were up to no good.") Shell, interview by JJF, HC-LMNO transcript p. 8, timecode 14:15:10. This guy was, to me, a little different.")

3. Sonia Finkle, phone interview by TJC, October 18, 2012, Notebook #1.

4. Dan Hunt, phone interview by TJC, February 2, 2015, Notebook #2.

5. Gail Marks' Child Support Petition, Santa Cruz County. (Marks claimed that RWR threatened to blow up her car over child-support issues.)

6. Loduca, interview by JJF, TJCC DVD #16, transcript p. 112, timecode 14.50.18. (Loduca said, "I was executor of the estate" for her murdered stepfather, Philip. "Bob had given it up.") Calaveras County Superior Court, Estate of Philip George Rackstraw, Declination to Act, May 4, 1978, scanned article. (Facing the charge of murdering his stepfather, RWR declined to act as the victim's estate executor and nominated his sister.) Loduca, phone interview by TJC, July 15, 2013, Notebook #2. (As the estate executor, Loduca redirected the $7,000 due RWR from her stepfather's will to Gail Marks for child support; State Child Services redirected $10,000 for RWR's workers' compensation reward to Gail Marks for child support.)

7. California Franchise Tax Board Suspension Records, October 23, 2012, Contractor Licenses: First Team Construction, formerly doing business as American Construction Team (ACT)—Outstanding Liability Suspension; Federal Tax Lien Release on ACT, original filing September 16, 1991, release date April 4, 1994. (The lien was for the amount of $7,854.) Pudgy Hunt, interview by JJF, HC-LMNO transcript p. 14, timecode 12:21:27. (Pudgy said RWR "stole a job from Mike [Narro] in Hawaii" in 1977 and worked it with Narro's competitor Woods in Eugene, Oregon; RWR later told Pudgy, "Mike [Narro] and I kind of broke off.")

8. McGarity, phone interview by JJF, HC-LMNO transcript pp. 3–4, timecode 15:35:06; Loduca, interview by JJF, TJCC DVD #16, transcript pp. 46–47, timecode 12:13:13.

9. McGarity, phone interview by JJF, HC-LMNO transcript p. 4, timecode 15:37:27. (McGarity said, "[RWR] always had a way of soothing things over. 'I'm gonna take care of your family, don't worry.' But it was a shock to think that hearing my house was put up as [collateral], and one of my neighbors, he had swindled him out of putting up for his print shop. So we rented a [Valley Springs] house, and it was up on the hill maybe five miles from his parents' home.")

10. Calaveras County Archives Search, January 15, 2013. (There were two court judgments against Fargo Graphics and Printing: Doc BK4206PG342, December 13, 1976, Dick A B Company; and Doc BK4318PG313, October 17, 1977, JC Paper Company Inc.)

11. AP, "Hijacker Who Jumped from Jet Indicted," November 25, 1976, scanned article.

12. Susan Gilmore, "D. B. Cooper Puzzle: The Legend Turns 30," *Seattle Times*, November 22, 2001, http://community.seattletimes.nwsource.com/archive/?date =20011122&slug=cooper22m; George Tibbits, AP, "After 25 Years, Legend of D. B. Cooper Lives On," November 24, 1996. http://www.deseretnews.com/article/526865 /AFTER-25-YEARS-LEGEND-OF-DB-COOPER-LIVES-ON.html?pg=all.

13. McGarity, phone interview by JJF, HC-LMNO transcript p. 5, timecode 15:42:51. ("He had been gone probably four or five days on some venture that I have no idea what he was [working] on.)

14. Ibid., HC-LMNO transcript p. 6, timecode 15:45:15; Calaveras County Record of Funeral, June 3, 1977, Lucille Lillian Rackstraw, Number 225, scanned document. (Lucille Rackstraw's registered religion was Jehovah's Witness.)

15. McGarity, phone interview by JJF, HC-LMNO transcript pp. 8 and 7, timecodes 15:55:08 and 15:51:19. As soon as I got back to Texas, that's when I got the phone call from him, that his lawyer was mailing me, [asking] am I contesting the divorce. And I was like, of course I want a divorce.) McGarity, phone interview by TJC, August 21, 2013, Notebook #2. (McGarity packed for her parents' home, Houston, Texas.)

16. Yontel, phone interview by JJF, HC-LMNO transcript p. 12, timecode 00:56:14.

17. Loduca, interview by JJF, TJCC DVD #16, transcript pp. 20 and 25, timecodes 11.31.35 and 11.44.31. ("Mom always said that dad would never let her spank us. . . . When we became a family, the word stepfather, stepson never entered the house, never entered the conversation.")

18. Marks, phone interview by TJC, August 12, 2013, Notebook #2.

Chapter Ten

1. Pudgy Hunt, interview by TJC, TJCC DVD #1, transcript p. 1, timecode 00.01.31. ("Once [Dick Briggs] started runnin' around with Rackstraw, Rackstraw planned things. And Dick started following what Rackstraw was doin'.")

2. Flip Cordoba (pseudonym, coworker), phone interview by TJC, August 8, 2011, Notebook #2. (Cordoba stopped cooperating, saying, "he'd kill me.")

3. Pudgy Hunt, interview by TJC, TJCC DVD #1, transcript p. 1, timecode 00.01.31; Pudgy Hunt, interview by JJF, HC-LMNO transcript p. 15, timecode 12:25:37.

4. Gail Marks, interview by TJC, August 12, 2013, Notebook #2.

5. Pudgy Hunt, interview by TJC, TJCC DVD #1, transcript p. 1, timecode 00.02.06. ("Briggs told of another time with Rackstraw, stealin' a Volkswagen, puttin' it [in the] back of a two-and-a-half-ton truck, strippin' it, puttin' the carcass out on the, some side road between wherever they were and, and comin' in to San Francisco. And, uh, these were all done, you know, in the, the daylight.")

6. Yontel, phone interview by JJF, HC-LMNO transcript p. 9, timecode 00:40:27.

7. Dan Hunt, interview by JJF, HC-LMNO transcript p. 18, timecode 12:33:10. ("Mike Narro and Flip told me not to let him steal any vehicles.") Pudgy Hunt, interview by TJC, TJCC DVD #1, transcript p. 1, timecode 00.02.06.

8. Yontel, phone interview by JJF, HC-LMNO transcript p. 19, timecode 01:20:22.

9. John Bocciolatt, phone interviews by TJC, June 11, 2012, and June 15, 2012, Notebook #1. (Bocciolatt provided the background on Briggs's death report and discussed cocaine sweeping Portland in 1970s.) Ray Tursik (former sergeant and author), phone interview by TJC, May 2, 2012, Notebook #1. (Tursik provided background information about cocaine sweeping Portland in 1970s.)

10. Shell, phone by TJC, June 30, 2013, Notebook #2. ("I've kept out of the limelight . . . Dick [Briggs's] life was an open and closed book.") Shell, interview by JJF, HC-LMNO transcript p. 12, timecode 14:24:03. ("I remember one day we walked into the shop, and he'd throw us like bags, like full of diamonds. And I'd just go, Dick, I, I don't even wanna know.")

11. Carlson, interview by TJC, TJCC DVD #7, transcript pp. 1 and 4, timecodes 00.01.45 and 00.08.30. ("I was introduced to [Dick Briggs] by a longtime friend of his who'd gone to school with him, [Jim Shell], who had previously been our cocaine sup-

plier. And we [Carlson and Verne Burke] started selling larger quantities . . . All of a sudden this news alert came by. They found like $6,000 of DB Cooper's money buried. I wake up my partner. I say, Verne, get up, you got to see this.")

12. Pudgy Hunt, interview by JJF, HC-LMNO transcript p. 14, timecode 12:21:42. (RWR "came in one night [to Portland], just out of the blue, and he said, 'I'm working with a company out of California. We're doing a floor job up in Woodburn.' Herb Woods says, 'that son of a bitch [RWR], he stole all my equipment!' He said he ran a truck right through the door of our warehouse.") Steve Woods, phone interview by TJC. ("My father hired [RWR] to teach me and workers how to use the polyurethane pouring machine.")

13. Yontel, phone interview by JJF, HC-LMNO transcript p. 28, timecode 01:51:51.

14. Pudgy Hunt, interview by JJF, HC-LMNO transcript p. 14, timecodes 12:21:27 and 12:21:42. (RWR "stole a job from [his old boss] Mike Narro, in Hawaii. That was the one that he borrowed the machine from the Woods.") Steve Woods, phone interview by TJC.

15. California Franchise Tax Board Suspension Records; Federal Tax Lien Release on ACT; Loduca, interview by JJF, TJCC DVD #16, transcript p. 49, timecode 12:16:48. ("When Mom got sick, Dad was drinking a lot. Bob moving up there was supposedly [to] help Dad to take care of the business and keep it going and everything. And then he just kind of took it over, Bob did. Bob wasn't good to his word and that he was lying to customers.") George Hoeper, "War Hero Says Criminal Charges Part of Campaign 'to Get Him'"; (In the murder trial, RWR blamed envious contractors for the attacks and the murder.) Calaveras County Probate of Murder Victim Philip Rackstraw. (Page 7 of the probate is an unpaid fourteen-month insurance bill [August 31, 1976, to October 31, 1977] to 3R Engineering for $997.)

16. "First Rackstraw Case Witnesses," *Stockton Record*, July 14, 1978, scanned clipping. (The DA in the murder trial told the jury that RWR's stepfather, Philip Rackstraw, had "expressed fear of his stepson, and said he wished to sever their partnership in the construction business.") Loduca, phone interview by TJC, July 15, 2013, Notebook #2; Loduca, interview by JJF, TJCC DVD #16, transcript p. 51, timecode 12:19:31.

17. Loduca, interview by JJF, TJCC DVD #16, transcript pp. 51–53, timecode 12:20:28. ("During Mom's illness, [Philip Rackstraw] had been drinking a lot. And he had met this lady that was a sister of one of the neighbors. I was okay with him dating somebody else. He could not take care of himself, and his life and his business and everything else, without a woman to do it with him. I know that Bob was unhappy about Dad dating somebody else.")

18. McGarity, phone interview by JJF, HC-LMNO transcript p. 6, timecode 15:45:15; Loduca, TJCC DVD #16, transcript p. 15, timecode 11.23.28. (In discussion with RWR's fiancée Gail, Loduca said, "You shouldn't marry him. He's already lied to you. He's already got other women.")

Chapter Eleven

1. "Lucille Rackstraw," obituary, *Calaveras Prospect*, 12, scanned article.

2. Yontel, phone interview by JJF, HC-LMNO transcript p. 24, timecode 01:41:09. ("I went to the funeral service with Bob and, you know, it was . . . it was very sad.") Loduca, interview by JJF, TJCC DVD #16, transcript p. 52, timecodes 12:22:47 and 12:24:21. (Loduca said, "Quite frankly, what I told him was Mom and Dad's marriage ended when she was so sick, basically. And so, you know, say a year ago. It's been a year . . . Bob said, 'Mom hasn't been dead for two months and he's seeing this lady, the neighbor's sister.'")

3. Marks, phone interview by TJC, August 12, 2013, Notebook #2.

4. Dan Hunt, interview by TJC, TJCC DVD #1, transcript p. 18, timecode 00.37.01. ("He said he was kicked out of the army because he had an affair with his commanding officer's wife. And I found that out later that that wasn't true.")

5. Loduca, interview by JJF, TJCC DVD #16, transcript pp. 53–54, timecode 12:24:21.

6. "First Rackstraw Case Witnesses." (The article covers the beginning of RWR's murder trial and includes quotes from Philip Rackstraw's friend Ben Brooks and his neighbor Pat Lombardi.)

7. Loduca, interview by JJF, TJCC DVD #16, transcript p. 54, timecode 12:26:48; Calaveras County Probate of Murder Victim Philip Rackstraw. (Page 5 of the probate includes PI Immendorf's July 3, 1978, invoice for six months of investigative work for Bill Rackstraw.)

8. Immendorf, "D. B. or Not D. B.?"

9. Loduca, interview by JJF, TJCC DVD #16, transcript p. 64, timecode 12:41:37. ("It was pretty tough. My friends and, and people around me really helped me through it. Plus I kind of find myself [crying]; I was a single mom at the time, too.")

10. Immendorf, "D. B. or Not D. B.?"; Tim Reiterman, "Skyjacking Suspect in Big, Big Trouble," *San Francisco Examiner & Chronicle*, February 4, 1979, 8, phone photo.

11. Immendorf, "D. B. or Not D. B.?"

12. Ibid.; Steve Woods, phone interview by TJC. (In March 1977, Rackstraw worked in Lahaina, Hawaii, with Steve Woods on a floor job.)

13. Yontel, phone interview by JJF, HC-LMNO transcript p. 14, timecode 01:01:58.

14. "Testing the Evidence," *Stockton Record*, April 25, 1979, photo caption. (In a test for a jury's consideration, the San Joaquin DA set off a similar amount of explosives that RWR had "allegedly shipped to a friend in Texas.") Yontel, phone interview by JJF, HC-LMNO transcript p. 20, timecode 01:26:25. ("Two packages were received . . . one didn't make it" and was intercepted by authorities in Stockton.) Loduca, interview by JJF, TJCC DVD #16, transcript p. 77, timecode 12:59:33. (RWR "had evidently also mailed some explosives back to Texas, somebody in Texas.")

15. San Joaquin County Court Archives, May 31, 1979, explosives trial. (TJC hired Calaveras County archivist Shannon Van Zant to dig for records in neighboring San Joaquin County regarding RWR's 1979 explosives case; old court and DA documents revealed three charges, four strong witnesses, and writing-style forensics comparing RWR's check signatures to lettering on a returned Texas-bound UPS package containing dynamite caps; the evidence convinced Rackstraw to plead "no contest" in the preliminary hearing.) "Rackstraw Pleads No Contest," *Stockton Record*, May 31, 1979, scanned clipping.

16. Loduca, interview by JJF, TJCC DVD #16, transcript p. 60, timecode 12:34:51; McGarity, phone interview by JJF, HC-LMNO transcript pp. 3 and 4, timecodes 15:32:27 and 15:35:06.

17. Loduca, interview by JJF, TJCC DVD #16, transcript p. 62, timecode 12:37:53. ("Oh, they were knocking. The most interesting one at that time was when the FBI agent came to my door.")

18. Remington and Flynn, "How 2 First Suggested Rackstraw-Cooper Link."

19. Gail Marks, phone interview by TJC, August 8, 2013, Notebook #2; Pudgy Hunt, interview by JJF, HC-LMNO transcript p. 13, timecode 12:19:03; Townsend, "Airplane Crash Could Be Hoax."

20. Loduca, interview by JJF, TJCC DVD #16, transcript p. 77, timecode 12:59:33. ("There were what we call fanatical groups that were blowing up PG&E plants. The FBI

guy was asking me about a connection because they thought that these explosives came from somebody in Santa Cruz. And Bob could have provided them. I said, 'You know, Bob would do things for money, but he won't do it for a cause.'") Bob Keefer, "Flyer Quizzed in D. B. Cooper Probe,"; *Long Beach Independent Press Telegram*, February 3, 1979, scanned article. (The county DA said he learned through the FBI that RWR "had been investigated for a possible role" in a 1975 PG&E power-line bombing.) AP, "San Francisco Has Become Belfast of North America," July 1, 1977, scanned article. ("The NWLF [New World Liberation Front] has claimed 53 bombings in the last few years, most of them directed at PG&E installations, and has been drawing on a cache of thousands of pounds of explosives stolen from the Felton Quarry," where Rackstraw was a named suspect.)

21. Loduca, interview by JJF, TJCC DVD #16, transcript p. 62, timecode 12:38:17.

22. Ibid., transcript p. 62, timecode 12:38:49.

23. Ibid., transcript p. 64, timecode 12:41:37.

24. Ibid., transcript p. 71, timecode 12:51:50; Immendorf, "D. B. or Not D. B.?" (Immendorf recalled Sheriff Leach making a similar statement, which is written in his RWR case narrative: "There's a thousand abandoned mine shafts . . . where it'd be easy to dump a body. Drop a stick of dynamite behind it and we have a no-fuss, no-evidence burial.")

25. Immendorf, "D. B. or Not D. B.?"; "Testimony of Witnesses in Murder Trial Continues." (On the murder case stand, new property owner Kelly Cline confirmed that both of the victim's dogs were still at the crime scene months after Philip went missing.)

26. "Explosives, Guns Discovered in Warehouse Here," *Stockton Record*, January 26, 1978, scanned clipping; Loduca, interview by JJF, TJCC DVD #16, transcript p. 78, timecode 13:01:43. ("Doesn't everybody store TNT in their storage lockers?")

27. Cline, phone interview by TJC, notes in Non-Perps folder. (Cline provided details on the ten-acre sale of Philip's property and Cline's personal involvement in the recovery of the murder victim's body.) "Testimony of Witnesses in Murder Trial Continues." (The article confirms Cline's verbal story of a property walkabout with RWR.)

28. Loduca, interview by JJF, TJCC DVD #16, transcript p. 59, timecode 12:33:16. (RWR "told the kid that he could buy it if he kept the payments up, and [if] Dad returns the deal's off.")

29. Ibid., transcript p. 59, timecode 12:32:47. ("They were going to be putting [Mary Yontel's] house up for sale. As a matter of fact, it was my neighbor who was a real estate person who handled the transaction to sell the house up in Valley Springs.") "Explosives, Guns Discovered in Warehouse Here." ("Investigators said Bekins trucks had picked up some boxes and also had done some packing of boxes at Rackstraw's home on December 9, about the time he disappeared.")

30. Calaveras County Archive, San Diego power of attorney document from Mary Yontel to her sister Pauline, December 21, 1977.

31. Sueyres, "Declaration in Support of Increased Bail," October 12, 1978, scanned document. ("A friend, Patrick Ebert, holds twelve-thousand dollars for Rackstraw which was part of the proceeds of the [1977] bank fraud here in Stockton.")

32. "Explosives, Guns Discovered in Warehouse Here"; "'Biggest Project' Means Trouble for Contractor." (Police have "sworn out warrants for Rackstraw's arrest for allegedly 'building' bank accounts of more than $75,000 with phony checks, withdrawing the money and fleeing to Hawaii.") Loduca, interview by JJF, TJCC DVD #16, transcript p. 67, timecode 12:47:33. ("I knew [Mary Yontel] was with him [in Hawaii], yes. Like I said, my neighbor sold the house for her.)

33. Immendorf, "D. B. or Not D. B.?"; Maloney, BHI Security Letter Synopsis. (Maloney notes the FBI's warrant for RWR's unlawful flight to Iran on page 6, and the connection to Immendorf is noted on page 1.)

34. "Valley Springs Contractor Facing a Murder Charge"; Maloney, BHI Security Letter Synopsis.

35. Maloney, BHI Security Letter Synopsis. (FBI Agent Warren Little's involvement in finding RWR and arranging to bring him home is mentioned throughout the document.) "Fugitive Believed in Iran."

36. Maloney, BHI Security Letter Synopsis. (In the synopsis, Maloney refers to the couple as "Mr. and Mrs. Rackstraw." The company security team documented the whole plan—between the FBI, US Embassy, State Department, French officials, and BHI—to bring RWR home.)

Chapter Twelve

1. Maloney, BHI Security Letter Synopsis.

2. "'Biggest Project' Means Trouble for Contractor"; "Fraud Suspect's Stepfather was Slain, Buried."

3. Yontel, phone interview by JJF, HC-LMNO transcript p. 22, timecode 01:32:34. (Yontel told the story of her and RWR's arrival in Iran and their short life in the neighborhood.)

4. Maloney, BHI Security Letter Synopsis.

5. Overturf, e-mails to TJC; Daggett, phone interview; Reiterman, "Skyjacking Suspect in Big, Big Trouble." (Detective Lawrence said RWR "claimed to be CIA, but we don't know it for a fact.")

6. Reiterman, "Skyjacking Suspect in Big, Big Trouble"; Maloney, BHI Security Letter Synopsis.

7. Yontel, phone interview by JJF HC-LMNO transcript p. 15, timecode 01:08:22. ("I tried to get him off the plane in Paris.") "$350,000 Bail Continued." ("They put him on the plane in Iran and handed his passport to the pilot to prevent Rackstraw from getting off the plane in Paris when it stopped there.")

8. Remington and Flynn, "How 2 First Suggested Rackstraw-Cooper Link." ("The two Stockton investigators said they have since learned that FBI agents questioned Rackstraw about being D. B. Cooper when they arrested him as he stepped off the airplane.")

9. Jones, phone interview by TJC.

10. Dennis Roberts (Oakland attorney), professional website, case histories, last accessed April, 2014, http://www.dennisrobertslaw.com. (In 2016, Roberts's website was down, but the postings are available); "Speaker Bios: 2007–2014," Norml, last accessed June 5, 2016, http://norml.org/about/item/speaker-bios-archive-2; "Oakland Criminal Defense—Dennis Roberts Attorney at Law (510) 465-6363," YouTube, last accessed June 5, 2016, https://www.youtube.com/watch?v=_dihdX0ggBE; "Dennis Roberts Attorney at Law," Yelp, last accessed June 5, 2016, http://www.yelp.com/biz/dennis-roberts-attorney-at-law-oakland-3.

11. Jones, phone interview by TJC.

12. Dennis McDougal, *The Last Mogul: Lou Wasserman, MCA, and the Hidden History of Hollywood* (Boston: Da Capo Press, 2001); McDougal, phone interviews by TJC, June 24, 2013, and March 21, 2014. (McDougal was consulted in 2013 and 2014 regarding Hollywood and how the early cocaine years [covered in his book] helped finance film projects.)

McDougal, professional website, http://www.dennismcdougal.com/, last accessed June 17, 2016.

13. Hoeper, "War Hero Says Criminal Charges Part of Campaign to 'Get Him'"; Maloney, BHI Security Letter Synopsis; Loduca, interview by JJF, July 13, 2013, TJCC DVD #16, transcript p. 14, timecode 11.21.55 ("He insisted it was always somebody else's fault. Never his own," Loduca said.)

14. "Body of Local Man Identified—Stepson Charged with Murder." ("Then the rain came . . . and they found a suspected depression in the ground.") "Testimony of Witnesses in Murder Trial Continues." ("Cline also stated that one of the dogs, which were still on the property, spent 'quite a bit' of time on that hill.")

15. Cline, phone interview by TJC; "Valley Springs Contractor Facing a Murder Charge." ("Detectives found [Philip] Rackstraw's body in a grave near his home.") John Crawford (former Calaveras County Sheriff's Office detective), e-mails to TJC, December 3, 2012, to December 7, 2012. (Crawford stated that as a rookie detective, he was assigned to help pull out Philip's body.)

16. Deck, "Jury Says Rackstraw Not Guilty of Murder."

17. Loduca, phone interview by TJC, July 5, 2013, Notebook #2. (Loduca discussed her father's time as a POW of the Japanese in World War II, how he survived the death pit, and how proud he was of RWR joining military.)

18. Cline, phone interview by TJC; Deck, "Jury Says Rackstraw Not Guilty of Murder"; "Blood-Stained Jeans Introduced at Trial."

19. Thomas R. Kinberg (former FBI agent), phone interview by TJC, January 14, 2014, notes in FBI Consults folder; "Suspect Returned," *Stockton Record*, March 6, 1978, scanned clipping.

20. "$350,000 Bail Continued." ("Rackstraw was wheeled into court in a wheelchair but was chained and shackled." Sueyres told the paper, "Doctors say they can't find anything wrong with him, and we suspect that he wants to go to the hospital from the jail in an attempt to escape.") "Suspect Arraigned on Murder, Theft Charges," *Calaveras Enterprise*, March 15, 1978, scanned article; Loduca, interview by JJF, TJCC DVD #16, transcript pp. 92–93, timecode 14:27:36.

21. "DA Takes Time," *Stockton Record*, March 9, 1978, clipping copy; Maloney, BHI Security Letter Synopsis; Kinberg, phone interview by TJC, notes in FBI Consults folder.

22. Yontel, phone interview by JJF, HC-LMNO transcript p. 10, timecode 00:45:09.

23. Jones, phone interview by TJC, Notebook #2; Loduca, interview by JJF, TJCC DVD #16, transcript p. 88, timecode 14:20:19. (Loduca heard the same story from RWR: "The FBI had come and they wanted his palm print. And so Bob said, 'Talk to my attorney.' And the attorney said, 'Yeah, I'd be pretty stupid if I let you do that!'") Cook, phone interview by TJC.

24. Loduca, interview by JJF, TJCC DVD #16, transcript p. 93, timecode 14:26:56.

25. Yontel, phone interview by JJF, HC-LMNO transcript p. 11, timecode 00:50:11.

26. Jones, phone interview by TJC, Notebook #2.

27. "Rackstraw Acquitted of Slaying in Lode." (The article covers why the jury didn't buy the prosecution's case.) Deck, "Jury Says Rackstraw Not Guilty of Murder."

28. Loduca, interview by JJF, TJCC DVD #16, transcript p. 97, timecode 14:31:35. ("To tell you the truth, I really, really thought that they had a very weak, weak case. I never thought and I still to this day don't think they should've ever had brought that to trial on the evidence that they had.")

29. Roberts, e-mails to TJC directly or through TJC's lawyer, Mark Zaid, June 10, 2013, to June 17, 2013.

30. Immendorf, "D. B. or Not D. B.?"

31. Betty Rackstraw (RWR's aunt), phone interview by TJC, February 17, 2016, notes in Rackstraw Relatives folder.

32. Jones, phone interview by TJC, Notebook #2.

Chapter Thirteen

1. Jones, phone interview by TJC, Notebook #2.

2. Loduca, interview by JJF, TJCC DVD #16, transcript p. 112, timecode 14:48:45.

3. Best and Clever, "Rackstraw Talks from County Jail."

4. Jones, phone interview by TJC, Notebook #2.

5. "Rackstraw Military Records Ordered," *Stockton Record*, September 16, 1978, scanned article; Loduca, interview by JJF, TJCC DVD #16, transcript pp. 92–93, timecode 14:27:36. (Regarding the wheelchair stunt, Loduca said, "That's the way Bob is. He would do that to, you know, make everybody else's life miserable . . . [and get] sympathy.") "Rackstraw Acquitted of Slaying in Lode"; Deck, "Jury Says Rackstraw Not Guilty of Murder"; "Leach Retirement Dinner," *Calaveras Enterprise*, November 30, 1978; Mike Taylor, "Law Enforcement Legend Leach Dies," *Calaveras Enterprise*, March 11, 2005, http://www.calaverasenterprise.com/news/obituaries
/article_2c7b3ed3-f9db-5b1e-924d-afd9162aef23.html.

6. "Rackstraw Military Records Ordered"; San Joaquin County Superior Court, Assignment and Transfer of Personal Property, September 15, 1978, scanned document. (In a dated and signed order, RWR transferred his gun collection to his sister, Linda Lee Loduca.)

7. Loduca, interview by JJF, TJCC DVD #16, transcript p. 111, timecode 14:47:42.

8. "Rackstraw, Plane Are Still Missing." ("Investigators say they are sure the 34-year-old Valley Springs contractor fled to avoid a state prison sentence on check-kiting charges he is facing.") Sueyres, "Declaration in Support of Increased Bail." ("On October 3, 1978, the case was pre-tried before Judge William Biddick of the Superior Court, who indicated that the defendant would be sentenced to prison" should he enter a plea.) Yontel, phone interview by JJF, HC-LMNO transcript p. 25, timecode 01:42:01. (When asked why RWR ran again, Yontel replied, "Because we didn't have any more money and he was going back to jail again.")

9. Loduca, interview by JJF, TJCC DVD #16, transcript p. 102, timecode 14:38:08.

10. "Bay Search Launched for Plane," *San Jose Mercury News*, October 12, 1978, phone photo; "Coast Guard Ends Search for Plane," *San Jose Mercury News*, October 13, 1978, phone photo.

11. "Rackstraw, Plane Are Still Missing."

12. Loduca, interview by JJF, TJCC DVD #16, transcript p. 103, timecode 14:39:22.

13. Immendorf, "D. B. or Not D. B.?"

14. Townsend, "Airplane Crash Could Be a Hoax"; Marks, phone interview by TJC, August 8, 2013, Notebook #2.

15. Jones, phone interview by TJC, Notebook #2.

16. Sueyres, "Declaration in Support of Increased Bail"; "Rackstraw, Plane Are Still Missing"; "Rackstraw's Bail Price Raised to $200,000," *Stockton Record*, October 17, 1978, scanned article. (Sueyres repeated his suspicions that RWR "is probably in Mexico.")

17. Yontel, phone interview by JJF, HC-LMNO transcript p. 25, timecode 01:42:01.

18. Sueyres, "Declaration in Support of Increased Bail."

19. AP, "Placard Could Be Link to Unsolved Skyjacking," January 18, 1979, https://news.google.com/newspapers?nid=1876&dat=19790118&id=P0EsAAAAIBAJ&sjid=v80EAAAAIBAJ&pg=5454,3109035&hl=en.

20. Loduca, interview by JJF, TJCC DVD #16, transcript p. 112, timecode 14:49:44.

21. Ibid., transcript p. 113, timecode 14:51:17.

22. Jones, phone interview by TJC, Notebook #2.

23. Shell, phone interview by TJC, Notebook #2. (After Shell told the story of RWR arriving in Portland in 1974 for a meeting with Briggs and "a duffel bag of cash," TJC asked him if his trafficker had Krugerrands, to which he replied, "Yes, he had them.")

24. Jones, phone interview by TJC, Notebook #2. (Jones said her attorney referral to RWR, Dennis Roberts, agreed to take his murder case "for $10,000 and his Corvette.") Yontel, phone interview by JJF, HC-LMNO transcript p. 26, timecode 01:46:03. (Yontel confirmed the Corvette-and-cash deal.)

25. *Peoplefinders*, s.v. "Patrick Robert Ebert," October 19, 2015. (The search listed Ebert, DOB November 2, 1944, with a residency at a mobile home park at 17 Treasure Island.) San Joaquin County Sheriff's Jail Log, Robert W. Rackstraw, DOB October 16, 1943, scanned document. (The log starts from RWR's arrival on February 1, 1979, and the last entry is on April 9, 1979. The address listed at his Fullerton, California, arrest was "Treasure Island, Laguna Beach.")

26. "Police Believe Man in Custody is Rackstraw." ("Eastman" had RWR's pilot's license on him.) UPI, "D. B. Cooper Case May Have a Suspect."

27. Bocciolatt, background IRB search, May 7, 2013, part 3 of 4, page 1 of 15. (Bocciolatt found that RWR has records of three social security numbers, one of which was assigned in the year of his Mayday fugitive run, 1978–79.)

28. Reiterman, "D. B. Cooper Suspect Is, in Any Case, a Lot of Trouble." ("Using a map drawn by Rackstraw, investigators went to Meadowlark Airport in Huntington Beach and located the Cessna. Its green stripe and numbers had been painted over brown.") "Rackstraw Due Back; Plane Found," *Stockton Record*, February 1, 1979, scanned clipping. ("Information on where the plane was hidden came from Rackstraw.") Yontel, phone interview by JJF, HC-LMNO transcript p. 18, timecode 01:16:23. ("It was taken to a smaller airport. It's a problem when you're trying to hide a plane.)

29. Mark Saylor, "Hijack Mystery Probe Points to Daredevil," *San Jose Mercury News*, February 3, 1979, front page, phone photo. ("Rackstraw was arrested—alias Robert Eastman—on January 26 for allegedly attempting to duplicate a pilot's license and medical certificates at a Fullerton print shop.")

30. UPI, "D. B. Cooper Case May Have a Suspect"; "Police Believe Man in Custody is Rackstraw."

31. "Prints Tell the Tale—It Is Rackstraw," *Stockton Record*, January 30, 1979, front page, scanned clipping. ("Within minutes after state fingerprint officials flashed the news . . . word was sent to local law enforcement officials to come and get him.")

32. Yontel, phone interview by JJF, HC-LMNO transcript pp. 16–17, timecode 01:11:55. ("I went to see Bob and I took an attorney with me. They put me in a cell. They didn't lock it, but they were coming in and out.")

33. Reiterman, "D. B. Cooper Suspect Is, in Any Case, a Lot of Trouble."

34. Ibid.

35. Saylor, "FBI Refuses to Deny D. B. Cooper Probe," *San Jose Mercury News*, February 3, 1979, front page, phone photo.

36. Bunting, "Defendant Vanishes; Police Doubt 'Mayday.'" (Loduca "said FBI agents had questioned her and some of his friends about the possibility he is D. B. Cooper.") UPI, "D. B. Cooper Case May Have a Suspect." (Ken Davis, a sergeant in the Fullerton police department, told a reporter, "[The] FBI requested and received fingerprints of Rackstraw. I understand they think he might be this person D. B. Cooper.") Reiterman, "D. B. Cooper Suspect Is, in Any Case, a Lot of Trouble." ("[The] FBI has investigated Rackstraw as a suspect in the hijacking to indict him or to eliminate him." More articles about RWR's suspected link to DBC are available upon request.)

37. UPI, "D. B. Cooper Case May Have a Suspect"; Reiterman, "D. B. Cooper Suspect Is, in Any Case, a Lot of Trouble."

38. Best and Clever, "Rackstraw Talks from County Jail." (RWR complained of the "unnecessary use of solitary confinement.")

39. Loduca, interview by JJF, TJCC DVD #16, transcript p. 108, timecode 14:44:49.

40. Shell, phone interview by TJC, January 22, 2015, Notebook #2. (This is the first of sixteen of RWR's documented trips to the Northwest. After telling the story of RWR arriving in Portland in July of 1974, Shell confirmed that his trafficker had Krugerrands.) Jones, phone interview by TJC. (Confirming RWR's own stash of Krugerrands, Jones said that "Bob felt bad" about jumping bail and Jones getting stuck with the $60,000 bond in 1978, so he offered up his gun collection in exchange and paid the balance in "Krugerrands from South Africa.") Yontel, phone interview by JJF, HC-LMNO transcript p. 26, timecode 01:46:17. (Confirming RWR's own stash of Krugerrands, "Yes ... I knew about them, [but] I can't tell you how many" RWR had.) Daggett, phone interview by TJC, notes in Non-Perps folder. (This is the second of sixteen of RWR's documented trips to the Northwest. When a Seattle-to-Portland airliner flight couldn't land on account of fog on January 16, 1975, the pilot went back to Seattle. RWR, another passenger, and Daggett all jumped into a rental car and headed to Portland. Daggett told TJC that Rackstraw claimed "he was CIA.") Steve Woods, phone interview by TJC. (Woods provided information on the third through the fourteenth of RWR's sixteen documented trips to the Northwest; RWR did twelve floor-laying jobs with the Woods family company, mostly in Oregon, from October 1976 to March 1977. The last job, in Lahaina, Hawaii, led to a violent falling out.) Pudgy Hunt, interview by JJF, HC-LMNO transcript p. 14, timecode 12:21:42. (This is the fifteenth of sixteen of RWR's documented trips to the Northwest. RWR "came in one night [to Portland in March 1977], just out of the blue, and he said, 'I'm working with a company out of California. We're doing a floor job up in Woodburn, Oregon.'") Briggs Jr., phone interview by TJC, April 13, 2013, Notebook #2. (This is the sixteenth of sixteen of RWR's documented trips to the Northwest. After viewing photos and a video of RWR, Briggs Jr. adamantly stated that the Mayday fugitive was in Portland in December 1978, meeting his father on their driveway. That was two months before drug runners Carlson and Burke alleged that Dick Briggs started claiming to be DBC and fourteen months before the runners witnessed Dick Briggs planning the Cooper cash stunt along the Columbia.) "Is Rackstraw D. B. Cooper?" ("Calaveras County sheriff officers said they had heard the rumor that Rackstraw may be Cooper. Other sources in San Joaquin law enforcement said [RWR] was reputed to have made frequent visits to the Northwest.")

41. "Is Rackstraw D. B. Cooper?" ("A former Calaveras County building contractor whose wild escapes have him facing years in prison is being investigated by the FBI as a possible suspect in the near-legendary D. B. Cooper skyjacking in 1971 in the Northwest.")

42. Saylor, "Hijack Mystery Probe Points to Daredevil." (Reporter Saylor describes RWR as a "world-hopping" and "chain-smoking perpetrator.")

43. Keefer, "Flyer Quizzed in 'D. B. Cooper' Probe."

44. Hoeper, "War Hero Says Criminal Charges Part of Campaign to 'Get Him.'"

45. Reiterman, "Skyjacking Suspect in Big, Big Trouble."

46. "Is Rackstraw D. B. Cooper?"

47. AP, "Suspect Linked to D. B. Cooper," February 2, 1979, scanned article; Zahler, "California Suspect Apparently Ruled Out as D. B. Cooper."

48. Zahler, "California Suspect Apparently Ruled Out as D. B. Cooper."

49. "Rackstraw Still Suspect in Hijacking," *Stockton Record*, February 4, 1979, scanned clipping. (Thomas Kinberg, a senior FBI agent in Stockton, California, told the paper that he strongly disputes the leaked Seattle claim.)

50. "Is Rackstraw D. B. Cooper?"

51. McGarity, phone interview by JJF, HC-LMNO transcript p. 7, timecode 15:49:12.

52. Dan Hunt, interview by JJF, HC-LMNO transcript p. 13, timecode 12:18:06.

53. Yontel, phone interview by JJF, HC-LMNO transcript p. 10, timecode 00:47:36.

54. Todd, phone interview by TJC, October 2, 2015, Notebook #2.

Chapter Fourteen

1. Shell, phone interview by TJC, January 22, 2015, Notebook #2; Dan Hunt, interview by TJC, TJCC DVD #1, transcript pp. 12–13, timecode 00:23:43. ("I knew that he was running around with different drug people. I would be with Briggs in northwest Portland, sittin' in a bar early in the morning. Doing cocaine . . . when he had his Rolls Royce.")

2. Nevin, phone interview by TJC.

3. Shell, interview by JJF, HC-LMNO transcript p. 6, timecode 14:10:13. ("Dick just went berserk and literally threw this guy through a plate-glass window.") Pudgy Hunt, interview by TJC, TJCC DVD #1, transcript p. 1, timecode 00.02.06. ("Briggs told of another time with Rackstraw, stealin' a Volkswagen, puttin' it [in the] back of a two-and-a-half-ton truck, strippin' it, puttin' the carcass out on the, some side road between wherever they were and, and comin' in to San Francisco. And, uh, these were all done, you know, in the, the daylight.")

4. Briggs Jr., phone interview by TJC, April 13, 2013, Notebook #1.

5. Carlson, interview by TJC, TJCC DVD #7, transcript p. 2, timecode 00.03.22. ("Almost from the time we met, he was telling us that he was in fact D. B. Cooper. I mean, he felt comfortable. We had a circle of friends and, and all these other people, uh, had been told the same thing.")

6. Verlan C. "Vern" Burke (drug runner), phone interview by TJC, August 3, 2013, notes in Perps folder.

7. Carlson, interview by TJC, TJCC DVD #5, transcript p. 4, timecode 00.10.19. ("We seen, I mean, looked like big military guns, antitank guns, he had a hundred of them laid out. And they were all neatly laid out, too. . . . It looked like we'd walked into a gun show.)

8. "FBI Enters Armory Bombing, Weapons Theft Case in SC"; Marks, phone interview by TJC, August 8, 2013, Notebook #2; Pudgy Hunt, interview by JJF, HC-LMNO transcript p. 13, timecode 12:19:03.

9. Carlson, interview by TJC, TJCC DVD #7, transcript p. 3, timecode 00.06.06; Burke, phone interview by TJC, notes in Perps folder.

10. Shell, phone interview by TJC, January 22, 2015, Notebook #2.

Chapter Fifteen

1. Loduca interview by JJF, TJCC DVD #16, transcript p. 103, timecode 14:39:22; Sueyres, Argument for Consolidating Charges, March 9, 1979, scanned document. ("Wherefore, the People respectfully request the Court order the consolidation of all three [grand theft charges] for trial on April 23, 1979.")

2. Pudgy Hunt interview by JJF, HC-LMNO transcript pp. 16–17, timecode 12:21:42. ("Mike [Narro] had some influence. He went to law school; he was an ABC officer and a Narc officer." Dan Hunt, Pudgy's brother, was in Narro's office "when Governor Brown called, wanted him to head up the California Alcohol and Beverage Division, and he said, 'No, I'm making too much money!' But anyway, I think Bob perceived that he had political pull and could possibly get him out" of state prison.)

3. Pudgy Hunt, interview by JJF, HC-LMNO transcript p. 17, timecode 12:29:15.

4. Ralph Himmelsbach (former FBI agent), phone interview by TJC, December 30, 2011, Notebook #2.

5. Fuentes, phone interview by TJC, April 16, 2016, Notebook #2. (After a videotaping session at the Seattle FBI office, Fuentes shared how "extensive" RWR's file was; there were seventy-seven "major" prints, most from plastic cups that Tina Mucklow had "taken and put aside.") Cook, phone interview by TJC, February 3, 2014. (Cooper "had gloves at jump.") UPI, "Skyjacker Eludes FBI." ("Dark-complexioned with black hair; very courteous; very relaxed; FBI and police indicated the hijacking had been carefully and minutely planned.")

6. Best and Clever, "Rackstraw Talks from County Jail." ("Now don't laugh, you son of a gun.")

7. San Joaquin County Sheriff's Jail Log, Robert W. Rackstraw. (The log notes that the first KNBC call from RWR was on March 7, 1979.)

8. Noyes, interview by Don Ray. TJCC DVD #8, timecode 00:00:40; Noyes, The Real L.A. Confidential (CreateSpace, 2010), 89. (Chapter 9 is titled "Breaking the Manson Case.") Ray, interview by TJC, April 13, 2012, TJCC DVD #9, transcript p. 5, timecode 00:06:30. (Ray claimed that in 1979, Noyes told him, "A guy up north in jail who [called] says he's D. B. Cooper, and to prove it, he says, he has an uncle named Ed Cooper who lives in Arizona.") Nicholas Chen, "The Don Ray Experience," Santa Monica College Corsair, May 28, 2003, scanned article. (The article, covering Ray's journalism class, discusses how he "tracked down a Cooper relative" in 1979, with details matching the story relayed to TJC in 2012.)

9. RWR, interview by Doug Kriegel (KNBC News reporter), March 21, 1979. (TJC has the video and transcripts.) RWR, interview by Olney. (TJC has the video and transcripts.) Kriegel, interview by Don Ray, April 13, 2012, TJCC DVD #8, timecode 00:37:49; Noyes, interview by Don Ray, April 13, 2012, TJCC DVD #8, timecode 00:00:40.

10. Remington and Flynn, "How 2 First Suggested Rackstraw-Cooper Link"; Loduca, interview by JJF, TJCC DVD #16, transcript
p. 31, timecode 11.52.06.

11. Remington and Flynn, "How 2 First Suggested Rackstraw-Cooper Link." (RWR claimed that right after the 1971 skyjacking, his suspicious Army brass at Fort Cronkhite "questioned him about the hijacking, shortly before he was discharged from the service." But Buck and Murray learned that at the time of the jump, RWR had been out of uniform for five months.)

12. RWR, interview by Kriegel; RWR, interview by Olney; Kriegel, interview by Ray, TJCC DVD #8, timecode 00:37:49; Noyes, interview by Ray, TJCC DVD #8, timecode 00:00:40.

13. Noyes, interview by Ray, TJCC DVD #8, timecode 00:00:40. (Noyes discussed the bomb squad photos, which were later gifted to TJC.) "Testing the Evidence," *Stockton Record*, April 25, 1979, scanned photo with paragraph. (This is a Stockton Bomb-Arson Unit photo of the old car that was blown up for the coming jury presentation; TJC has twelve more of these original photos.)

14. Helen Flynn, "Rackstraw Guilty on Five Felony Counts," *Stockton Record*, May 19, 1979, front page, scanned clipping.

15. RWR's San Joaquin County Court Appeal Letter, undated, scanned document.

16. Sueyres, e-mail to TJC, October 12, 2012; Sueyres, phone interview with TJC, April 30, 2016, Notebook #1.)

17. "Rackstraw Pleads 'No Contest.'" ("The explosives charge involves a cache of dynamite reportedly found in a warehouse and traced to Rackstraw in 1977.")

18. RWR, letters to Pete Noyes, June 26, 1979, and June 27, 1979, ownership given to TJC on June 15, 2012.

19. "Not D. B. Cooper, Rackstraw Insists."

20. "Rackstraw Gets 3-Year Term." (RWR's former commander said that he was "one of two worst lieutenants I have ever seen in my 29 years of service.")

21. RWR, interview by Kriegel; RWR, interview by Olney; Noyes, interview by Ray, TJCC DVD #8, timecode 00:00:40.

22. Noyes, interview by Ray, TJCC DVD #8, page 11, timecode 00:30:49. ("[Another editor] and I had reservations about the story. . . . The *Times* wouldn't have wasted their time. . . . He seemed to be a very bright, intelligent, charming rogue.")

23. Noyes, interview by Ray, TJCC DVD #8, timecode 00:00:40.

Chapter Sixteen

1. Carlson, interview by Kashanski, February 2, 2011, TJCC DVD #7, transcript p. 3, timecode 00.05.38.

2. William M. Baker (assistant special agent in charge at the river money find, 1980), e-mail to TJC, April 2, 2016. ("Please find as an attachment a statement I authorize you to use as you deem fit.")

3. Richards, "Part of Cooper Cash Uncovered"; Zahler and Johnston, "More D. B. Cooper Cash Sought." (A backhoe and scientific experts were brought in to search the area where three bundles of decomposing twenty-dollar bills were discovered.) Georger, comment on "Tina Bar Money Find," April 11, 2015, 4:47 p.m., *DB Cooper Forum*, http://www.thedbcooperforum.com/index.php?topic=4.955;wap2 (Georger provides details on the Tina Bar money find, bundles, and rubber bands.)

4. Carlson, interview by Kashanski, December 6, 2011, TJCC DVD #5, transcript p. 15, timecode 00.40.55. ("Briggs portrayed himself as D. B. Cooper, and having done all these amazing things during the years, when it was actually Bob Rackstraw.")

5. "Muddy Clue to D. B. Cooper."

6. Richards, "Part of Cooper Cash Uncovered."

7. Zahler and Johnston, "More D. B. Cooper Cash Sought."

8. Ibid.; Larry Batson, Scripps Howard Wire, "Stalker of Legendary D. B. Cooper Claims He's Closing In," November 9, 1986.; Sidney Tipper (fisherman), interview by David Dow, CBS Evening News, February 13, 1980.

9. Georger, comment on "D B Cooper," July 1, 2008, 8:07 p.m., http://www.dropzone .com/cgi-bin/forum/gforum.cgi?post=3256266;guest=209075951#3256266.

10. Ingram, interview by TJC, TJCC DVD #3, transcript pp. 9–11, timecode 00.29.50.

11. Brian and Dwayne Ingram, interview by JJF, September 15, 2015, HC-LMNO transcript p. 8, timecode 15:18:56.

12. Fuentes, on-camera interview by TJC, October 17, 2015. (Schotz provided TJC with the full transcript.)

13. Carlson, interview by Kashanski, December 6, 2011, TJCC DVD #5, transcript p. 4, timecode 00.10.06; Ron Sterrett (former Phoenix detective), e-mail to TJC, November 1, 2011. (The DEA gave Sterrett, who had joined an Arizona financial crimes task force, the confirming February 1, 1980, details on Carlson's drug-raid incident.)

14. Bocciolatt, interview by TJC, June 11, 2012, Notebook #1. (Through a former deputy medical examiner with records at home, Bocciolatt got details on Briggs's accident and death. The examiner also found an adhesive note from IRS Criminal Investigations Division agent Mike Maney, who wanted details on Briggs's demise.) Nevin, phone interview by TJC. (On the night before his death, Briggs's last phone comment to Nevin was, "Gotta run; they're after me.") Briggs Jr., phone interview by TJC, November 9, 2011, Notebook #1. (On the night before his father's death, John got a call from him and "sensed his uneasiness.")

15. "Convictions Upheld." (Rackstraw was paroled to Ohio, the home state of his mother's family.)

16. Shell, phone interview by TJC, June 30, 2013, Notebook #2. (Shell confirmed his cocaine-money-man role for Briggs. He said he was busted on September 12, 1980, and received five years' probation; he confirmed that it was because of Carlson's DEA bust in Phoenix on February 21, 1980. He claimed not to be a federal informant.)

17. Jim Hollingsworth, interview by TJC, October 30, 2011, Notebook #1. (Later the next day, Hollingsworth was told in a bar that "somebody killed [Briggs].")

18. Nevin, phone interview by TJC.

19. Daryl Headland (former classmate of Briggs), interview by TJC, October 15, 2011, Notebook #1.

20. Pudgy Hunt, interview by TJC, November 25, 2011, TJCC DVD #2, transcript p. 7, timecode 00.13.21. Hunt also said, "The thing I heard was that he got a call, and he thought somebody was after him.")

21. Bocciolatt, phone interview by TJC, June 11, 2012, Notebook #1; "Traffic Accident Kills Portlander," Oregonian, December 13, 1980, scanned article.

22. Briggs Jr., phone interview by TJC, December 11, 2014, Notebook #2. (John, who was thirteen at the time of his father's death, still believes it was a "covered-up murder.")

23. Pudgy Hunt, interview by TJC, November 25, 2011, TJCC DVD #2, transcript p. 7, timecode 00.13.21; Dan Hunt, interview by TJC, November 25, 2011, TJCC DVD #1, transcript p. 14, timecode 00.27.12. ("I heard it was an accident, but I don't believe that's what happened.")

24. Bocciolatt, interview by TJC, June 11, 2012, Notebook #1.

25. Briggs Jr., phone interview by TJC, December 11, 2014, Notebook #2. (John described the odd mix of people at his father's funeral.)

26. Shell, phone interview by TJC, June 30, 2013, Notebook #2.

27. "Funeral Notices," *Oregonian*, December 14, 1980, E9, scanned article; Phyllis Briggs-Meyers and her husband, Doug, e-mail to TJC, August 27, 2015. (Briggs's sister, Briggs-Meyers, and his brother-in-law discussed the trafficker, his lifestyle, and his demise.)

Chapter Seventeen

1. Kentucky Marriage Records Search, Department of Libraries and Archives, January 19, 2014. (Dorothy B. "Dottie" Klayer and Robert W. Rackstraw were registered on December 26, 1981, in Kenton, Kentucky, certificate #31305. Records show that it was a third marriage for them both.)

2. Marks, phone interview by TJC, August 8, 2013, Notebook #2.

3. Ray, e-mail to TJC, March 23, 2012. (Ray forwarded a twenty-page California public document search that lists RWR's corporation, California Aviation Transportation Systems, which was filed on August 3, 1982, filing #01154512.)

4. Ibid. (Dorothy Rackstraw was a California state masonry inspector, License #5298, until October 1, 2013.)

5. Ibid. (The document lists a franchise tax board suspension, filed on September 4, 1984.)

6. Patsy Lamberson, phone interviews by TJC, February 6, 2014, and February 7, 2014, Notebook #2, signed rights agreement. (TJC received a copy of the San Bernardino County Sheriff's Department traffic report, which shows the couple's separate addresses, lawyer suit documents, photos of crashed cars, accident diagrams, a Rancho Cucamonga civil subpoena; in his suit, RWR claims the city failed to "adopt a street plan of signing, marking, and designation of turning movements.") Peter Eggertsen (president of arbitration mediation services at IVAMS), phone interview by TJC (under the alias "Joseph Richards"), November 9, 2012, notes in Perp-Rackstraw Folder. (At Spoke.com, RWR listed his employment at IVAMS in Rancho Cucamonga; Eggertsen confirmed he worked there "long ago," for three years.)

7. Van Zant, e-mail to TJC, January 24, 2013. (Reading the 1978 murder trail files, Van Zant discovered an "order to destroy all documentary evidence introduced to the jury trial" from April 26, 1983, on page 285, and an order to destroy "1 pair of old Levis in a brown bag" [the bloody pants] on page 291.)

8. "25 Years Ago," *Canyon Lake News*, 2009 edition of "Friday Flyer News," http://fridayflyer.com/stories/view/daa459fb-bd13-4026-99e1-151989a8c348?print=1. ("Four incumbent POA Directors, as well as a new resident, threw their hats into the local political ring . . . newcomer Robert Rackstraw.")

9. Ray, e-mail to TJC, May 17, 2012. (Ray forwarded a National Student Clearing House search for education verification from May 11, 2012. (The document shows RWR's attendance at the University of San Francisco from June 11, 1983, to September

26, 1995; he was awarded a bachelor of science in applied economics on December 22, 1991.)

10. Lisa Warren (payroll representative, University of California, Riverside Extension), phone interview by TJC, November 13, 2012, notes in Perp-Rackstraw folder. (Warren confirmed RWR's nearly ten years teaching at UCR, including two years, 1990–92, as the interim director of law, public policy, and research.)

11. R. W. Rackstraw vs. Child Support Division, Case CIV215745, Santa Cruz, December 9, 1991, petition, copy of action summary. (RWR applied for a waiver of court fees; in a June 1, 1993, status hearing, the child-support order was vacated.)

12. Ray, e-mail to TJC, March 23, 2012. (Ray forwarded a twenty-page California public document search. A summary of RWR's estate property transfers is available.) Marks, phone interview by TJC, August 8, 2013, Notebook #2. (Marks called RWR's divorce of Dottie a "scam"; it put RWR's property and money in Dottie's name.)

13. Ray, e-mail to TJC, June 21, 2014. (Ray forwarded twenty-one pages of RWR's Riverside County Superior Court "Legal Separation" documents. (The legal separation was filed on September 16, 1991.)

14. Loduca's daughter (anonymous), e-mail to TJC, January 21, 2014. (After Loduca's death, her daughter sent TJC a 1991 family photo from the wedding of RWR's son that shows RWR and Dottie still together, more than three years after their January 1, 1988, "estrangement" and their "separating all assets.")

15. Loduca interview by JJF, TJCC DVD #16, transcript p. 133, timecode 15.27.04. Loduca said, "I saw him and his current wife, Dottie," there.)

16. Ray, e-mail to TJC, November 26, 2012. (Ray forwarded RWR's 1993 juris doctor and master of laws in international law and economics from Northwestern California University School of Law, Sacramento, California. This online law school only confirms degrees with students' permission; the degrees are posted on RWR's LinkedIn profile and in his 1997 California Department of General Services arbitration application.)

17. Loduca, interview by JJF, TJCC DVD #16, transcript p. 135, timecode 15.29.42.

18. "Blood-Stained Jeans Introduced at Trial."

19. Loduca, interview by JJF, TJCC DVD #16, transcript p. 135, timecode 15.31.06.

20. Last Will and Testament of Linda Lee Loduca, signed August 9, 2013, scanned document. (Nine days after signing her will, Loduca died of recurring cancer.)

21. Riverside County, California, Superior Court Criminal Records, December 15, 1997, obtained through the service Instantcheckmate.com. (RWR was convicted for resisting arrest, driving under the influence of drugs, and providing a false ID to a peace officer.)

22. Ray, e-mail to TJC, June 21, 2014. (Ray forwarded twenty-two pages of RWR's Riverside County Superior Court divorce documents. After half a year in court, the divorce was filed on May 28, 1998.)

23. Marks, phone interview by TJC, August 8, 2013, Notebook #2.

24. Ray, e-mail to TJC, June 21, 2014.

25. TJC's PI records and surveillance footage show that the couple still live together in San Diego, California, now in a condo under her name on Bankers Hill.

26. Ray, e-mail to TJC, May 11, 2012.

27. Freeze, e-mail to TJC. (Freeze forwarded RWR's July 13, 1999, revocation of his California contractor's license for First Team Construction. In 1997, RWR applied to be a certified court mediator for "engineering and design disputes," but he allegedly "misrepresented facts" in the 1997 application.

28. Robert W. Rackstraw, Petitioner, v. Togo D. West, Jr. Secretary of Veterans Affair, Re No. 99-2152, United States Court of Appeals for Veteran Claims, "2000 U.S. App. Vet. Claims Lexis 167," February 28, 2000. (A copy of RWR's Petition for Extraordinary Relief is available. On February 28, 2000, the US Court of Appeals for Veterans Claims rejected RWR's argument.)

29. Warren, phone interview by TJC. (Warren confirmed that RWR's last day of teaching was October 31, 1999.)

30. Bocciolatt, Background IRB Search, May 7, 2013, part 1 of 4, p. 3 of 5. (Bocciolatt's database search revealed RWR's new address history in San Diego city and county, beginning on December 16, 2003.)

31. Ray, e-mail to TJC, April 25, 2012. (Ray forwarded RWR's FAA details; in the accessed FAA database, Ray learned that RWR was required to wear glasses and had his last medical exam in August 2003.)

32. Overturf, e-mail to TJC, May 14, 2015. (Overturf e-mailed an eleven-year-old letter to RWR's PTSD attorney: "Statement of Mission Requirements & Performance in Vietnam, March 1969–March 1970." The letter states that aerial surveillance duties for intelligence-gathering in PLB required "nap-of-the-earth reconnaissance flights.")

33. Overturf, e-mails to TJC, May 12, 2015 to July 2, 2015. (RWR's former PLB commander recalled seeing him head without orders into the jungle with a CIA agent, sometimes for days.) Manley Jr., phone interview by TJC. (Manley Jr. provided details on Vietnam, RWR, and seeing RWR in a stolen Jeep with Special Forces.) Olmstead, e-mail to TJC, May 27, 2015. (Olmstead provided stories of RWR and the CIA.)

34. Daniel Dewell (United States Department of Homeland Security, US Coast Guard), e-mail to TJC, December 26, 2013. (TJC received ownership records of RWR's forty-five-foot yacht, *Poverty Sucks*, which began on March 6, 2006; the bill of sale amount was $86,400.)

35. Bocciolatt, Background IRB Search, June 21, 2014, part 3 of 15, p. 3 of 5. (Dottie Rackstraw purchased a condo on Bankers Hill in San Diego; a database search revealed that RWR is "associated with this address.")

36. Mike Unser, "D. B. Cooper Notes Make $37K at Heritage's Americana Memorabilia Auction," June 13, 2008, front page, http://www.coinnews.net/2008/06/13/db-cooper-notes-make-37k-at-heritages-americana-memorabilia-auction/.

37. LC, Dropzone.com blog thread from September 7, 2007, to March 30, 2008. (LC, a.k.a. Ckret provides facts, theories, and answers to old questions. TJC has the full thread.) "In Search of D.B. Cooper: New Developments in the Unsolved Case," FBI.gov, March 17, 2009, https://www.fbi.gov/news/stories/2009/march/in-search-of-d.b.-cooper/dbcooper_031709. (The article provides a background of LC.)

38. Kaye, interview by TJC, November 26, 2011, TJCC DVD #4, transcript pp. 1–11, timecodes 00.01.30, signed rights agreement. (This interview about the forensic team focused on the team's river money investigation.)

Chapter Eighteen

1. Investigative Report. (A five-year, ninety-plus-page summary of the DBC research is available.) Evidence List. (An eleven-page summary of the evidence, in bullet form, is available).

2. RWR, e-mail to JJF, November 6, 2012. (TJC has a copy.)

3. JJF, e-mail to TJC, 2014.

4. Skyjacking Statute of Limitations. (To stop the five-year statute of limitations from expiring on DBC's November 24, 1971, skyjacking, the FBI's lead Portland agent, Ralph P. Himmelsbach, and Assistant US Attorney Jack G. Collins assembled a federal grand jury to get an indictment in absentia against "John Doe," AKA "D.B. Cooper," for air piracy. Hijacking is no longer a capital offense with a death penalty.)

5. RWR, phone interview by JJF, February 19, 2013, in JJF notebook.

6. US Coast Guard, e-mail to TJC, December 26, 2013.

7. San Diego PI Team, "Alternative Solutions Offered." (Eighteen days of surveillance and armed protection, notes, and surveillance photos are available.)

8. Cook, e-mail to TJC, November 9, 2012.

9. RWR, letters to Noyes, June 26, 1979, and June 27, 1979.

10. Patty Mott, e-mail to TJC, September 10, 2014. (Mott e-mailed two letters from NdW to her husband during college, postmarked September 2, 1971, and September 17, 1971.)

11. Cook, interview by George Noory.

12. Erik A. Kleinsmith, e-mail to TJC, June 21, 2014. (Kleinsmith forwarded the Lockheed Martin Link Chart, which documents the forty-five-year trail of RWR and his alleged crime partners, coworkers, families, and other associates.)

Chapter Nineteen

1. Roberts, e-mail to TJC, May 23, 2013. (Contrary to RWR's claim on May 21, 2013, that he was talking to his lawyer, Roberts clarified two days later that he had been away during the May 21 face-off on "a two-week vacation which has caused many fires which need to be extinguished.")

2. San Joaquin County DA Petition for Writ of Habeas Corpus. (Sueyres said FBI agent Warren Little told him that fourteen of RWR's medals and awards were phony, including all his Purple Hearts).

3. "Valley Springs Contractor Facing a Murder Charge." ("Detectives found [Philip] Rackstraw's body in a grave near his home.") "Rackstraw Acquitted of Slaying in Lode"; Deck, "Jury Says Rackstraw Not Guilty of Murder."

4. "Rackstraw Due Back; Plane Found." (The article lists RWR's pending San Joaquin charges for plane theft, check kiting, and illegal explosives.) Reiterman, "D. B. Cooper Suspect Is, in Any Case, in a Lot of Trouble." (The end of the article states that RWR was "charged with grand theft of an airplane, possession of explosives, check forgery and writing checks with insufficient funds.")

In Conclusion

1. Ted Skillman, e-mail to TJC, September 5, 2015. (Skillman mentioned his recent "initial contact" with the FBI's Seattle field office, from which he later updated TJC in two phone calls that both RWR and the field office had asked, "Is Tom Colbert involved in this?")

2. Susan McKee (FBI Investigative Publicity and Public Affairs Unit chief) e-mail to TJC, August 15, 2012. (The e-mail was cc'd to Katherine W. Schweit, Steven E. Grassie, Michael P. Kortan, Curtis J. Eng, and Ayn S. Dietrich and said, "The FBI welcomes any

further information that you uncover, and you can provide that to SA Eng through Public Affairs Specialist Ayn Sandalo Dietrich.")

3. The FBI's unofficial most important rule is "Don't Embarrass the Bureau." (Jack Trimarco and Tom Fuentes confirmed that this is an FBI code of conduct.)

4. Remington and Flynn, "How 2 First Suggested Rackstraw-Cooper Link." (Both of RWR's 1978 alibis were explained in the article.) Loduca, interview by JJF, TJCC DVD #16, transcript p. 31, timecode 11.52.06.

5. "Documentary Revelations," video-recording by LMNO Productions, April 15, 2016.

6. Jeff Renz (professor) e-mail to TJC, December 3, 2014.

7. Cami Green (technician), Sorenson Forensics Case Report, December 2, 2014, scanned document.

8. Renz, e-mail to TJC.

9. Bill Mitchell (passenger and witness), interview by JJF for HC-LMNO, September 21, 2015, Portland, Oregon.

10. Todd, phone interview by TJC, September 20, May 2015, Notebook #2.

11. Kris Mohandie (psychologist), e-mail to TJC, December 13, 2015. (Mohandie's analysis was also video-recorded for the LMNO-History documentary.)

12. Tina Mucklow (stewardess and witness), video-recording by HC-LMNO, April 11, 2016, Portland, Oregon.

13. Bruce Smith, "The Hunt for DBC—Looking for Tina Mucklow, the Primary Witness," *Mountain News*, February 8, 2011, 1–2.

14. Bernie Rhodes, research by Russell Calame, *D.B. Cooper: The Real McCoy* (Salt Lake City: University of Utah Press, 1991), 124.

15. Richard Tosaw, *D. B. Cooper: Dead or Alive?* (Ceres, CA: Tosaw Publishing, 1984); Smith, "The Hunt for DBC—Looking for Tina Mucklow, the Primary Witness."

16. Florence A. Schaffner, senior stewardess, phone interview by TJC, May 27, 2016. (Schaffner appeared to have serious memory loss and paranoia; she thought she was only the one who sat with Cooper and that no college student [Mitchell] was ever there.) Alice F. Hancock, first-class stewardess, phone interview by TJC, June 2, 2016. (No memory of her documented discussions with or observations of Cooper.)

17. Thomas P. Mauriello (professor), e-mail to TJC, June 15, 2016. (In his e-mail, the professor noted two sources: Mauriello, "Criminal Investigations Handbook, 2015: 15-5; and Elizabeth Loftus, Eyewitnesses Testimony, [Cambridge: Harvard University Press, 1996]: 153–156.)

18. Todd, phone interview by TJC, May 15, 2014, Notebook #2.

Photo Credits

The photo on page 1 is reproduced by permission of the *Record*, Calixtro Romias, photographer.

The photo on page 33 is reproduced by permission of Lonnie Long, courtesy of Lonnie M. Long and Gary B. Blackburn.

The photo on page 40 is reproduced by permission of Getty Images, courtesy of Patrick Christian/Getty.

The photo on page 69 is reproduced by permission of AP, courtesy of AP Photo.

The photo on page 77 is reproduced by permission of AP, courtesy of AP Photo.

The photo on page 81 is adapted from Google Maps mapping service, map data © 2016 by Google, used with permission. Google and the Google logo are registered trademarks of Google Inc.

The photo on page 83 is reproduced by permission of the *Province*, courtesy of the *Province*.

The photo on page 99 is reproduced by permission of the *San Bernardino Sun*, courtesy of *Sun Telegram*/Jan Cleveland.

The photo on page 149 is reproduced by permission of the *Record*, Calixtro Romias, photographer.

The photo on page 173 is reproduced by permission of the *Record*, Calixtro Romias, photographer.

The photo (on page 182 is reproduced by permission of NBC Archives, courtesy of NBC.

The photo on page 186 is reproduced by permission of Getty Images, courtesy of Getty Images/Bettmann.

Index

Note: Page numbers in *italic* refer to photos and accompanying captions. "RWR" refers to Robert W. "Bob" Rackstraw.

About the Authors

Thomas J. Colbert is a former senior media executive with thirty-six years of management and editorial experience in the national news, television entertainment, publishing, and motion-picture fields. He began his career in journalism research at the CBS flagship news station, KCBS, in 1980. From there he was recruited by Paramount Television in 1988 to be a story editor. In 1992, Colbert  launched his own true-story research company, Industry R&D (IRD), to serve national networks, studios, and publishing houses. Nineteen of his breaking stories became movies for the big and small screen, with a like number of published books. He sold IRD in 2009 but still pursues the occasional book, movie, and series project through his firm, TJC Consulting, LLC.

In his off hours, Colbert has always found time to conduct talks and classes on media relations, disaster preparedness, and crisis management. That resulted in an invitation in 1983 to become a rotating instructor at the California Specialized Training Institute, a state Office of Emergency Services academy at Camp San Luis for public servants. Colbert provided his unique expertise in courses there for eighteen years to thousands of students wearing badges and uniforms. It is from these law enforcement alumni, and old news sources, that Colbert created his elite cold case team for the Cooper investigation.

Tom Szollosi is a veteran writer for episodic television and movies with over thirty-five years of experience. His television credits include work on shows such as *The Incredible Hulk, Quincy, M.E., The A-Team, Hardcastle and McCormick, Hunter, Star Trek: Voyager, The Outer Limits, Amazing Stories*, and many more. Feature films include *Three O'clock High, Snow White: A Tale of Terror*, and *Bone Daddy*.

He has written four novels, *The Proving, The Space He Filled, Dead Set on Tuesday*, and the forthcoming *Treachery*. He is a clinical assistant professor of screenwriting at Loyola Marymount University in Los Angeles.